Do-It-Yourself

Includes online audio & instructional video

BASS GUITAR

BY TRAVIS DYKES

I0803441

PLAYBACK+
Speed • Pitch • Balance • Loop

To access audio and video visit:
www.halleonard.com/mylibrary

Enter Code
5588-7991-6434-0450

ISBN 978-1-70513-784-0

HAL•LEONARD®
A Muse Group Company

Visit Hal Leonard Online at
www.halleonard.com

World headquarters, contact:
Hal Leonard
7777 West Bluemound Road
Milwaukee, WI 53213
Email: info@halleonard.com

In Europe, contact:
Hal Leonard Europe Limited
Dettingen Way
Bury St Edmunds, Suffolk, IP33 3YB
Email: info@halleonardeurope.com

In Australia, contact:
Hal Leonard Australia Pty. Ltd.
4 Lentara Court
Cheltenham, Victoria, 3192 Australia
Email: info@halleonard.com.au

CONTENTS

About the Author

After getting his start in the professional music industry at an early age, Travis has been a full-time touring and studio musician for many years in Nashville, Tennessee. From the start of his music career, he has always felt a passion for teaching and has taught hundreds of bass and guitar students. This passion prompted the start of a YouTube channel to provide bass lessons and a behind-the-scenes look at the professional music industry. Over the past few years, Travis' YouTube channel has grown to over six figures in his subscribers count, and he continues to create videos weekly. Although many of his lessons and insights come through video, Travis authored *Do-It-Yourself Bass Guitar* to give bassists a unique and practical approach to learning. Travis continues to travel and work as a musician, touring with artists such as Gone West, Carrie Underwood, Colbie Caillat, Cece Winans, Eric Paslay, Charity Gayle, Riley Clemmons, Stephen Day, James Wilson, and many others. Outside of his music career, Travis enjoys being home with his wife and ministering at his local church every Sunday.

Introduction

Wanting to Learn Bass?

Let me guess the answer to the question above: You saw a bass player groovin' and making some faces that made you laugh and dance at the same time? Even if it's not the answer, that is part of the reason many bass players (including myself) wanted to learn to play bass because of the power of the low-end groove.

Many books focus on only teaching technique, but one of the things that we wanted to do with this book is teach you not only how to play with good technique, but also understand how it's used in the music you listen to every day. To start things off, we will be going through some of the basic parts of the bass, a quick explanation of key terms, and some fundamental concepts that all bass players should know about how the bass works.

Returning to Bass?

If you're someone who has played the bass for years but had to pull back from it for a while because of the many things that can happen in life and you feel the urge to pick up the bass again, then this book is designed to help you get back in the groove. If you already know some of the beginning techniques, that is totally fine! You can use the table of contents to skip around and start where you feel the weakest and build from there.

About the Audio and Video

This book features accompanying audio and video files that are accessible by going to **www.halleonard.com/mylibrary** and inputting the code found on page 1. These media files are essential for you to view and hear while working through the book.

How to Learn from This Book

Practical Song-to-Song Learning

In this book, we will learn techniques of how to play bass by using popular songs that you have likely heard before. Most people want to learn to play bass because they heard a bass line someone played or felt something "in their bones" when they heard a bass line in a song.

Song-to-song learning makes mastering the bass more practical outside of just learning isolated techniques that you may or may not use. This type of learning lets you learn how to play all those techniques in context of what you hear in common popular songs while also learning how you can put them into your own playing. In this book, you'll learn songs by artists such as Bruno Mars, John Mayer, Coldplay, the Killers, Kacey Musgraves, and many more.

How to Approach Practicing

There are several misconceptions about practicing for any instrument. For instance, some claim that you must practice at least three hours a day while some say if your hands don't hurt when you're done practicing, you didn't really practice—the claims go on and on. The main thing about learning and practicing the most effectively is to consistently grow every day you practice. The way growth happens is by playing and learning things that are hard for you to play until you master them. When you approach practicing this way, the amount of time that is needed becomes a lot more doable than you think. Practicing effectively is not just about the quantity of your practice time—it's about the quality of it. If you have a busy life and cannot spend hours of time every day practicing learning a new instrument, then set a timer and take around 15 to 30 minutes per day to work on the things you cannot play well and practice consistently until you can. Remember this: You don't climb Mount Everest in one big step, but by many small steps.

Basics of the Bass

If you're completely new to learning how to play the bass, there are a few different pieces of the instrument you should familiarize yourself with.

You'll first need to learn the general parts of the bass that you may hear mentioned in the book and when playing with other musicians as well. Here is a quick diagram of the different parts of the bass.

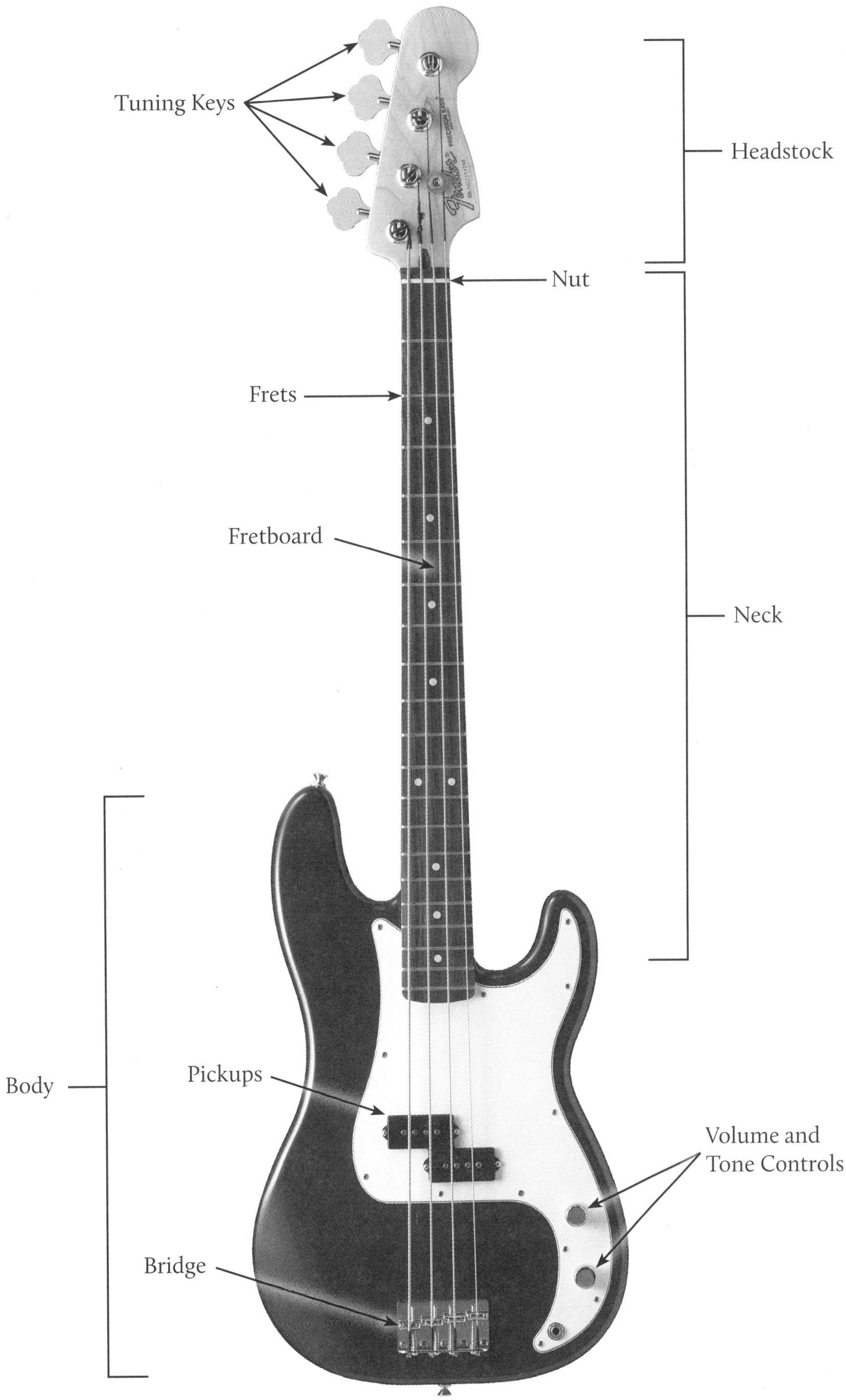

Your bass may or may not look exactly like this one, but most basses share all these same general parts.

Tuning

If you already know how to tune your bass, then you can definitely skip to the next section. If you don't, here are the string names and numbers for the most common bass configurations you will possibly encounter. To help you find each of these strings, the list below indicates which string is thickest down to the thinnest. Here are the most common bass configurations:

The Four-String Bass

- 1st string = G (thinnest string)
- 2nd string = D
- 3rd string = A
- 4th string = E (thickest string)

The Five-String Bass

- 1st string = G (thinnest string)
- 2nd string = D
- 3rd string = A
- 4th string = E
- 5th string = B (thickest string)

So let's say you do not have access to the online audio with the tuning notes; how should you tune then? Well, there are a couple of ways you can solve this problem. You can first buy a tuner from any local or online music store (most recommended) and use that to tune. Another way is to use a piano (if there is one around) and play the notes associated with the different strings labeled in the chart above and match the pitch/sound of each of your bass strings to that particular note.

Notes on the Bass

When first starting to learn the bass, you may hear bass players and musicians refer to different letters in the alphabet when talking about a bass line or melody; these are what we call *notes*. This is where the language of music starts. Just like the actual alphabet, they are the foundation of the musical alphabet; the only difference is that it stops at the letter "G." As bass players, most of what we do begins and ends with single letters from the musical alphabet (notes) because of how low our instrument is in context of *frequency*. (Frequency refers to how pitch is measured in *hertz*. Generally, bass players should play notes with lower frequencies that are clear and provide a solid foundation.) With that being said, here are two charts of all of the notes that are on the neck of the bass up to the 16th fret. (We'll cover this more in-depth later in the book, but for a quick tip, the "♭" sign means "flat" and the "♯" sign means "sharp.")

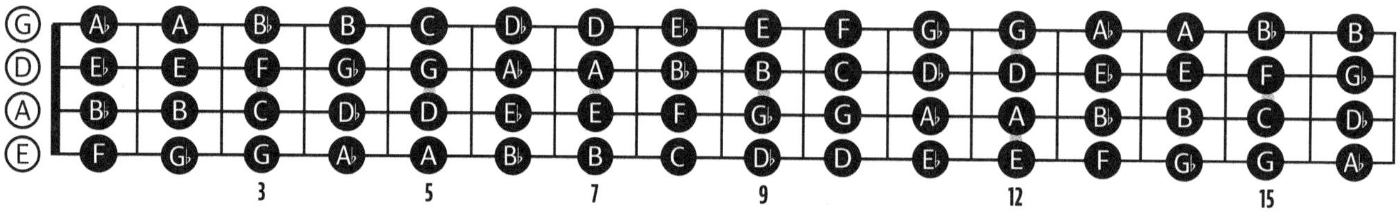

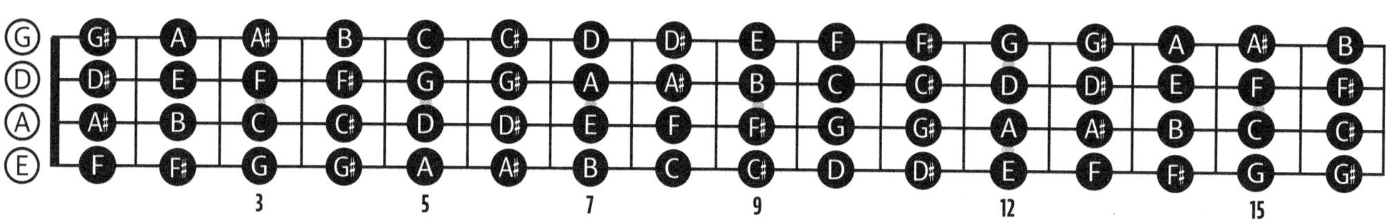

How to Hold the Bass

Holding the bass is very simple, but it can sometimes be confusing. The most common or comfortable ways to hold the bass are by either standing or sitting.

Standing

When standing, to find the best length for you on your strap, make sure your forearm can slightly rest on the top bevel of the body while being able to reach down to pluck the strings.

Sitting

Now, when sitting with the bass, you can rest the bottom bevel of the body on your leg while still resting your forearm on the top bevel so you can have ease of play. These ways of holding the bass are not set in stone; they're just common ways many players use when holding the instrument. Whatever feels the most comfortable to you when you play is most likely the best option for you to hold the bass.

Placement of the Bass in a Band

Learning how to play the bass is very important but learning where it fits in a band is the most important. When it comes to playing with other musicians, knowing where the bass fits musically and sonically can make or break how you sound when playing with others. Below is a diagram of how the bass fits in a band when it comes to frequency and its musical function.

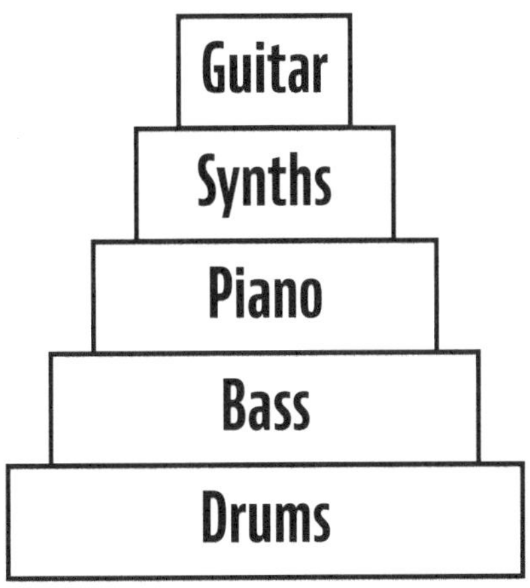

Chapter 1
Basics of How to Play Bass

Basic Right-Hand Technique

*Go to **www.halleonard.com/mylibrary** and input the code found on page 1 to access this video and others!*

When it comes to learning how to play bass, we have to acquire some basic techniques so we can get the proper sound out of the instrument by playing as clean as possible. The first thing we need to learn is the different ways you can pick or pluck the bass strings to get certain sounds and tones. (For our purposes, "right-hand playing" and "left-hand playing" refer to "pick-hand playing" and "fret-hand playing," respectively.)

Fingerstyle

This style of right-hand playing is the most common. The way you achieve this sound is by resting your thumb on the pickup of the bass and then pulling the tip (the fleshy part) of your index finger in an upward motion through the string, towards your thumb.

Try not to do this too hard because it can result in a very harsh, unpleasant sound. Instead, play it lightly at first. The stronger you play, the louder the bass will sound. Also, make sure you alternate your index and middle fingers when plucking so you can have consistent tone when playing faster or more complex lines. This way of playing with your right hand also allows you to develop speed and dexterity.

Picking Style

Using a pick is not as common as fingerstyle when it comes to right-hand playing, but it is a very valuable technique that every bass player should learn in order to be versatile. Picking gives you a very clear and biting attack when used correctly. Most bass players that use this technique play rock or indie styles of music.

To achieve this sound, you first need to choose the right pick. Since we are playing a bass with thick strings, we need to use a heavy-gauge pick (which means a thicker pick). This is because the gauge of the pick can affect the tone of the bass immensely. Thinner picks produce a slightly floppy or sloppy sound, while a thicker pick results in a tighter and punchier sound.

When picking, you will need to hold the pick between your index finger and thumb very snugly, but not too tight. Rest the tip of the pick flatly onto a string to press down and through to the next string; this is called a *downstroke*. When performing the same technique, going upwards to the string above, it's called an *upstroke*.

TOOLBOX

Make sure to practice picking and plucking each string evenly each time you play—this will make your bass lines in songs very clean and professional sounding.

Music Literacy

Before starting our picking exercises, we need to cover the basics of reading music. When learning how to play music, you are introduced to a language that you have never spoken before, and because of that, you have to learn how to read and write it. In music, there are several ways musicians communicate with each other when it comes to playing together. We won't tackle learning all of them in this book; we'll only cover the most common ways that you will encounter often when playing bass.

Common Ways to Read Music (That We'll Use)

- Tablature
- Chord Charts
- Nashville Number System

As we progress in this book, we will learn how to read and understand each of the three common ways to read music. To start, let's learn the first way of reading music that you will encounter the most when working through this book: *tablature*.

How to Read Tablature for Bass

TOOLBOX

Tablature ("tab/tabs" for short) is the most basic visual representation of music that shows exactly what fret to play while also telling you which string to play at the same time. When playing by tabs, the horizontal lines represent the strings on the bass. It looks like this:

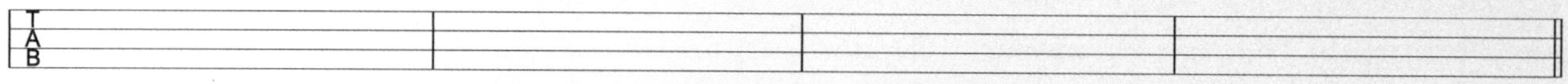

The most common bass tab configuration, which we will use very often in this book, shows four strings, as opposed to five. The way that it works is the lowest line (at the bottom of the graphic) represents the lowest-pitched string (E). It follows suit as you ascend the lines, with the highest line (at the top of the graphic) representing the highest string (G).

Simple enough right? The next step is learning what these numbers mean on a normal bass tab.

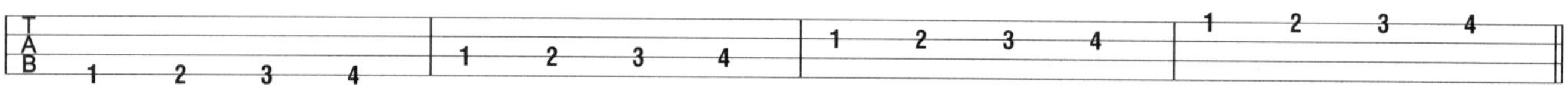

Each number that is represented is telling you which bass fret to play on each string. So when you look at the first four notes on this tab (1, 2, 3, 4), basically all it is saying is to play the 1st, 2nd, 3rd, and 4th fret on each string.

Whenever you see the number 0 on a bass tab, this means that you play an open string without pressing down any of the frets.

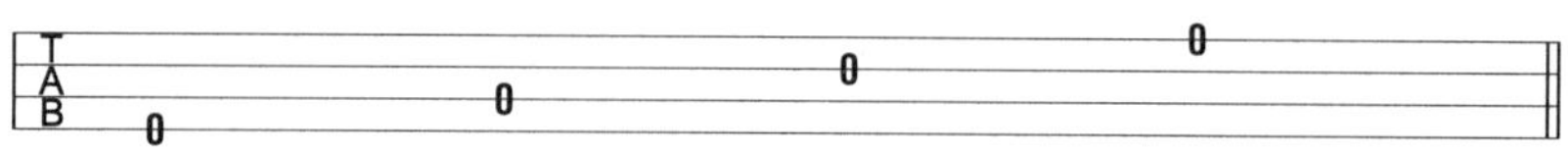

When learning from this book, you will need to know these basic techniques about how to read tablature so you can successfully take on the lessons that come next.

Practical Exercises

Here are some open-string progressions for you to practice right-hand techniques. First, practice the exercises with fingerstyle plucking, and then move to using a pick.

Track 1

Go to ***www.halleonard.com/mylibrary*** *and input the code on page 1 of this book to access this audio track and others!*

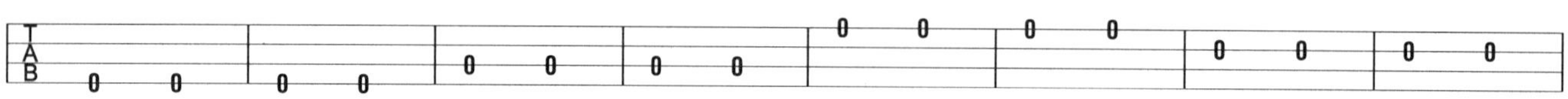

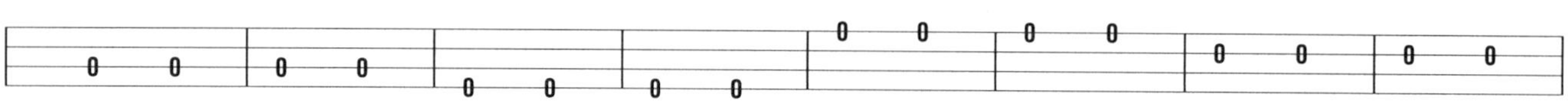

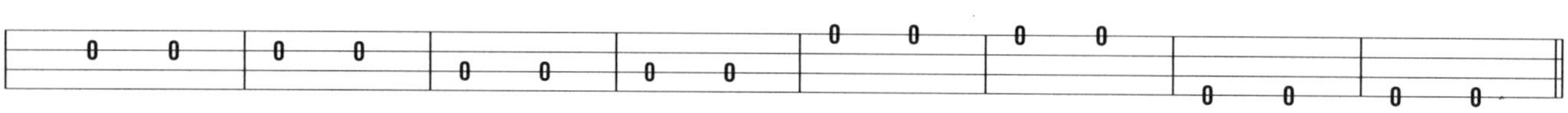

Basic Left-Hand Technique

Now that we have learned basic right-hand technique, the next step in starting to play bass lines is learning how to use our left hand to play different notes on the fretboard.

To start playing notes on the fretboard, take your index finger and press down on the first fret of the bass firmly and pluck using your right hand to hear the note that is being pressed. You may hear a buzz when pressing down; if so, then experiment with your pressure to see if the buzz goes away. (Your thumb should be placed firmly against the back of the neck.)

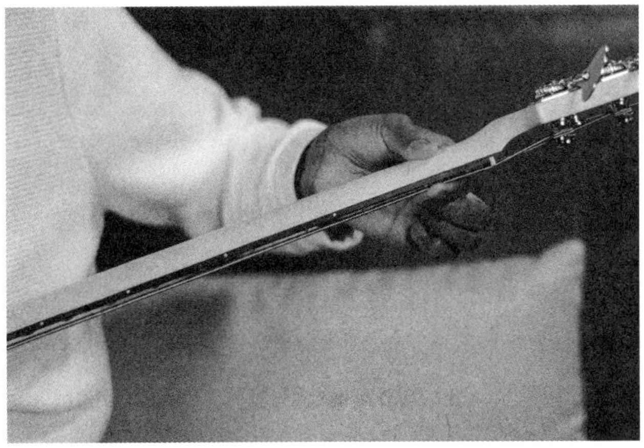

One of the most important things to grasp when using your left hand is to find the correct balance of pressure when placing your fingers on the fretboard.

Now, after learning how to press down with your index finger, practice the same technique with your middle, ring, and pinky fingers. A very effective method to use for your left hand is called the "one-finger-per-fret" system. Basically, this system helps you achieve effective economy of motion, which means that your hand is moving the least distance possible to play the notes you are reaching for. The way you use this technique is by only using one finger per fret within four frets of each string, shown in the photo below.

By using this technique, you can develop very clean means of playing that will make it easier for you to work through any musical passage.

Using Right- and Left-Hand Techniques Together

So now, let's put our left- and right-hand techniques together to play our first notes on the fingerboard!

Track 2

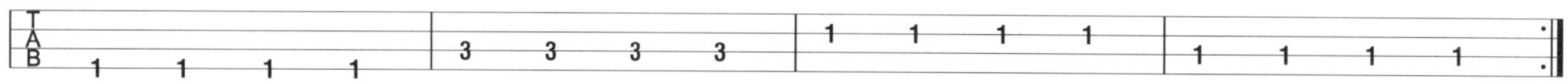

Track 3

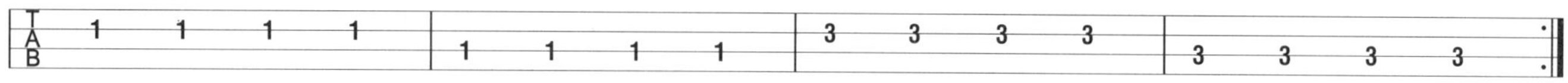

Track 4

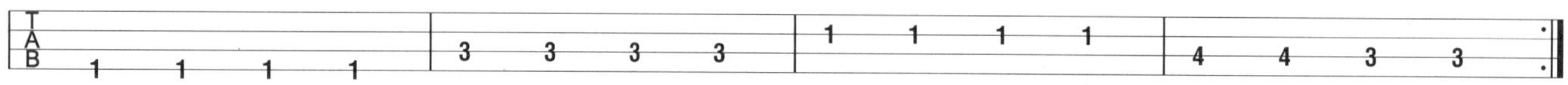

Track 5

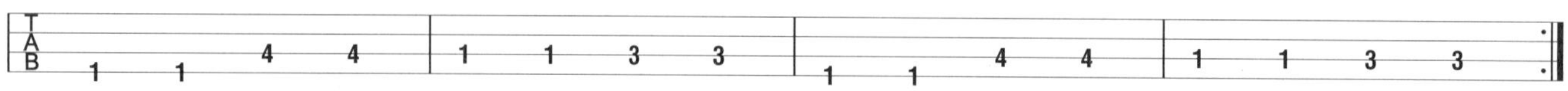

Track 6

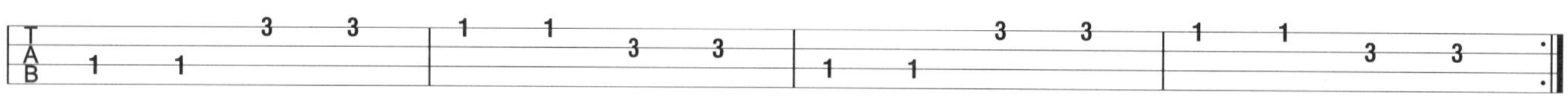

Track 7

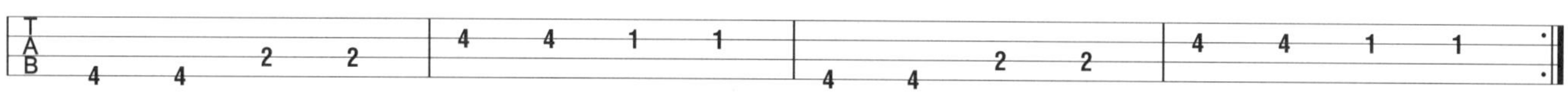

Chapter 2
Pitch and Rhythm

Basic Music Theory

Learning music theory can seem daunting to any person who takes on a new instrument, but it isn't too difficult if you start with solid fundamentals. Music theory gives you more power to create music in an easier way and more intention in realizing your ideas. Our first step in theory will be learning about notes on the bass.

Notes

Music, in theory, is a collective sequence of audio vibrations that create sound. When we organize those sounds and give them names, we call them *pitches*, or as we've already mentioned, notes. On the piano, every note looks unique like this:

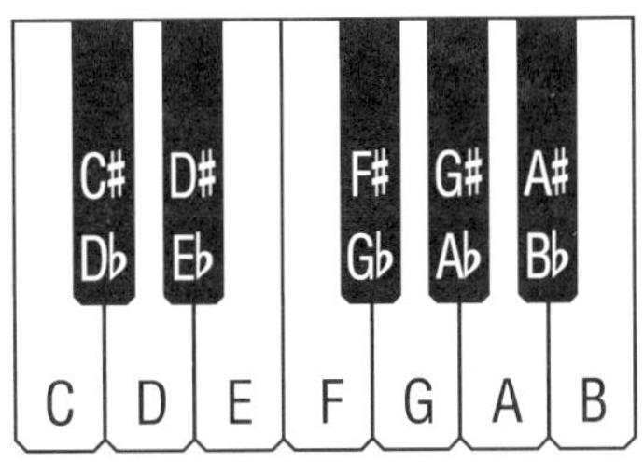

Here, each note only occurs in a single sequence that is repeated, either lower or higher in pitch. These notes are the same on bass, but they are arranged differently.

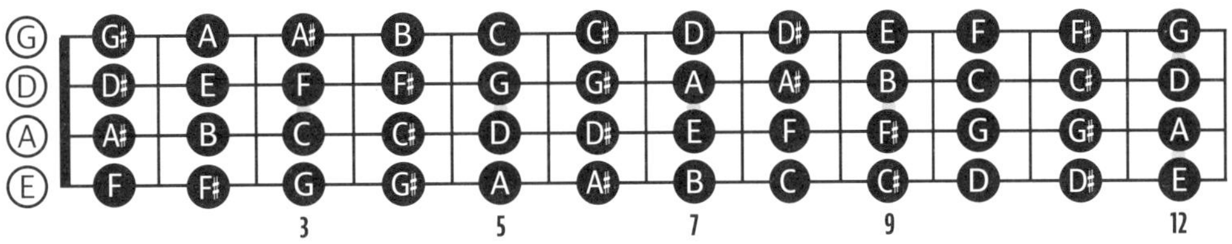

The biggest difference between these two diagrams is that the bass notes don't match the spacing and shape of the notes arranged on the piano. What this tells us is that the bass is a multi-pattern-based instrument, as opposed to the piano, which uses a single layout to arrange the notes. This means that when learning and creating music on the bass, applying multiple patterns are going to be essential to understand the instrument.

In modern music, there are 12 notes that we use to create music. The seven main musical notes are called A, B, C, D, E, F, and G (called *naturals*), and the other five notes are variations of the naturals, called *sharps* (indicated with a ♯ symbol; you'll also see a "#" used instead, usually in music typed in some type of word processor) and *flats* (indicated with a ♭ symbol; you'll also see a lowercase "b" used instead, much like how the # relates to the ♯ symbol). These notes are arranged in *half steps*, which we see as moving fret by fret on the fingerboard.

A sharp note is one half step higher than one of the naturals, and a flat note is one half step lower than one of the naturals. For example, A would become **A#** (pronounced "A sharp") or **A♭** (pronounced "A flat"). If we wanted to return to an A natural in the same measure as an A# or A♭, then we would use this symbol: ♮. Otherwise, if there is no symbol, assume it is natural. Here is that same chart, but this time we've changed the sharp notes to flats, known as *enharmonic equivalents*.

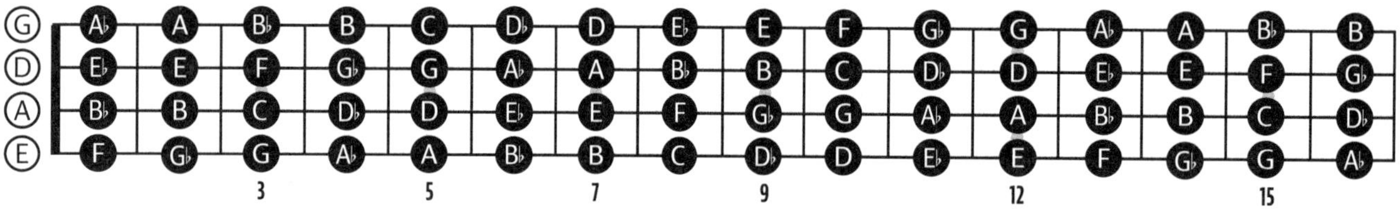

One of the easiest ways to learn and memorize all the notes on the bass is to learn them on the E and A strings first, and then find the rest by playing an *octave* (the same note, but eight letters higher or lower in pitch). To find octaves on the fretboard, you can locate a note on a given string, then move two strings down and two frets up. This gets you the higher octave, while the opposite is used to find lower octaves. The diagram below shows the arrangement of notes on the fretboard to the 16th fret, with all of the A natural notes highlighted in different octaves.

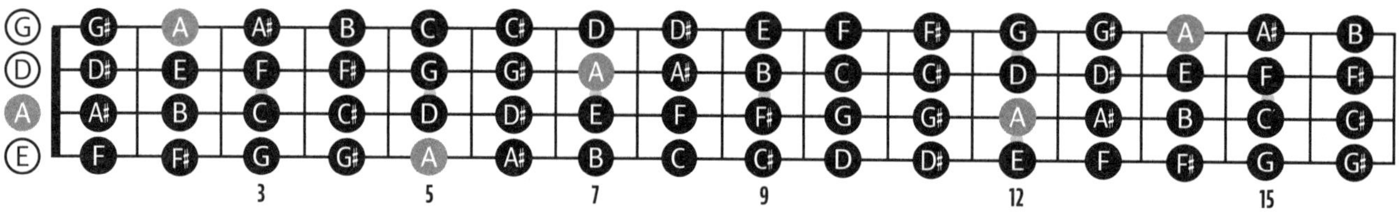

You'll notice some notes occur in different places on the neck but are exactly the same regarding their register. For instance, the A located on the fifth fret of the E string is the same exact note as the open A string. In the same way, the A located at the seventh fret of the D string is the same exact note as the one located at the second fret of the G string. (We'll explore octaves more in Chapter 8.)

This may seem like a lot of information to digest, but it's important to know when it comes to playing songs. Songs are created or arranged using different sequences of these notes. The effectiveness of your bass lines when playing through these progressions is up to how well you know the fretboard.

Fretboard Quiz (See Video)

1. ______________________

2. ______________________

3. ______________________

4. ______________________

5. ______________________

6. ______________________

Playing Rhythms

As bass players, we are the pulse, especially when playing with a drummer, in a band. How we play, understand, and follow rhythms can make or break a song. Having a solid grasp of rhythm helps us to effectively navigate and create the pulse of a song or bass line.

First, we need to understand what the building blocks of rhythm are. If you ever heard someone counting, "1, 2, 3, 4," those are what we call *beats*. In this case, counting to "4" is what we call a *bar* or *measure* of music. We use this terminology to help us understand what the pulse is of any given song we play. (Not every bar of music is made up of four beats, but we'll dive into more of this later.)

Now, let's address the elephant in the room: How does this help me play bass? Knowing this helps us determine what our note values (durations) are. The ToolBox below shows you the most common types of note lengths you'll encounter.

TOOLBOX

Whole Notes	A *whole note* is when you play a note and hold it down for the duration of four beats.
Half Notes	A *half note* is when you play a note and hold it down for two beats.
Quarter Notes	A *quarter note* is when you play a note on every beat in a bar.
Eighth Notes	An *eighth note* is when you play a note on every beat and between every beat in a bar. They can either be flagged or beamed together.

Note: These note values are given in context of a bar of 4/4 time. (More on this later.)

Here's a chart that breaks down one whole note into half, quarter, and eighth notes.

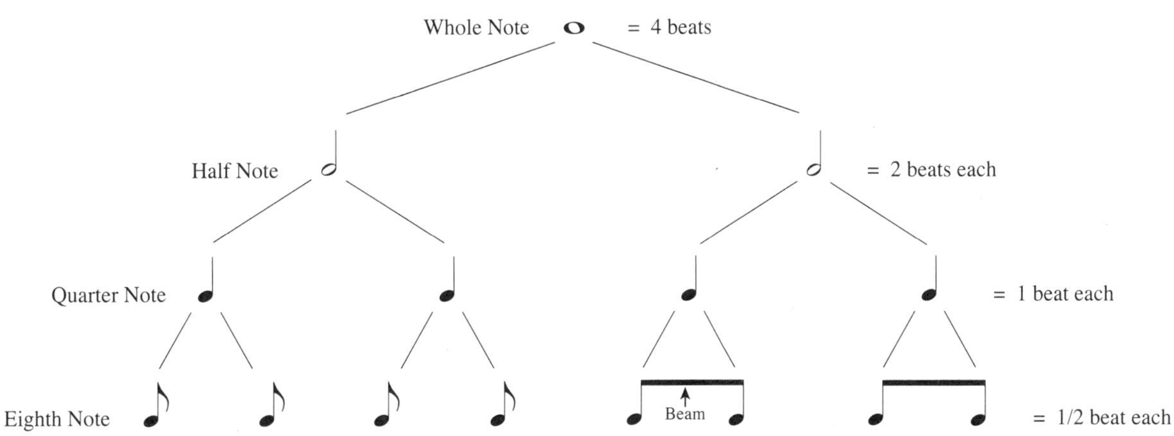

Song Examples

"JUST THE WAY YOU ARE"

Words and Music by Bruno Mars, Ari Levine, Khari Cain, Philip Lawrence and Khalil Walton

Let's play this popular song, using whole notes.

Track 8

Verse

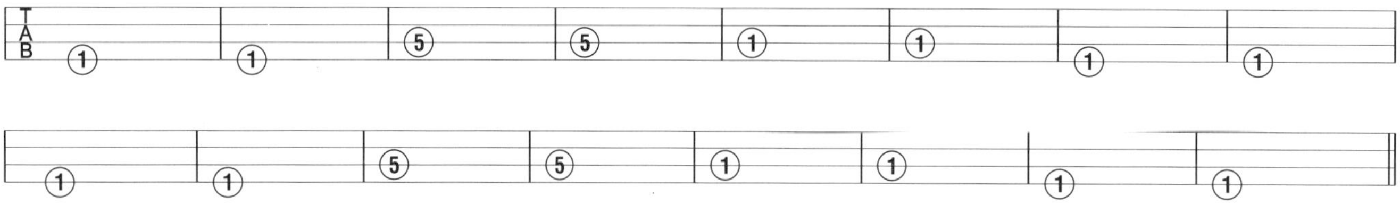

Chorus

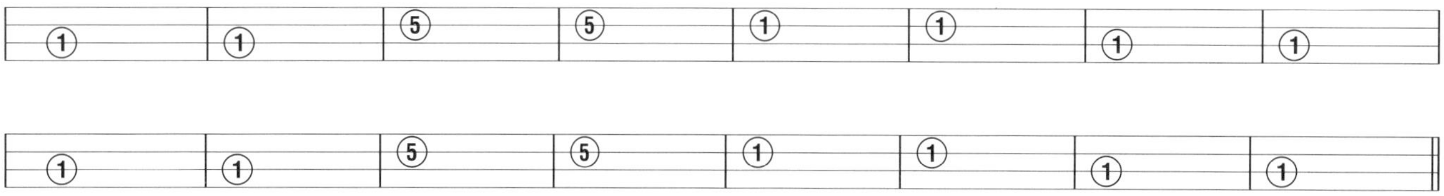

"SLOW BURN"

Words and Music by Kacey Musgraves, Ian Fitchuk and Daniel Tashian

We'll tackle this next tune with half notes.

Track 9

Verse

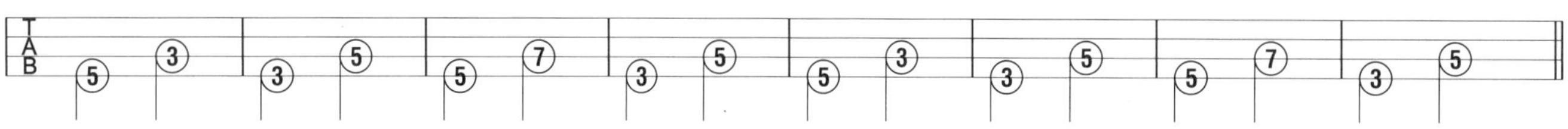

Chorus

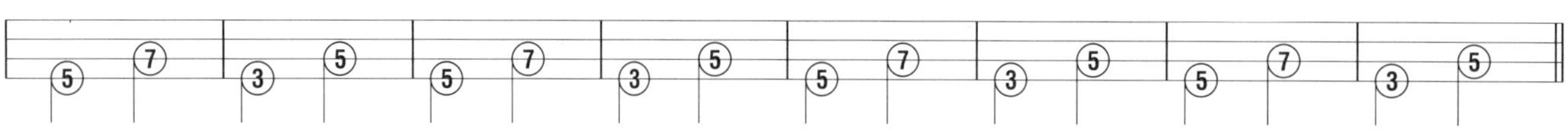

"EVERY TEARDROP IS A WATERFALL"

Words and Music by Guy Berryman, Jon Buckland, Will Champion, Chris Martin, Peter Allen, Adrienne Anderson and Brian Eno

Play through this song with quarter notes played on each beat of the measure.

Track 10

Verse

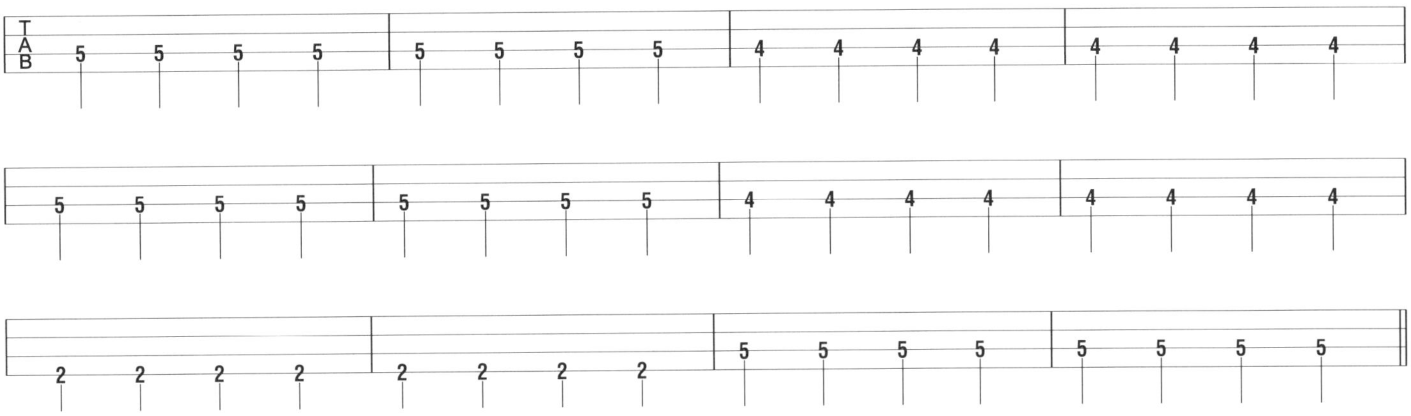

Chorus

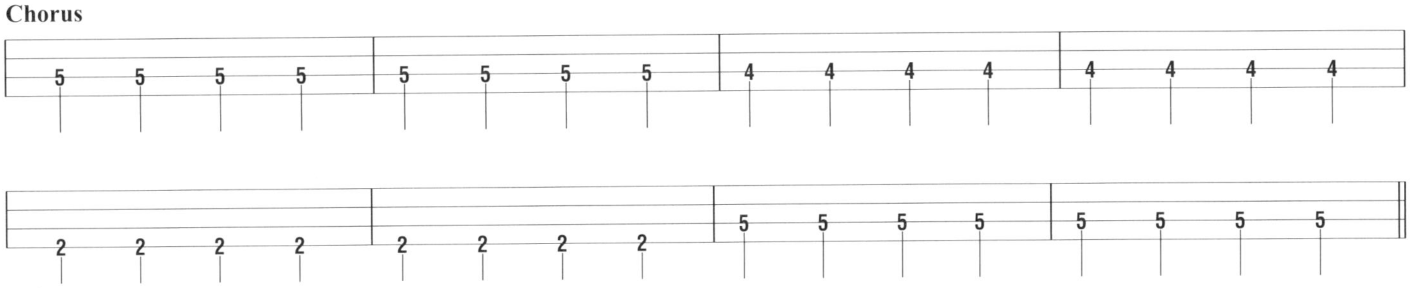

"YELLOW"

Words and Music by Guy Berryman, Jon Buckland, Will Champion and Chris Martin

Here's another tune by Coldplay where we'll use eighth notes to play through the progression.

Track 11

Verse

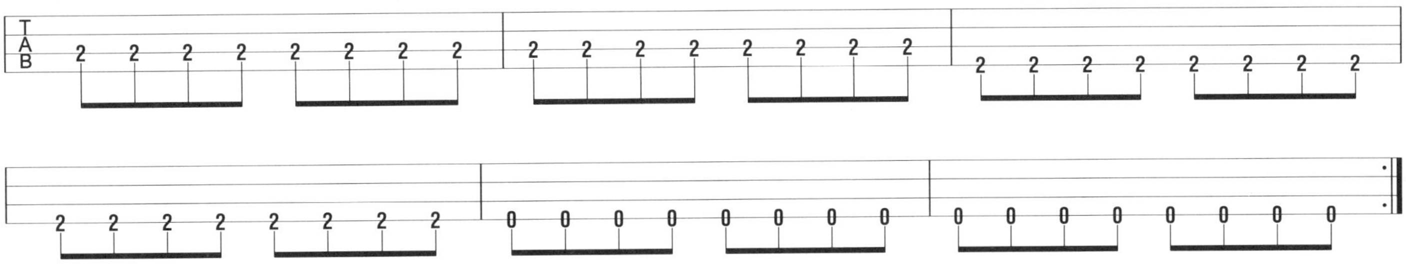

Chapter 3
Scales and Time Signatures

Basic Scales

So now that we know the basics of rhythms and how notes work and where they are, let's learn some of the foundational patterns, or scales, of music that will make it easy to create bass lines and play songs. *Scales* are a set of musical notes from which you can create melodies or harmonies easily. The first scale we're going to learn is the *major scale*. It's the foundational scale that makes it easier to learn all other scales you will encounter.

The Major Scale

Here is the C major scale on bass:

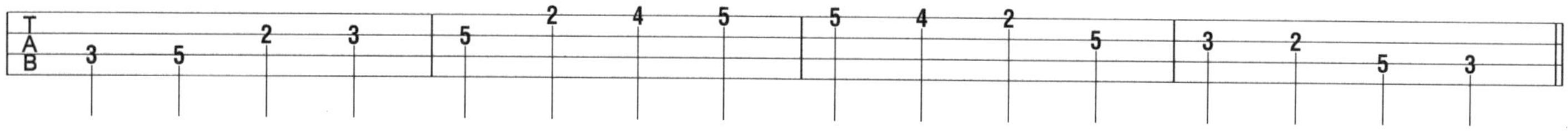

The notes of the C major scale are C–D–E–F–G–A–B. Note that we repeat the first note of the scale, one octave above where we started. This major scale pattern is the same when played at any place on the fretboard, but when you change the starting note, but keep the spacing the same, then the scale is named according to that particular starting note. For example, if you start this same pattern with the B note as the first note, or *root note*, it will be considered a B major scale.

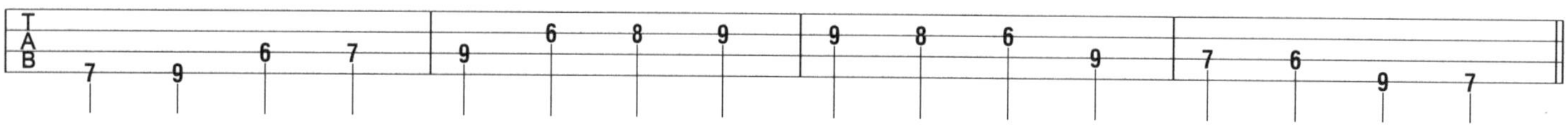

The notes of the B major scale are B–C#–D#–E–F#–G#–A#–B.

The Minor Scale

Now, before we learn the next pattern, we need to understand a very basic principle of *tonality*, or *key*, which is the difference between major sounds and others, such as the *minor scale*. The main difference between major and minor is that the third note of the scale (called the *3rd*) changes, depending on what sound you are going for. (The same can be applied to chords.) When you play a major scale or chord, you will play a *major 3rd*, which gives it a "bright" or "happy" sound. Here are the first five notes of the C major scale (C–D–E–F–G):

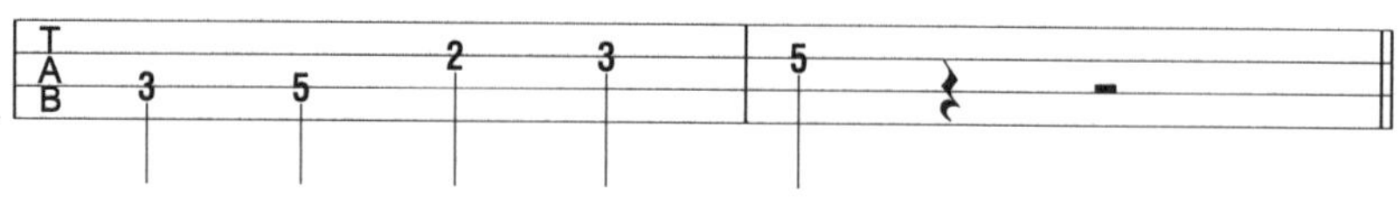

When you play a minor scale or chord, you will play a *minor 3rd* (sometimes called a *♭3rd* or *lowered 3rd*) which will give it a "dark" or "sad" sound. Here are the first five notes of the C minor scale (C–D–E♭–F–G):

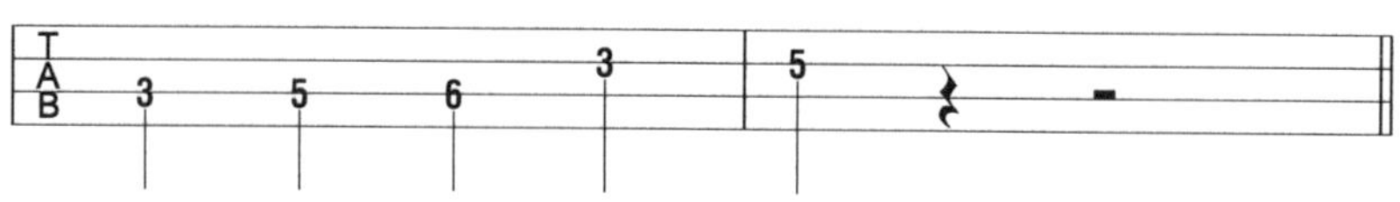

Here is the C minor scale in its entirety; the ascending notes are C–D–E♭–F–G–A♭–B♭–C:

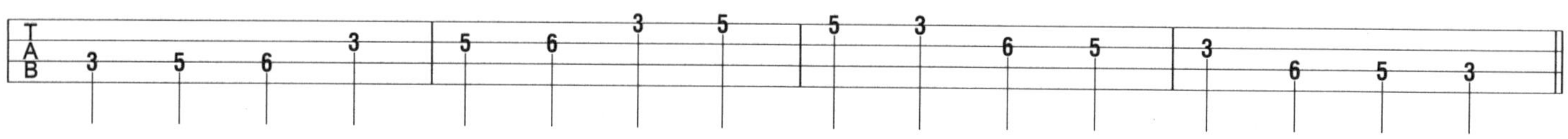

Once you get these patterns under your fingers, practice the following exercises to help you master them. In the end, you'll learn to play all of these patterns over the entire neck of the bass, from any spot you choose on the fretboard.

Major and Minor Scale Exercises

The following exercises have you playing each note twice, moving up and then down the scale. This is an excellent way for you to work on your right-hand technique, whether with fingerstyle or with a pick.

C Major Scale, Two Strokes per Note

Track 12

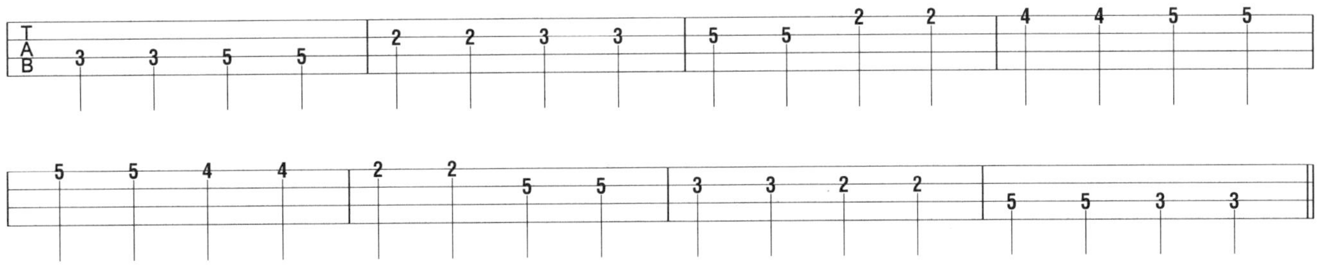

C Minor Scale, Two Strokes per Note

Track 13

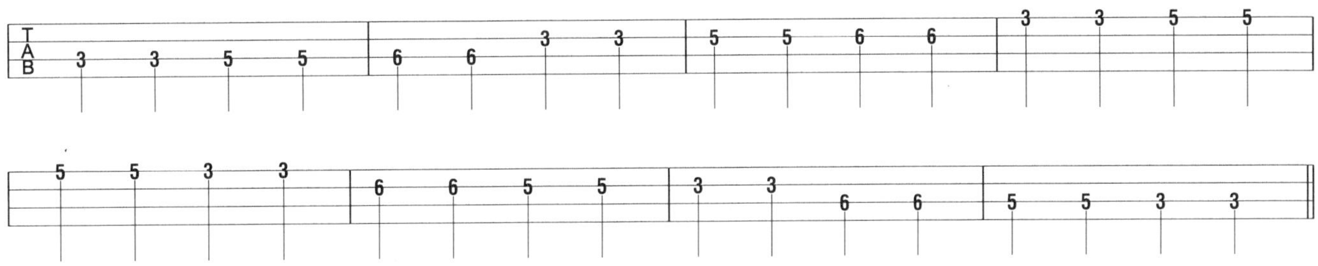

These exercises have you playing four-note groupings, moving up each scale degree and then back down.

C Major Scale, Groups of Four

Track 14

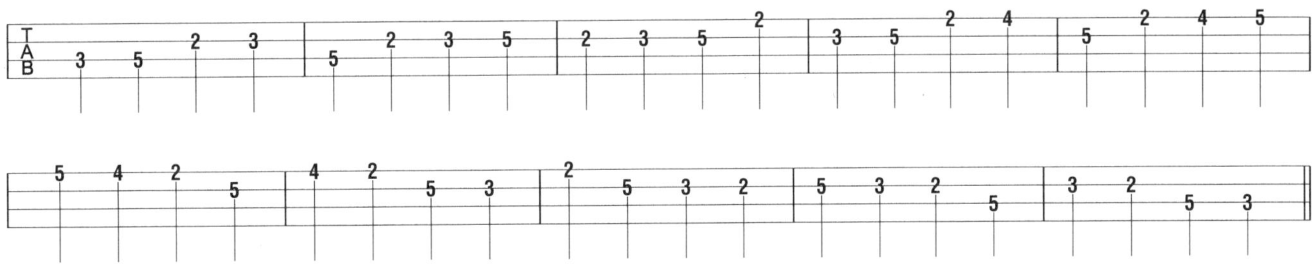

C Minor Scale, Groups of Four

Track 15

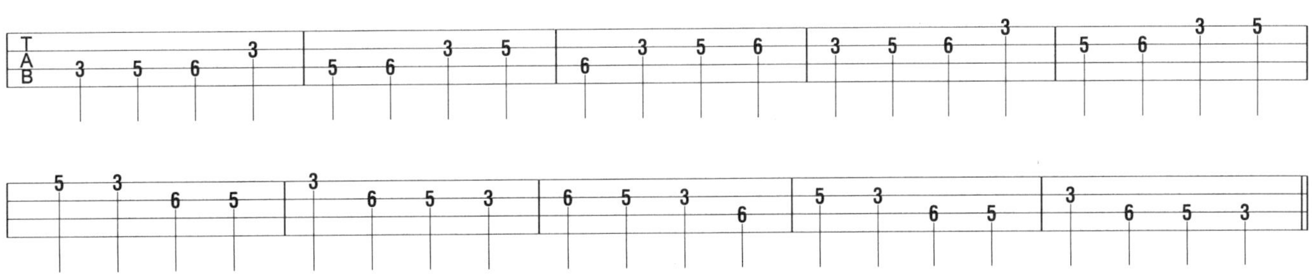

These exercises have you play the starting note of the scale, skip to the third, and then step down to the second, repeating the pattern to the end (1–3, 2–4, 3–5, etc.).

C Major Scale, Skip-Step

Track 16

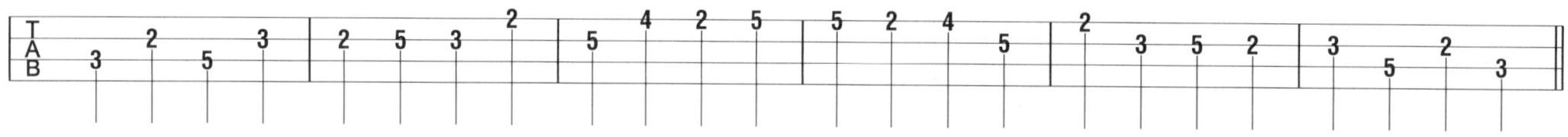

C Minor Scale, Skip-Step

Track 17

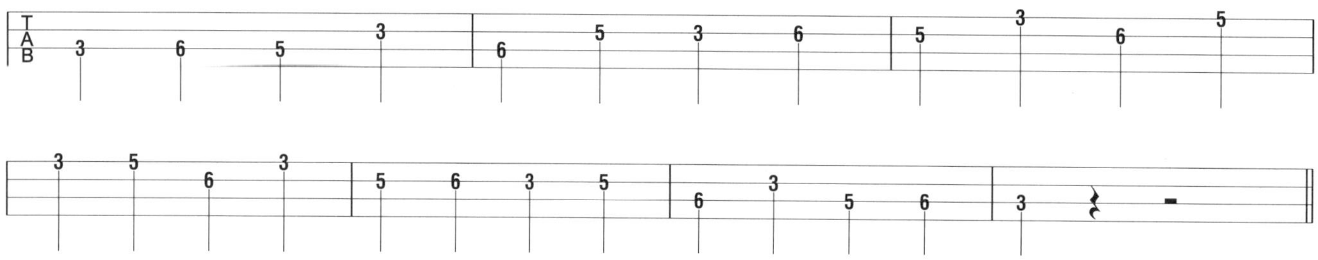

Time Signatures

Time signatures indicate how music is counted. When first reading a piece of music, or when a fellow musician gives you a verbal cue about the time signature, we instantly know how many beats are in a bar and which of our notes gets assigned to each beat. We've been playing exercises where one bar of music equals four beats, but the reason that it's four beats and not any other amount is indicated by the time signature.

4/4 Time

Here is the most common time signature you will encounter with most songs, 4/4:

$$\begin{matrix}4\\4\end{matrix}$$

The way this works is the top number indicates how many beats are in a bar, and the bottom number indicates which type of note gets the beat (just replace the top number with a "1" to determine this). In a bar of 4/4, there are four beats throughout, and the quarter note (1/4) gets the beat. You've played this next exercise previously, but here, the time signature has been added.

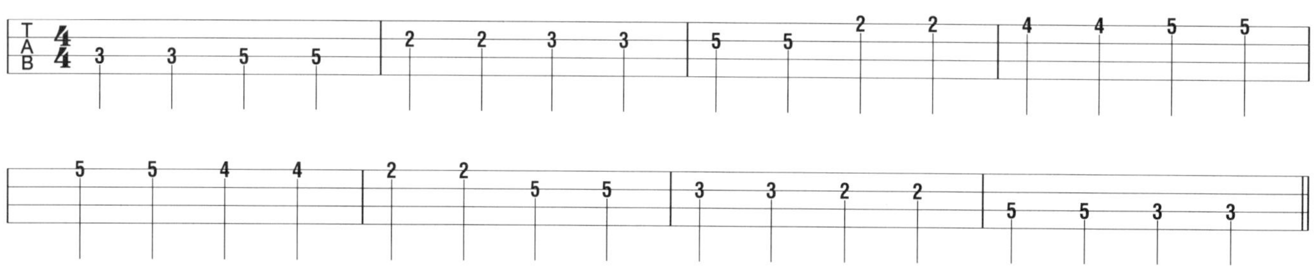

Here are a few popular songs that are in 4/4:

- "Dear Marie" by John Mayer
- "Paradise" by Coldplay
- "Rolling in the Deep" by Adele

Now, 4/4 isn't the only time signature that's used in music around the world. Let's check out another common time signature: 6/8.

6/8 Time

Now, let's say a song is in 6/8—what does that mean? All we have to do is count six beats instead of four, and we'll assign the eighth note to each beat. Here's an example of how a phrase of music in 6/8 is organized.

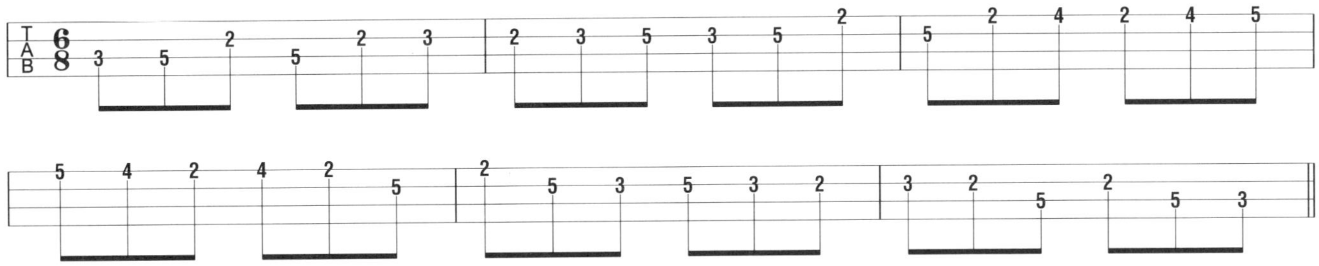

Here are a few popular songs that are in 6/8:

- "We Are the Champions" by Queen
- "Perfect" by Ed Sheeran
- "A Thousand Years" by Christina Perri

There are several other types of time signatures, some common and others that are not as common in popular music. This would include 3/4 and 2/4, and 5/4 and 7/8, respectively.

If you don't have music in front of you and the bandleader doesn't tell you the time signature of the song you're playing, you can find out what time signature a song is in by counting the beats as the song plays. It's all about the feel and where the emphasis is placed. If you get off the rhythm, or if you start repeating in weird places in the song, then that means you're probably not referencing the correct time signature.

Chapter 4

Song Structure and Dynamics

Basic Song Structure

How is a song structured? When listening to any song, our ears hear them in sections, even if we don't know what they are. This makes up what we call *form*.

Here are the typical common sections of a song:

- **Intro**: An instrumental or musical section that starts a song.
- **Verse**: Usually, the first section that features singing where the singer starts to tell the story of a song, setting up the main idea, or chorus.
- **Chorus**: The main thought or concept of a song; it's where most other sections lead to in the course of a song.
- **Bridge**: A contrasting section set apart from the others in melody and harmony; it functions as the takeaway point of a song or instrumental break.
- **End**: The final section of a song that works similarly to an intro.

Here are some other sections that you may encounter:

- **Pre-Chorus**: A section featuring a melody or thought that is different than the verse, and occurs right before the chorus.
- **Instrumental**: A musical break with no lyrics; it functions to help transition between the chorus and another following section.
- **Tag**: The catchy part of a song that usually happens after the chorus; it's usually repeated for emphasis.
- **Solo**: A section where an instrument plays a solo for the duration of another given section, usually over the same chords.

TOOLBOX

Some simple ways to hear these sections when listening to a song is by identifying melodies and lyrics that are repeated. So when listening to find song sections, listen if the singer repeats a melody or lyric again, or if an instrument or other musical element repeats a melody. Understanding the structure of a song and where the sections are within it makes learning, playing, and creating music a breeze. Below, I've created a chart to help you see and understand one of the most popular song structures you will hear.

Intro → Verse → Chorus → Verse → Chorus → Bridge → Chorus → End

Song Structure Quiz

Below is a list of songs to quiz yourself to see if you can hear and identify which of the popular song structures are used in each of them. (The answers are located in the Appendix at the end of this book.)

- "Hollow" by Tori Kelly
- "Blank Space" by Taylor Swift
- "Let It Go" by James Bay
- "Keep Your Head Up" by Andy Grammer
- "Don't Start Now" by Dua Lipa
- "Friends in Low Places" by Garth Brooks
- "Love Me Now" by John Legend
- "Sucker" by Jonas Brothers
- "Waiting on the World to Change" by John Mayer

Dynamics

When listening to any song, there are times where music is loud, soft, or somewhere in the middle; this is what we call *dynamics*. Learning dynamics can help make what you play be more effective to the listening experience in terms of intensity and mood. Although getting the notes right is half the battle, knowing how loud or soft to play them is the other half, equally important to making the entire performance sound good.

This concept on bass is very simple; all we have to do is listen. The best way to get better at this is listening to different types of songs that use a wide range of different dynamics and learning what those dynamics are (loud, medium, or soft).

TOOLBOX

In music theory, these dynamics are labeled like this:

- ***pp***: *pianissimo*, meaning "very soft"
- ***p***: *piano*, meaning "soft"
- ***mp***: *mezzo piano*, meaning "medium soft"
- ***mf***: *mezzo forte*, meaning "medium loud"
- ***f***: *forte*, meaning "loud"
- ***ff***: *fortissimo*, meaning "very loud"
- ***fff***: *fortississimo* (sometimes called *triple forte*), meaning "even louder"

The chart in the ToolBox above shows specific ways of identifying dynamics. Sometimes, it can be overwhelming to understand within the music you regularly hear. To simplify it, a really effective way to learn dynamics is to put them into three categories:

- Loud
- Medium
- Soft

By simplifying what you hear, these three dynamic categories will help you understand the general volume of sound in music while giving you space to be able to have your own interpretation.

To help develop your ear to hearing these dynamic ranges, listen to the same list of songs that you did before, but this time, identify what dynamic range each section is (loud, medium, or soft). You may hear some general nuances that happen in most songs, such as verses are usually medium or soft and that choruses are usually loud towards the end of a song, etc. Quiz yourself on all of these, and it will strengthen your ability to hear and create music effectively.

Chapter 5
Chord Charts

Chord charts are a printed collection of chords aligned above the lyrics of a song that allow note- or chord-playing instruments to learn and follow songs easily. You will see these types of charts in several performance environments; they're very common in churches.

Chord charts lean more to chord-heavy instruments, but as bass players, we need to know how to identify and read them so that we are never unaware of what we need to play. Most of the time, chord charts look like this:

"AMAZING GRACE"
Traditional American Melody
Words by John Newton

Verse 1

```
 C                F         C
Amazing grace how sweet the sound

                         G
That saved a wretch like me

  C                   F       C
I once was lost but now am found

    Am        G6     F   C
Was blind but now I see
```

Verse 2

```
      C                    F        C
'Twas grace that taught my heart to fear

                     G
And grace my fears relieved

     C                 F       C
How precious did that grace appear

    Am     G6     F        C
The hour I first believed
```

Verse 3

```
     C                    F        C
When we've been there ten thousand years

                      G
Bright shining as the sun

      C                 F          C
We've no less days to sing God's praise

      Am        G6    F    C
Than when we'd first begun
```

Chord charts like the one shown previously aren't the only ones you'll run into. Here's a similar format, called a *rhythm chart*, that looks like this. (This is also called *slash notation*; the slashes simply mean to compose your own rhythm—it just needs to fit the groove and mood.)

"AMAZING GRACE"

Traditional American Melody

Words by John Newton

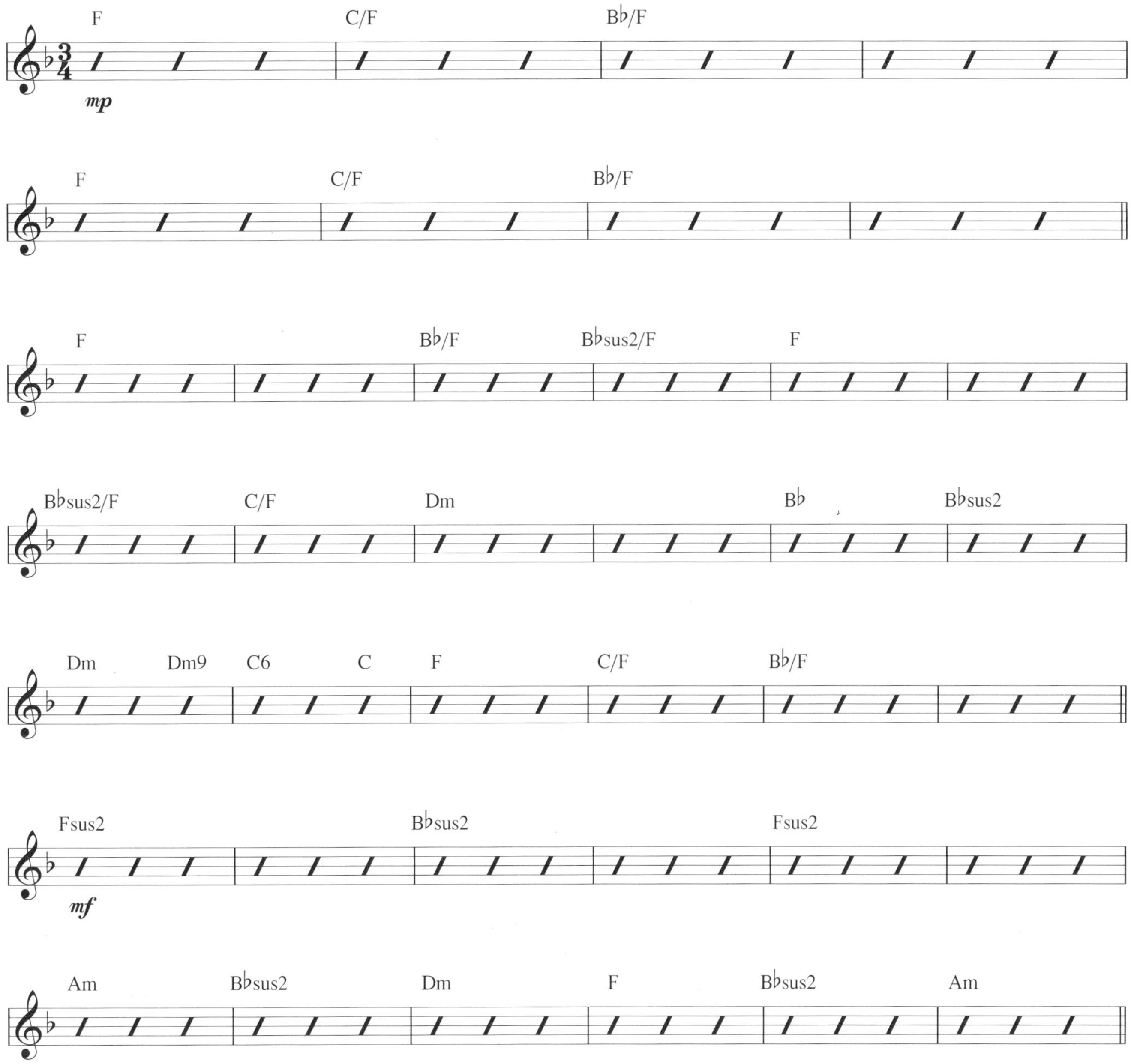

Both of these charts are similar because they use chords as a way of referencing the progressions and timing of songs. The way that we read this on bass is by reading the *root* of each chord. The root of a chord is what gives a chord its name. For example, the root of an F chord is, well F! On bass, we simply read the note name that appears in the chord symbol and play the corresponding pitch on the fretboard.

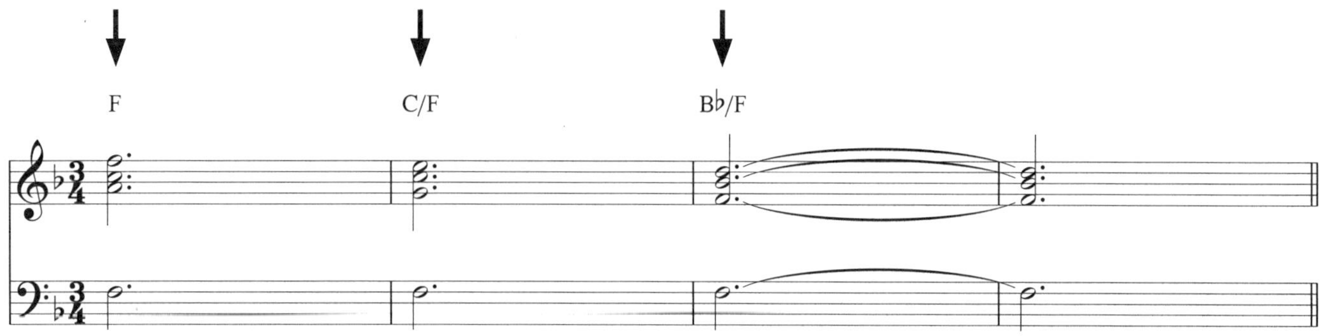

Now, sometimes this can be different if there is a *split chord* (sometimes called a *slash chord*).

A split chord is just a way of rearranging a chord where the bottom note differs from the root. Remember, it's our job as bass players to play those foundational notes, and sometimes, the music calls for notes other than the root to be played in the lowest register. So when you see split chords written horizontally like this...

C/E ←

...the lowest-sounding note (the one you play) will be the one on the right. If you see the symbol arranged like this...

C
E ←

...the note you play will be the one at the bottom.

The next question you may ask is, "When do I actually play the note?" A rhythm chart is pretty straightforward; you can see the exact place within the bar where the chords change. However, a chord chart with only lyrics and chord symbols can be tricky. On chord charts, the placement is usually indicated by what lyric or syllable the chord is over.

```
    Am      G6    F   C
Was blind but now I see
    ↑       ↑     ↑
```

Sometimes, the timing on chord charts can be incorrect, depending on the writer of the chart. A simple way to check if it's incorrectly written is to sing with the song as you play, or listen to the lyrics as the music plays to see if they match or not.

To practice this more, here are a few chord charts of songs for you to play through.

"DEAR MARIE"

Words and Music by John Mayer

Verse 1

```
A
Dear Marie,

D                                   A
Tell me what it was I was I used to be?

         D
Oh, dear Marie,

                                    A
Tell me what it was I was I used to be?

              E                            D                          A
And if you're further up the road, can you show me what I still can't see?
```

Verse 2

```
A
Remember me?

        D                                  A
I'm the boy you used to love when you were fifteen.

         D
Remember me?

                                           A
I'm the boy you used to love when you were fifteen.

      E                              D           A
Now I wonder what you think when you see me in a magazine.
```

Verse 3

```
             A
From time to time

        D                           A
I'll go looking for your photograph online.

                  D
From time to time

                                    A
I'll go looking for your photograph online.

         E               D                  A
But some county judge in Ohio is all I ever find.
```

"THINKING OUT LOUD"

Words and Music by Ed Sheeran and Amy Wadge

Verse 1

C C/E F G
When your legs don't work like they used to before

C C/E F G
And I can't sweep you off of your feet.

C C/E F G
Will your mouth still remember the taste of my love?

C C/E F G
Will your eyes still smile from your cheeks?

Pre-Chorus 1

C C/E F G C C/E F G
And darling I will be loving you till we're seventy.

C C/E F G C C/E
And baby my heart could still fall as hard at twenty-three.

F G Dm G C
And I'm thinking 'bout how people fall in love in mysterious ways,

Dm G
Maybe just the touch of a hand.

Dm G Am
Well me, I fall in love with you every single day

Dm G
And I just wanna tell you,

Chorus

N.C. C C/E
So honey now

F G C C/E
Take me into your loving arms,

F G C C/E
Kiss me under the light of a thousand stars,

F G C C/E
Place your head on my beating heart.

F G
I'm thinking out loud

Am G F C/E Dm G C
That maybe we found love right where we are.

Verse 2

C C/E F G
When my hair's all but gone and memory fades

C C/E F G
And the crowds don't remember my name.

C C/E F G
When my hands don't play the strings the same way,

C C/E F G
I know you will still love me the same.

Pre-Chorus 2

C C/E F G C C/E F G
'Cause honey your soul could never grow old; it's evergreen,

C C/E F G C C/E
And, baby, your smile's forever in my mind and memory.

F G Dm G C
I'm thinking 'bout how people fall in love in mysterious ways,

Dm G
And maybe it's all part of a plan.

Dm G Am
Well, I'll just keep on making the same mistakes

Dm G
Hoping that you'll understand.

Chorus 2

N.C. C C/E
That, baby, now,

F G C C/E
Take me into your loving arms,

F G C C/E
Kiss me under the light of a thousand stars,

F G C C/E
Place your head on my beating heart.

F G
I'm thinking out loud

Am G F C/E Dm G C
And maybe we found love right where we are.

Instrumental

```
     C      C/E      F      G

     C      C/E      F      G

     C      C/E      F      G

     C      C/E      F      G
```

Chorus 3

```
(G)              C      C/E
 So,  baby,  now,

 F   G                               C       C/E
     Take  me  into  your  loving  arms,

 F   G                                   C        C/E
     Kiss me  under  the  light  of  a  thousand  stars,

   F        G                                         C       C/E
Oh, darling, place  your  head  on  my  beating  heart.

                    F G
I'm   thinking  out  loud,

                Am  G      F     C/E    Dm    G    C
And  maybe  we  found  love  right  where  we  are.
```

Outro

```
                Am    G    F     C/E    Dm    G    C
That  maybe  we  found  love  right  where  we  are.

             Am   G     F     C/E   Dm    G    C
Oh, baby,  we  found  love  right  where  we  are.

        Am   G     F    C/E   Dm     G   C
And  we  found  love  right  where  we  are.
```

"ALL OF ME"

Words and Music by John Stephens and Toby Gad

Verse 1

Em   Cmaj7   G
What would I do without your smart mouth,

D   Em
Drawing me in, and you kicking me out?

C   G   D   Em
Got my head spinning, no kidding, I can't pin you down.

Cmaj7   G
What's going on in that beautiful mind?

D   Em
I'm on your magical mystery ride,

Cadd9   G   D   Am
And I'm so dizzy, don't know what hit me, but I'll be alright.

Pre-Chorus 1

Am   G
My head's under water,

D   Am
But I'm breathing fine.

G   D
You're crazy and I'm out of my mind.

Chorus

G
'Cause all of me

Em(add9)
Loves all of you;

Am/C
Love your curves and all your edges,

C/D   D
All your perfect imperfections.

G
Give your all to me;

Em(add9)
I'll give my all to you.

Am/C
You're my end and my beginning;

```
     C/D              D
Even when I lose, I'm winning.

                Em  C     G  Dadd9
'Cause I give you all, all of me,

                Em  C     G  Dadd9
And you give me all, all of you.
```

Verse 2

```
Em      C                      G
How many times do I have to tell you

                 D                    Em
Even when you're crying you're beautiful, too.

              C          G          D                    Em
The world is beating you down; I'm around through every mood.

           C                  G
You're my downfall, you're my muse,

              D                      Em
My worst distraction, my rhythm and blues.

               C         G        D           Am
I can't stop singing, it's ringing in my head for you.
```

Pre-Chorus 2

```
  Am           G
My head's under water,

  D          Am
But I'm breathing fine.

               G          D
You're crazy and I'm out of my mind.
```

Chorus

```
      G
'Cause all of me

     Em(add9)
Loves all of you;

           Am/C
Love your curves and all your edges,

           C/D    D
All your perfect imperfections.

           G
Give your all to me;
```

Am/C
You're my end and my beginning;

C/D **D**
Even when I lose, I'm winning.

Em C G Dadd9
'Cause I give you all, all of me,

Em C G Dadd9
And you give me all, all of you.

Pre-Chorus 3

Am G
Cards on the table,

D Am(add9)
We're both showing hearts,

Am G D
Risking it all, though it's hard.

Chorus

G
'Cause all of me

Em(add9)
Loves all of you;

Am/C
Love your curves and all your edges,

C/D D
All your perfect imperfections.

G
Give your all to me;

Em(add9)
I'll give my all to you.

Am/C
You're my end and my beginning;

C/D D
Even when I lose, I'm winning.

Em C G Dadd9
'Cause I give you all, all of me,

Em C G Dadd9
And you give me all, all of you.

Outro

Em C G Dadd9
I give you all, all of me,

Em C G Dadd9
And you give me all, all of you.

Chapter 6

Developing Speed and Strength

One of the fastest ways to get yourself playing bass is by gaining speed, strength, and dexterity in your hands. Being the fastest bass player in the world is not the purpose of this section, but instead, it's to help you be the most accurate and cleanest bass player. My rule of thumb is speed = accuracy.

Not all exercises are melodic. Some exercises are exactly that—exercises. Most of the time, when you go to the gym, you are doing exercises like arm curls, bench press, etc. But on a normal day, how often are you doing those exact motions? Probably not very often, but it hasn't stopped bodybuilders from gaining strength through those exercises. We must have the mindset that we have exercises to build actual strength versus melodic exercises you can put into your playing. So for those "workout" days, here are three effective speed and strength exercises that will help you grow fast in your technical facility and melodic sensibility.

Non-Melodic Speed Exercises for Right and Left Hands

Track 18

Track 19

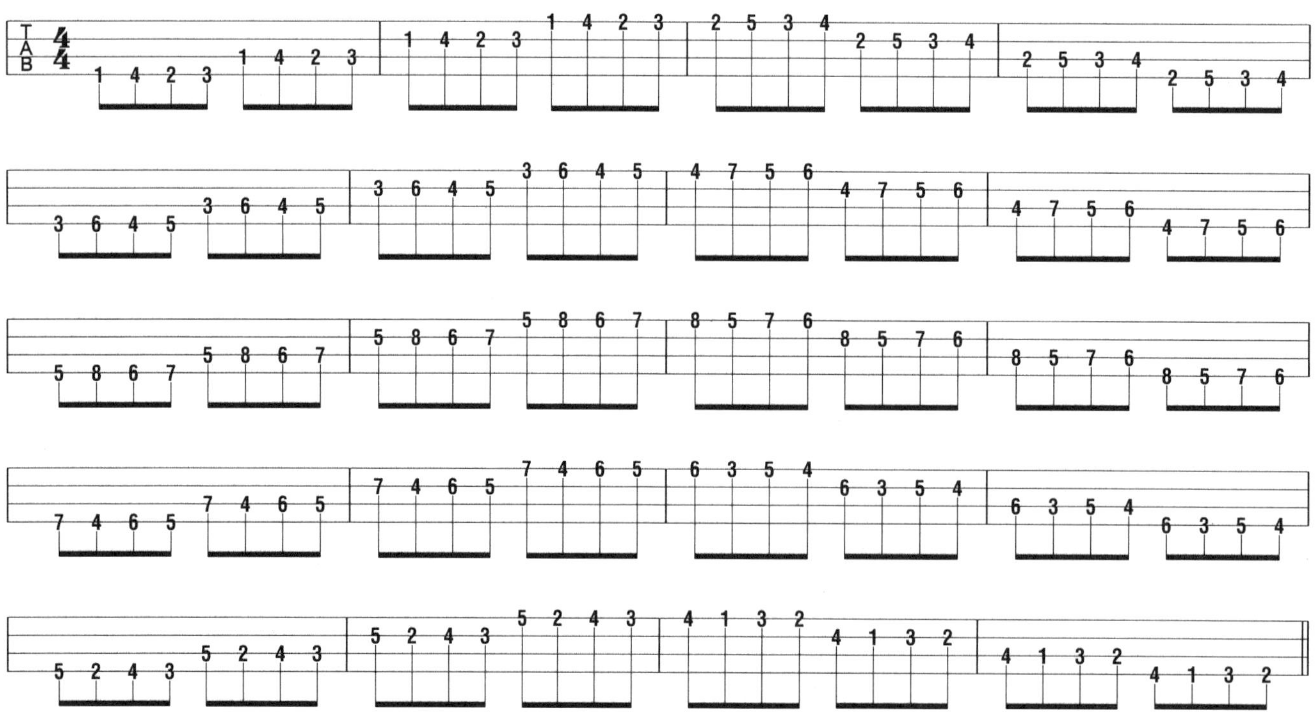

Track 20

Now, let's try some exercises that are a bit more melodic.

Melodic Speed Exercises for Right and Left Hands

Track 21

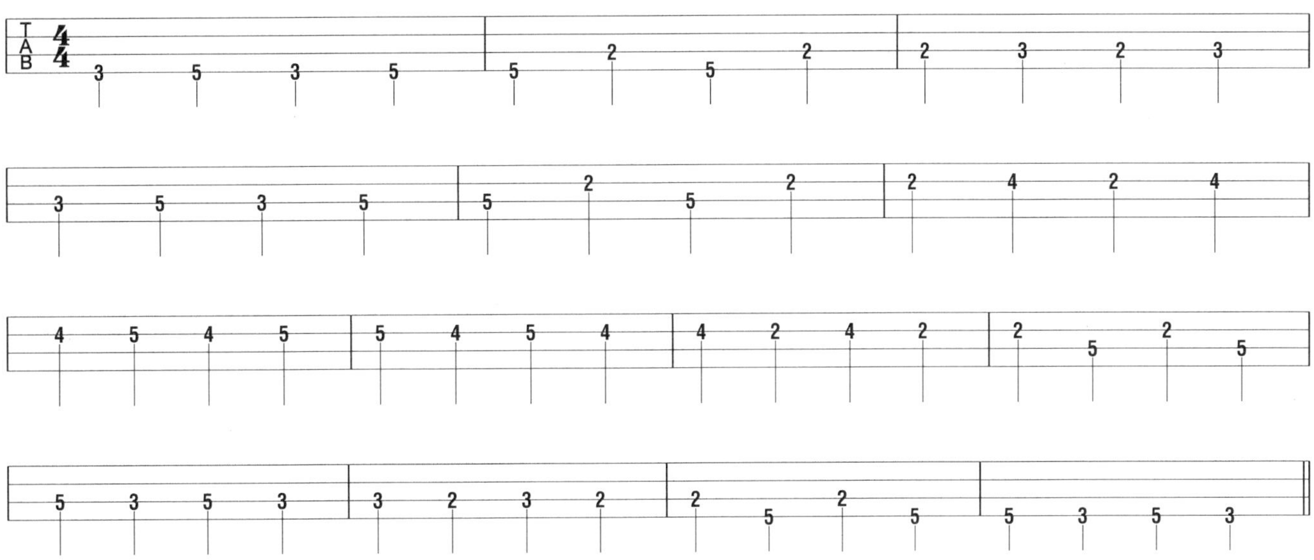

Track 22

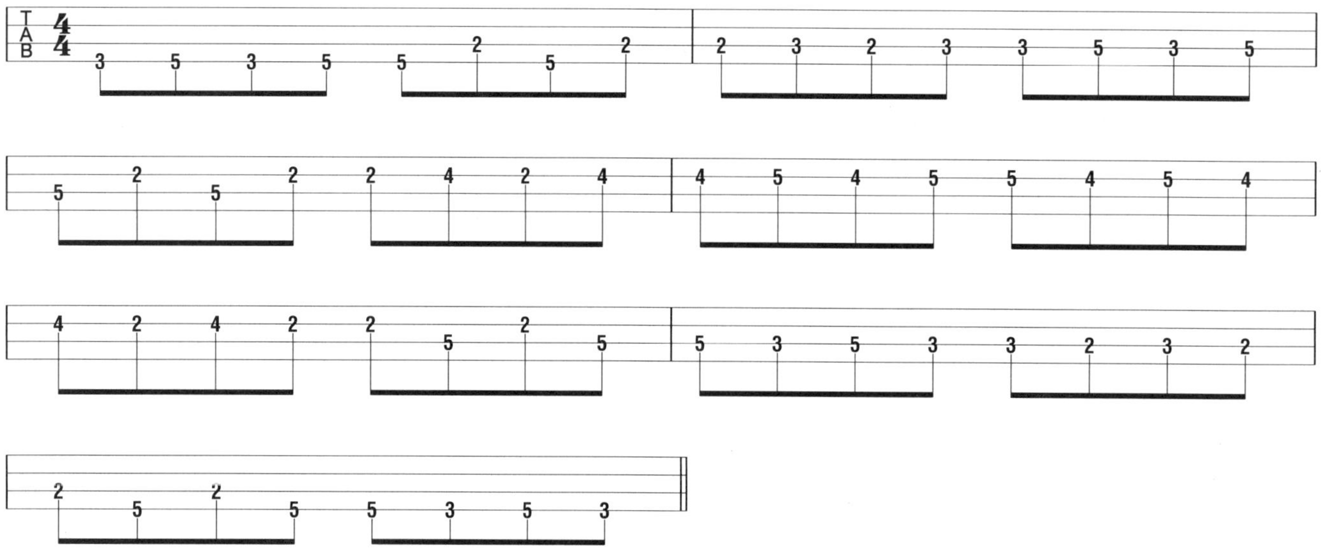

Track 23

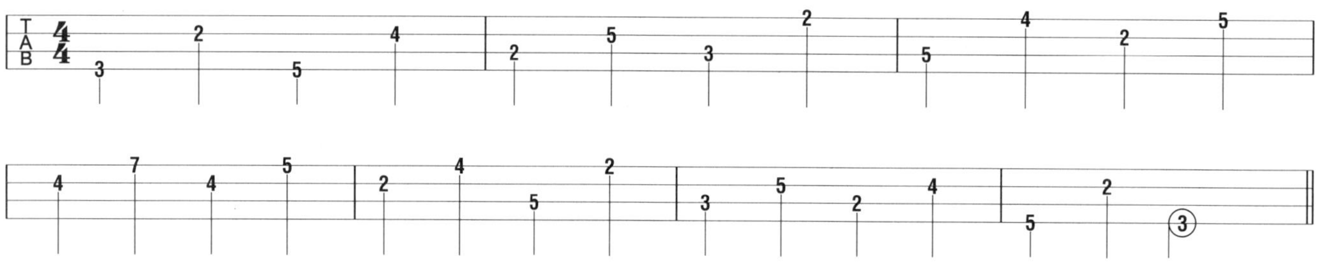

Track 24

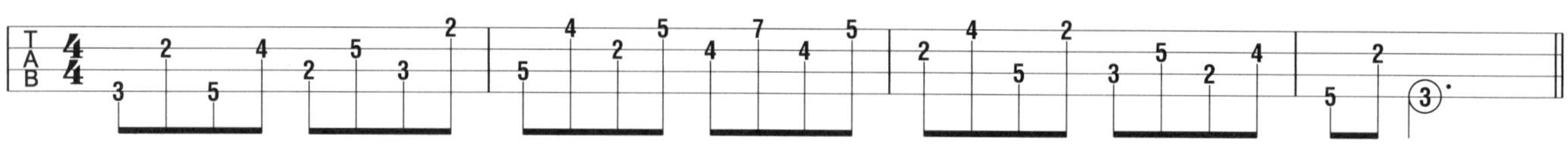

To get the most out of these exercises, play each of these patterns all the way up through the G string and then move them up a fret and go backwards back to the E string until you get to the 12th fret of your bass. If you want an extra workout, you can go backwards down the neck the same way.

TOOLBOX

A useful tool you can use to help improve your speed is called a *metronome*. A metronome is a device that provides a beat/click that can range from simple pulses to customized time signatures, all with adjustable speeds.

If you want to stretch or increase your speed, play with a metronome and increase the beats per minute (bpm) when your hands start to feel comfortable with the patterns. I recommend to start around 60 bpm and increase it in increments of 5–10 bpm every time you want to challenge yourself further.

Chapter 7
Exploring New Articulations

Muting

Palm muting is a technique that is used on bass to dampen the volume and change the tone of the strings when playing. The reason why many bass players use this technique is because it can make an electric bass sound like an upright bass, and it can sound really round and deep when played correctly. Muting can be created a couple of different ways. First, you can lay the fleshy part of the palm of your right hand on the bridge of the bass, like this:

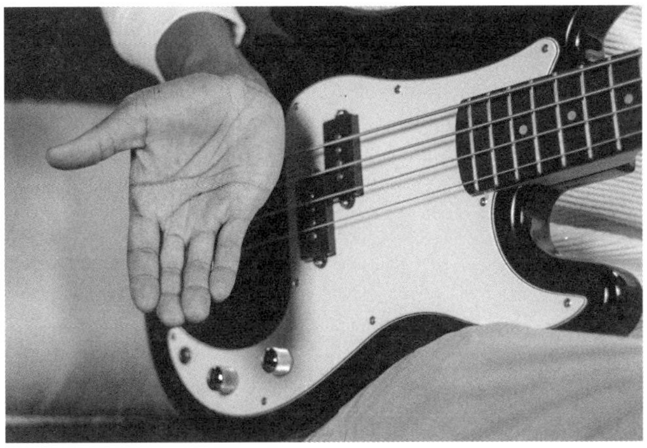

When muting with your right hand, use the side of your thumb to now pluck the strings.

Now, the other way of achieving a muted sound is to use the fingers of your left hand that aren't holding down any strings.

Using your left hand to mute allows you to have more attack from your right hand and play faster, but your left hand has to do a little more work.

Getting proficient in these two muting techniques will help you achieve a lot of tones that you hear on songs like "What's Going On" by Marvin Gaye or "I Don't Trust Myself" by John Mayer. To get your hands familiar with these techniques, here is a set of exercises to practice both types of muting techniques. The best way to practice this is to first learn all of the bass lines with fingerstyle plucking, then use right- and left-hand muting to get your hands familiar with the techniques.

Muting Exercises

Track 25

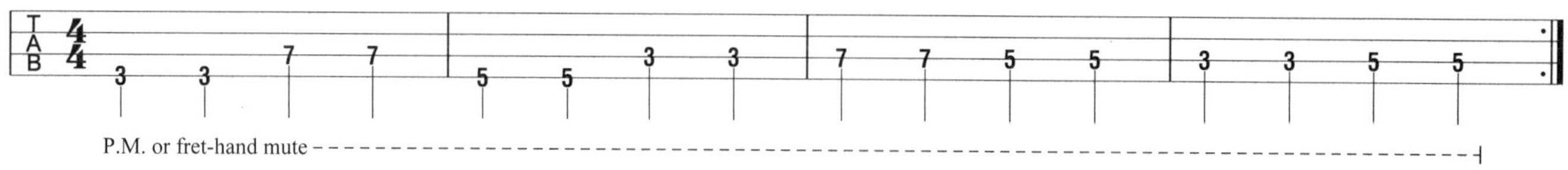

Track 26

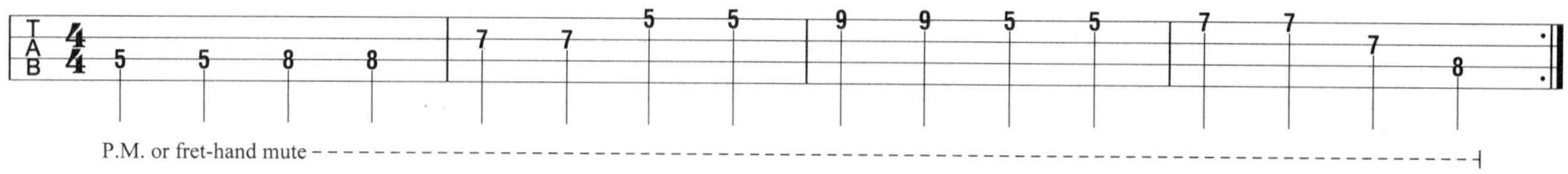

Track 27

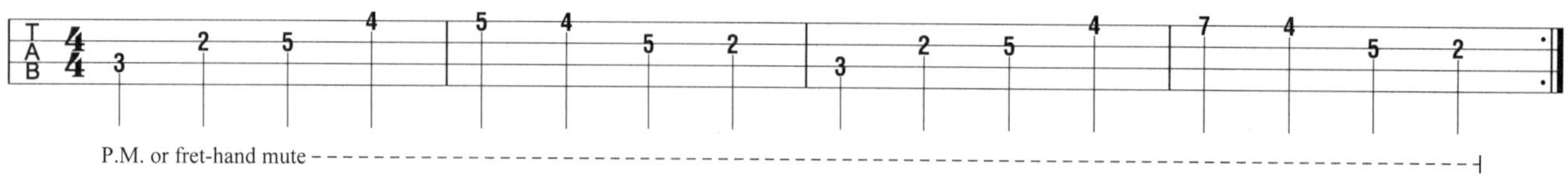

Track 28

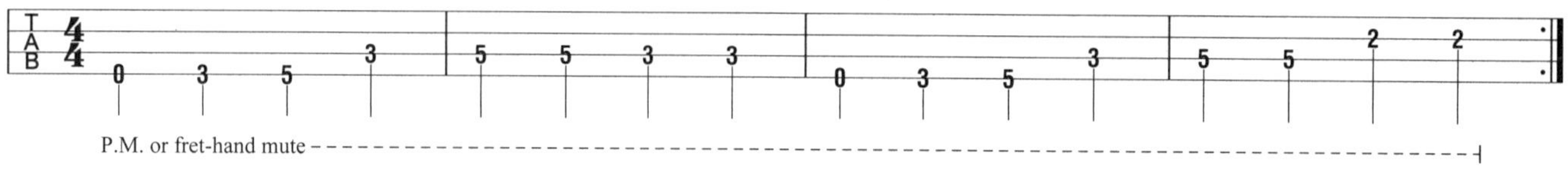

Track 29

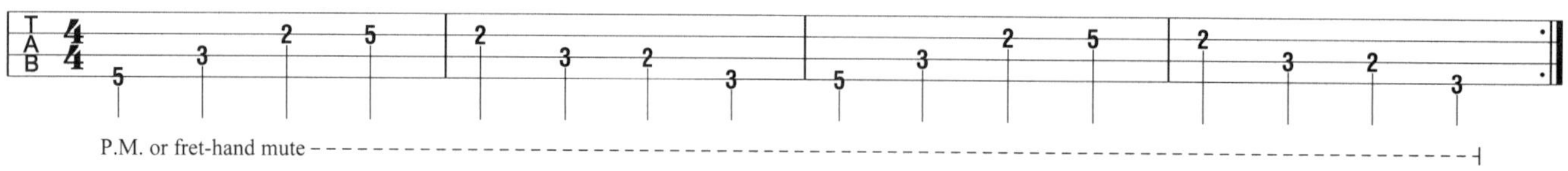

Track 30

Chapter 8

Introducing Intervals and Chords

It's time to explore *intervals*! An interval is the distance between two notes, and as bass players, we can use them to our advantage. Indeed, you've already played intervals in the previous sections of the book, but now, we'll dive into how they work to make our playing more effective. In this chapter, we'll talk about 3rds and octaves.

Playing Octaves

Now, we mentioned *octaves* (higher and lower pitches of a singular musical note) in Chapter 2, but here, we're going to explore them in more depth. If you have ever listened to '70s disco or funk music, you most likely have heard octaves played in bass lines. Octaves have a very distinct sound that, once you hear it, you most likely won't forget it. Songs like "YMCA" by the Village People use octaves in the bass to great effect.

For example, if you play a C note on the A string, then played a C note on the G string, you would be playing the higher octave of that C note. Basically, what you are doing is finding the higher and lower sounds of the same note. Finding your octaves on bass is actually very easy when you follow this simple octave rule.

The 2x2 Rule

To find the upper octave of any note on the bass, go up two frets and down two strings—the same is true in reverse to find a lower octave.

Octaves are used in almost every genre of music, but they are played with different techniques to connect them in more interesting ways: plucked and sliding.

Plucked Octaves

This method of playing octaves is primarily what you hear when you hear disco, funk, pop, etc. This is achieved through plucking a low octave and high octave like they are walking. To get this sound, you have to pluck with your right-hand index finger on the lowest sounding note and your middle finger on the octave above.

To practice and master this technique, here are some bass lines that utilize the plucked octave technique.

Track 31

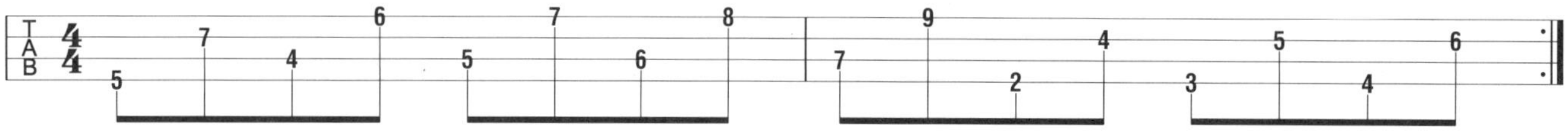

Track 32

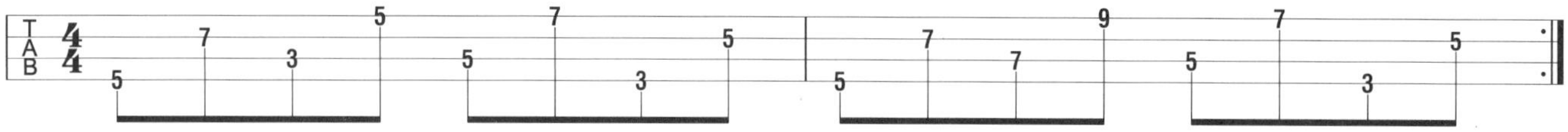

Track 33

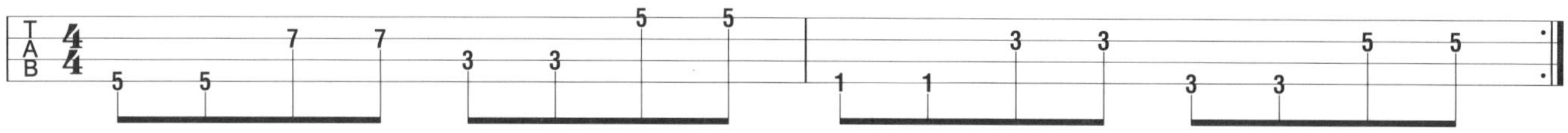

Track 34

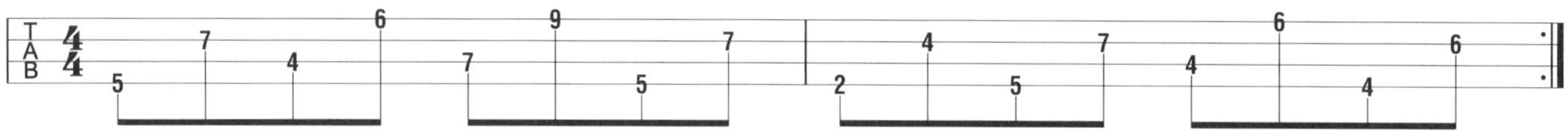

Track 35

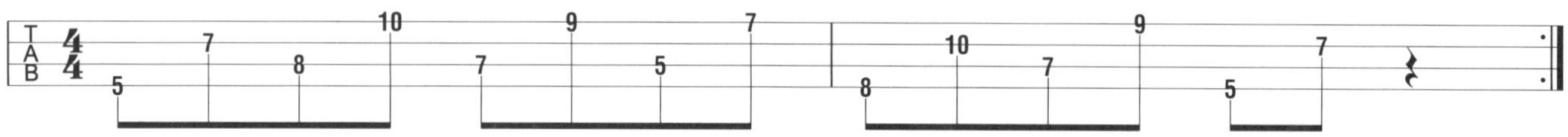

Sliding Octaves

The next method of using octaves is through *sliding*, which you will often hear in rock, CCM, pop, etc. Sliding is where you press down a left-hand finger below your target note and then move your hand to the target note. (We'll cover this more in-depth in Chapter 9.)

By using this technique, you can give more interest to your octave playing, rather than just going straight to them, such as the plucked method.

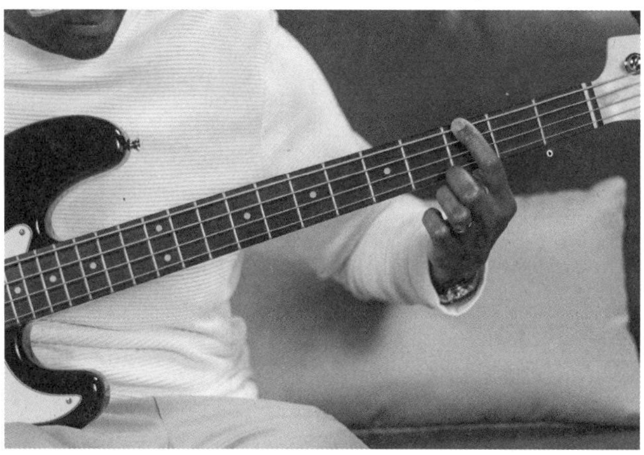

To play this technique, just place your finger on C on the A string, third fret, and slide up to the higher octave of C which is on the 15th fret of the same string. (Be sure to keep your fretting finger on the fretboard and string as you slide.)

A slide is indicated by this:

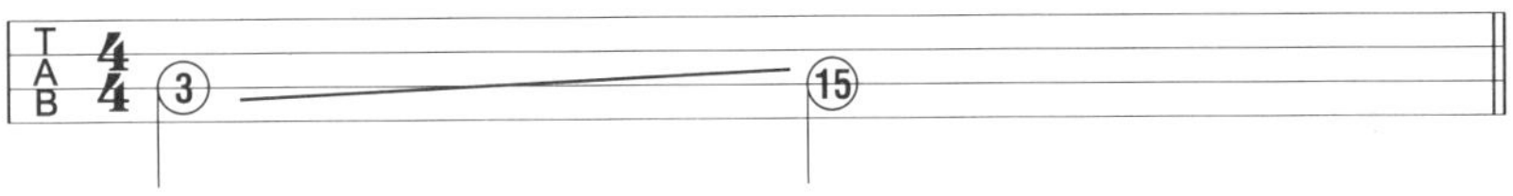

Here are some bass lines to practice this technique. Some of these lines end with a descending slide to close out with a bit of style, but others show you how to cleanly end a phrase without a slide.

Track 36

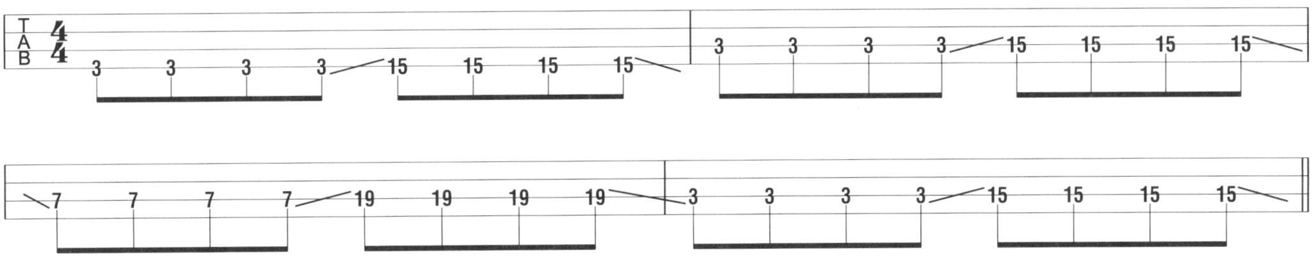

Track 37

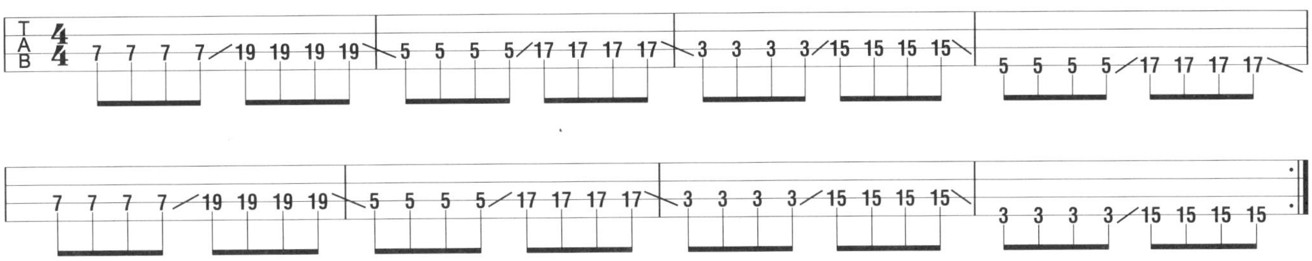

Track 38

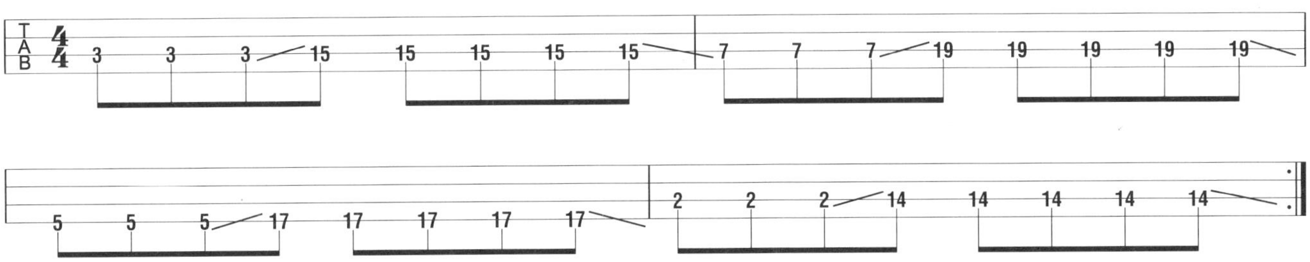

Track 39

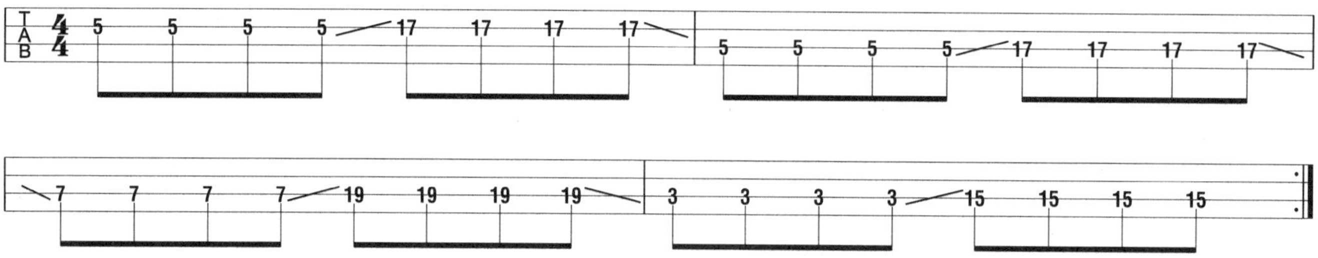

Playing 3rds

Bass players are usually relegated to playing single notes when creating bass lines, but after a while, most bass players want to spice up their single-note lines by adding chords. Chords are defined as multiple notes played simultaneously that create harmony. In the previous chapters of this book, we've understood chords to be played by other instruments, such as piano and guitar. As bass players, our main job is to keep rhythm and play the bass line, but a way that we can spice up our lines without taking away from them is by using 3rds. These are two-note chords (technically, *dyads*) that are easy to play and add to the bass without playing as many notes as the piano or guitar player. These intervals make up larger chords called *triads* (more on this in Chapter 13), that range from major to minor, dominant to diminished, and everything in between. Despite all these types, they're all made from two essential types of 3rds: the major 3rd and the minor 3rd.

The Major 3rd

When explaining chords and major/minor concepts, I will be referencing the major scale to identify which notes to target. To create a major 3rd, all you need to do is play the first note of the major scale and the third note of the major scale. For example, to play a major 3rd from C, you would play the C and an E above it.

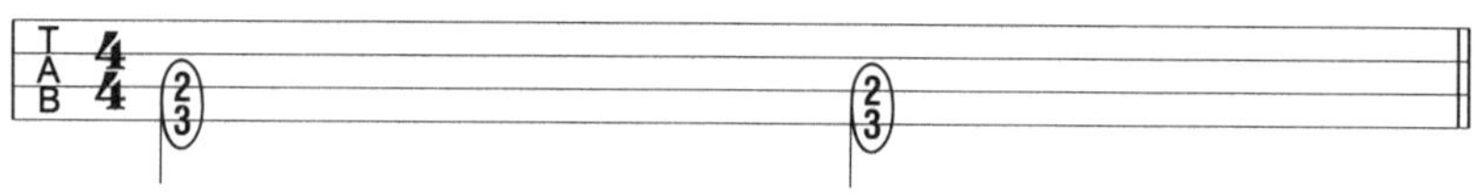

But when you play these notes at the same time, they may sound too "muddy." To fix this, we would need to move our E note up an octave to a higher E note. (This technically creates a *10th* interval, or an octave plus a 3rd.)

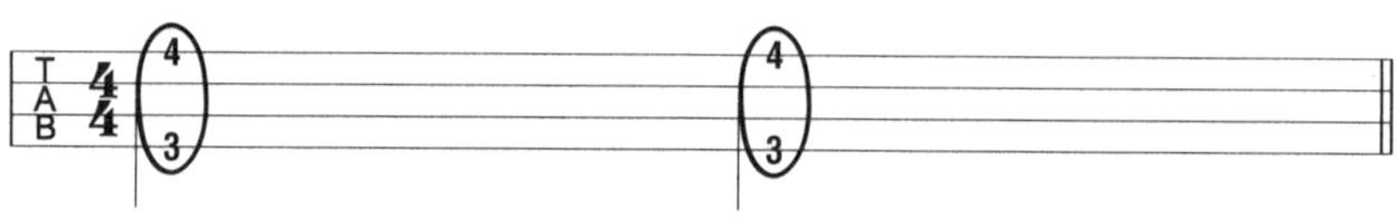

On your right hand, you can pluck with your index and middle finger.

Or, you can use your thumb and middle finger. Whichever pair you feel most comfortable with is the way to go!

The Minor 3rd

Finding a minor 3rd is almost exactly the same as finding a major 3rd. The only difference is the third note of the major scale goes down one fret to become a ♭3rd.

That's it! Just apply the other rules used in the major 3rd, such as playing the 3rd an octave higher and using the two plucking methods.

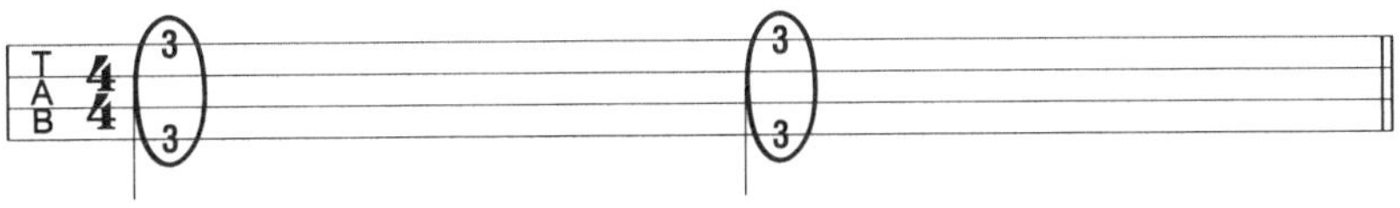

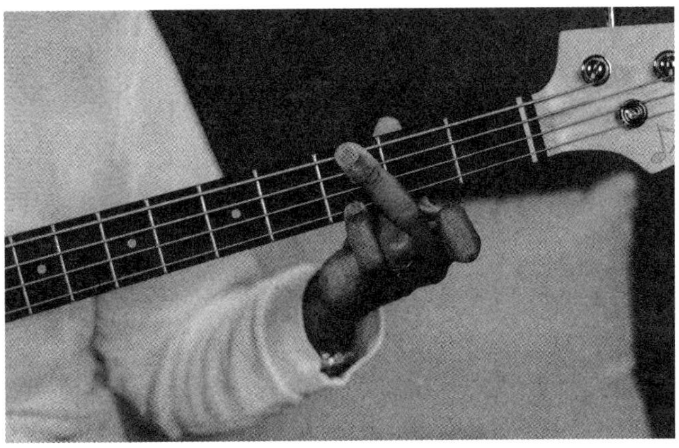

Here are some progressions to help get your hands familiar with playing 3rds.

Track 40

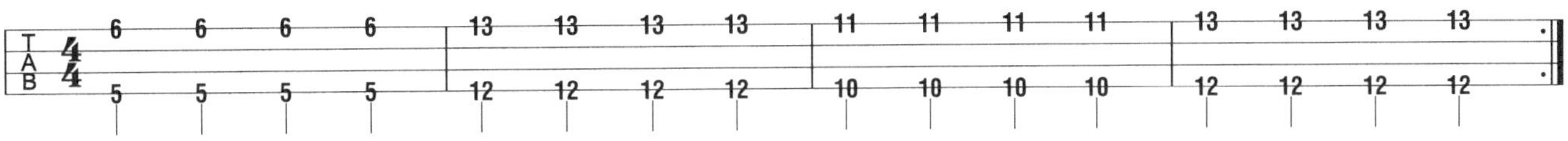

Track 41

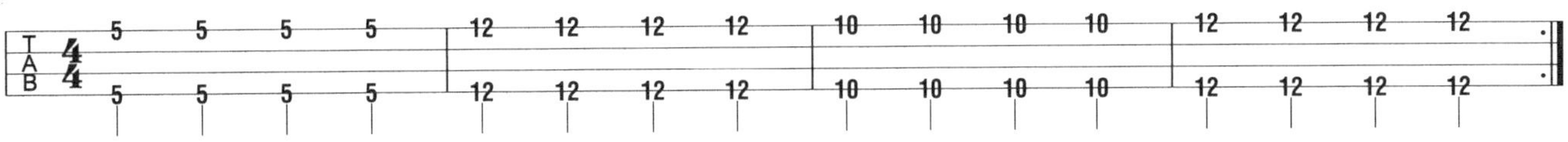

Track 42

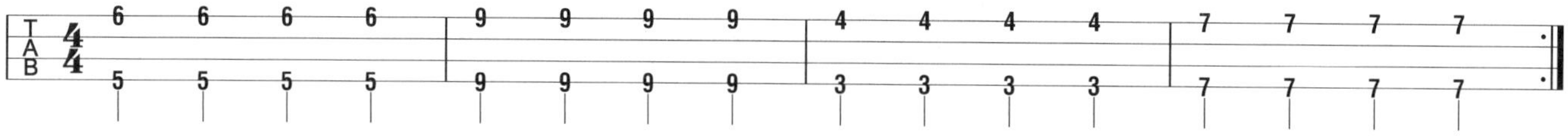

Track 43

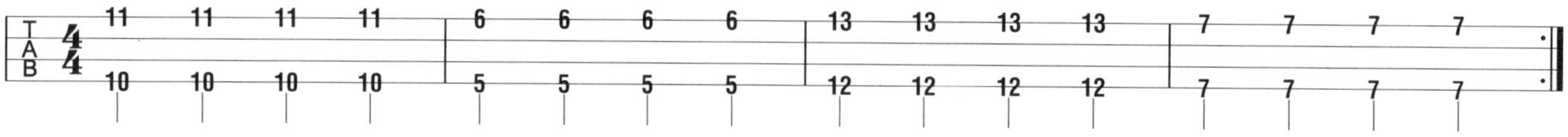

TOOLBOX

Before we get further, we need to discuss more complex rhythms that feature *16th notes*, *ties*, and *dotted rhythms*. Sixteenth notes divide eight notes by half, counted "1-e-and-a, 2-e-and-a..." Ties connect note values (don't re-pick the second note in a tie). Dots add half the value of the note they're attached to. These can all be used in combination to create really funky bass lines.

Now, here is a song that utilizes 3rds in its bass lines. (Don't worry about breaking down the counting; listen to the track for the *feel* of the bass line).

"BREAK EVEN"

Words and Music by Stephen Kipner, Andrew Frampton, Daniel O'Donoghue and Mark Sheehan

Track 44

Intro

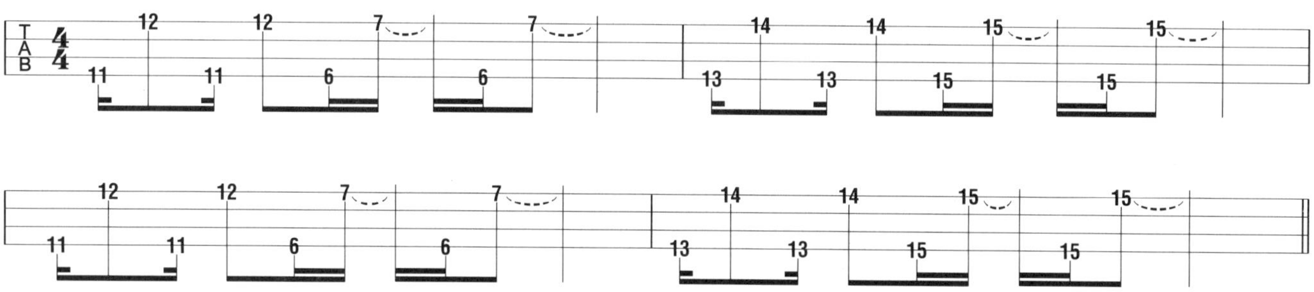

Verse

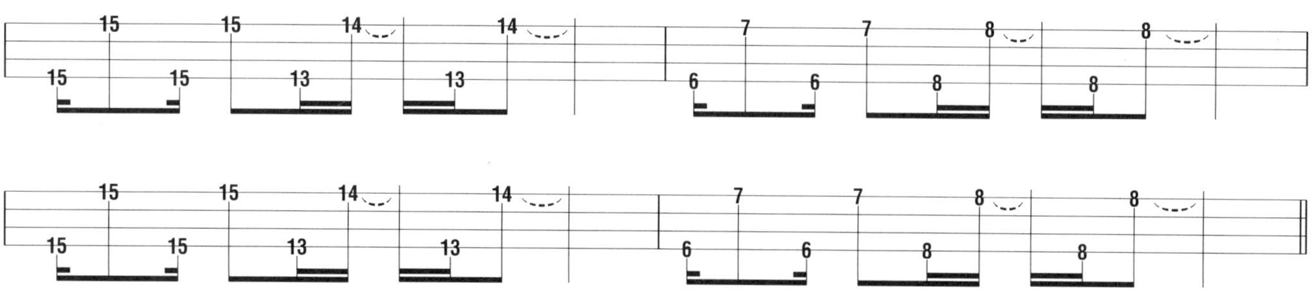

Power Chords

Using simple chords in bass lines really makes them stand out when performing or writing music. *Power chords* are simple chords that can fit with almost any kind of music you play.

These types of chords consist of two primary notes: the first and fifth notes of the major scale. A third note (the octave above the root) is optional, either placed above the main two notes or only in conjunction with the fifth note of the major scale.

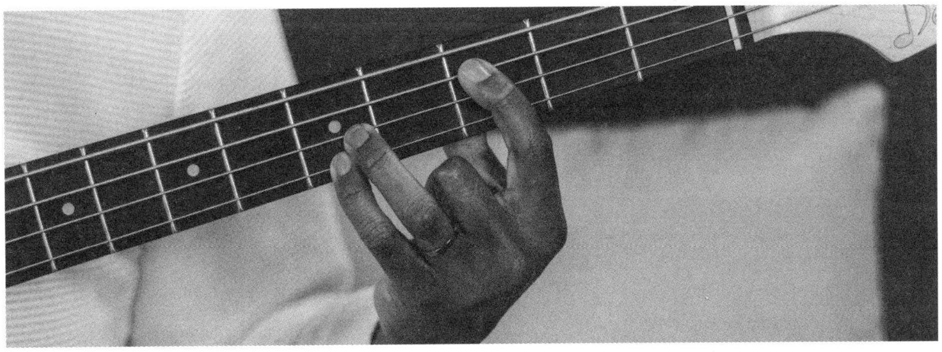

This technique is best utilized by playing the chord as an *arpeggio*, which means playing it one note at a time. (We'll talk about this more in-depth in Chapter 12.)

Here are some progressions to help get you familiar with this concept under your fingers.

Power Chord Exercises

Track 45

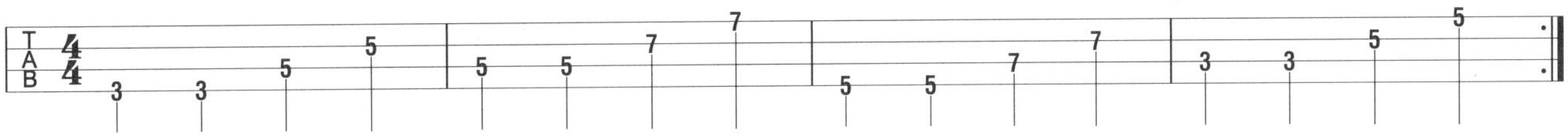

Track 46

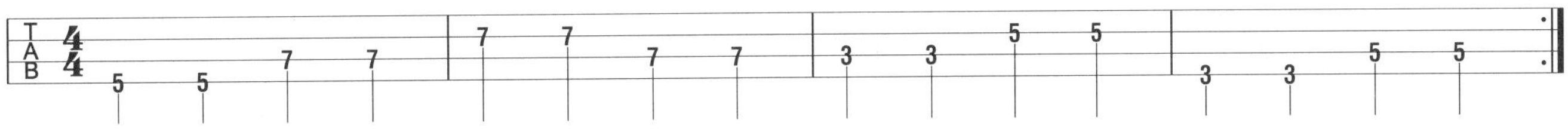

Track 47

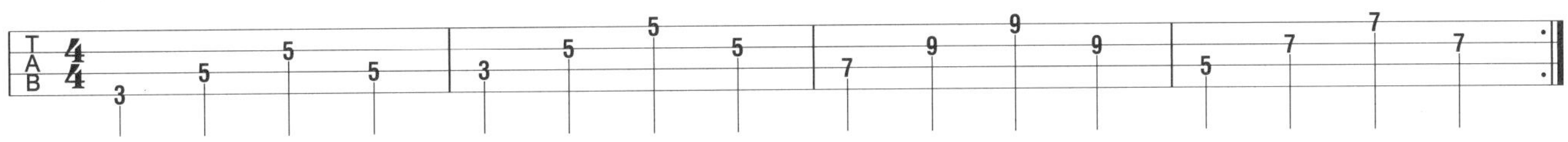

Track 48

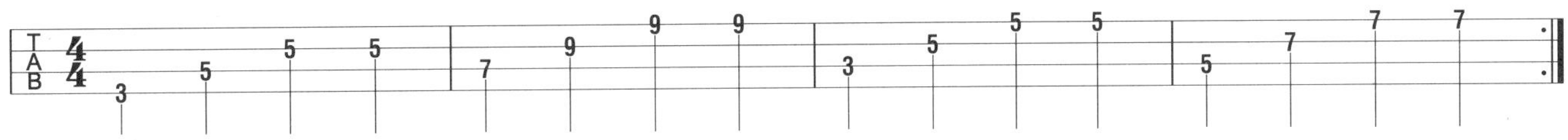

Track 49

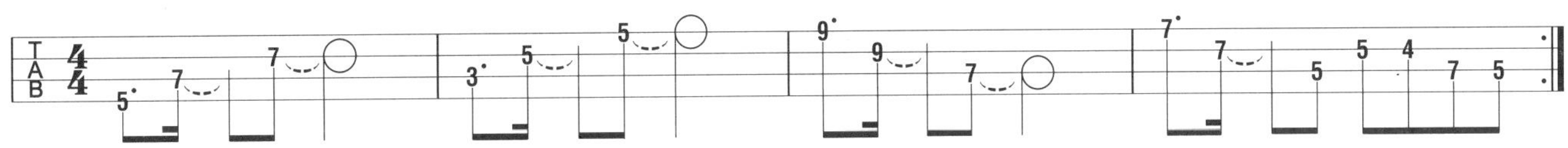

Chapter 9
More Left-Hand Techniques

Hammer-Ons and Pull-Offs

Playing with a good feel is very important when playing bass because it is an instrument that is mostly felt rather than heard much of the time. *Hammer-ons* and *pull-offs* give us ways to create great articulation and feel while also giving us shortcuts for our playing when performing scales and licks. These are notes produced by your left hand without using the right hand to pluck the string. These are common techniques used by many, if not all, stringed instruments. Both articulations are indicated by what's called a *slur*, which looks like this:

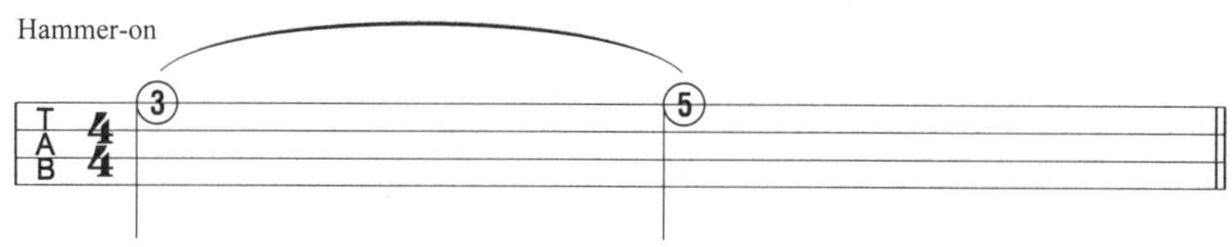

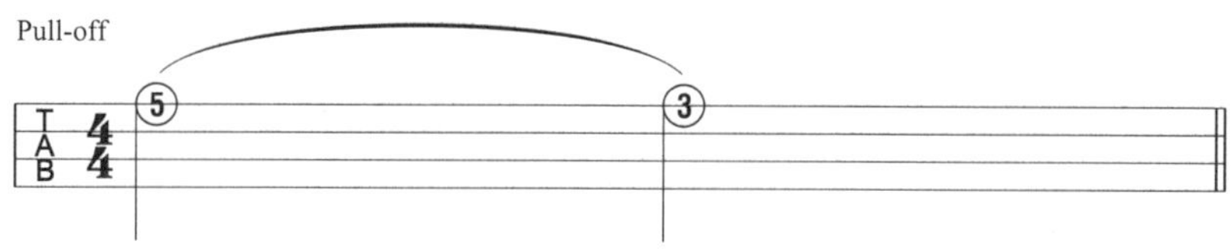

Hammer-Ons

The hammer-on is easy to understand, and with practice, it can be effective for your playing. Let's say if you played the 3rd fret of the G string with your left-hand index finger and wanted to play the 5th fret, just press down or "hammer on" that note with your ring finger to create the sound instead of plucking with your right hand.

Pull-Offs

These are the opposite of hammer-ons. Instead of hammering up to a higher note, you "pull off" from a note to play another note on a lower fret.

Using our previous example, but in reverse, hold down both the 3rd and 5th frets of the G string with your index and ring fingers, respectively. Pluck the string, and then "pull off" your ring finger from the fretboard to sound the note on the 3rd fret. (Make sure you pull with plenty of force to get an even sound from one note to the next.)

Hammer-On and Pull-Off Exercises

Track 50

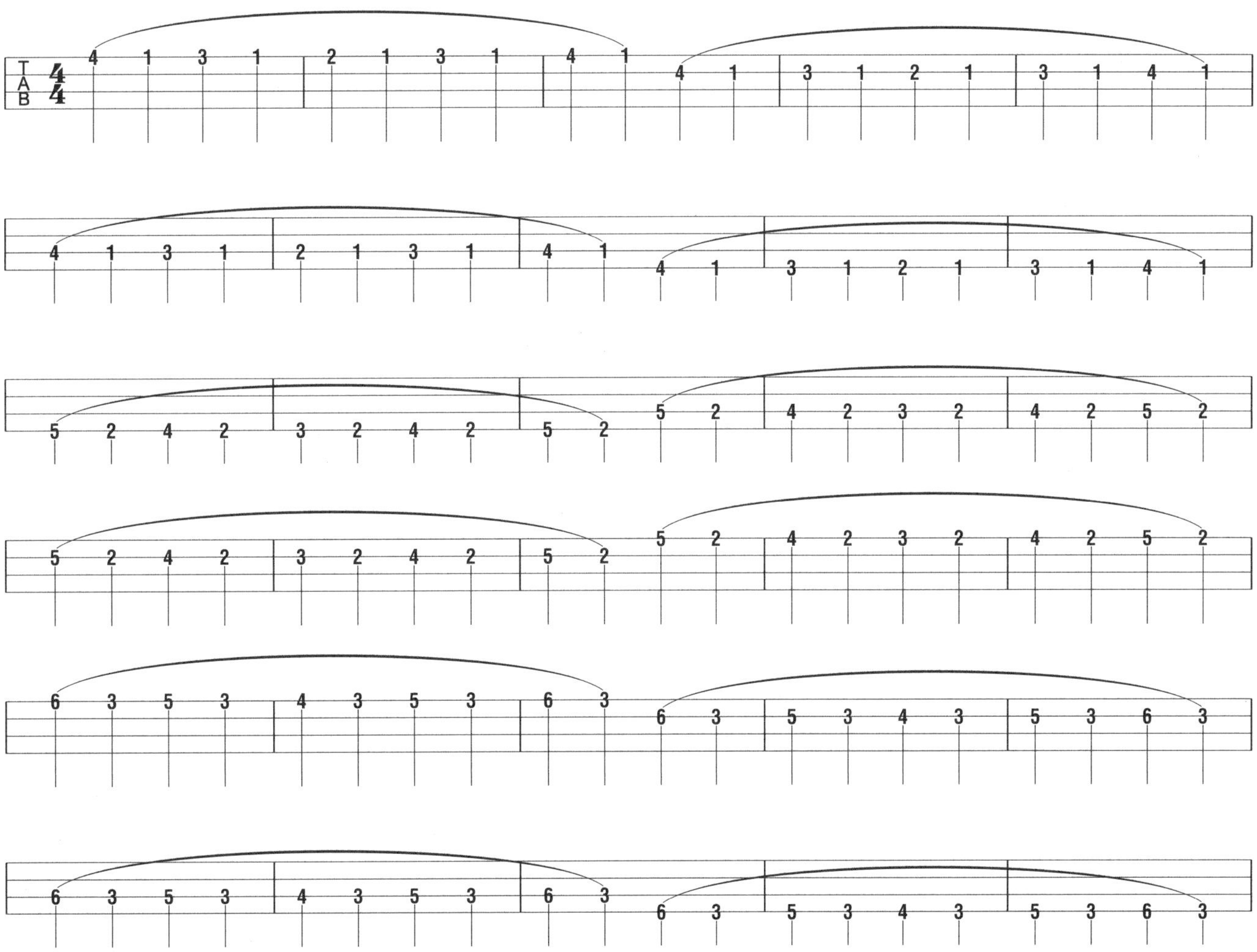

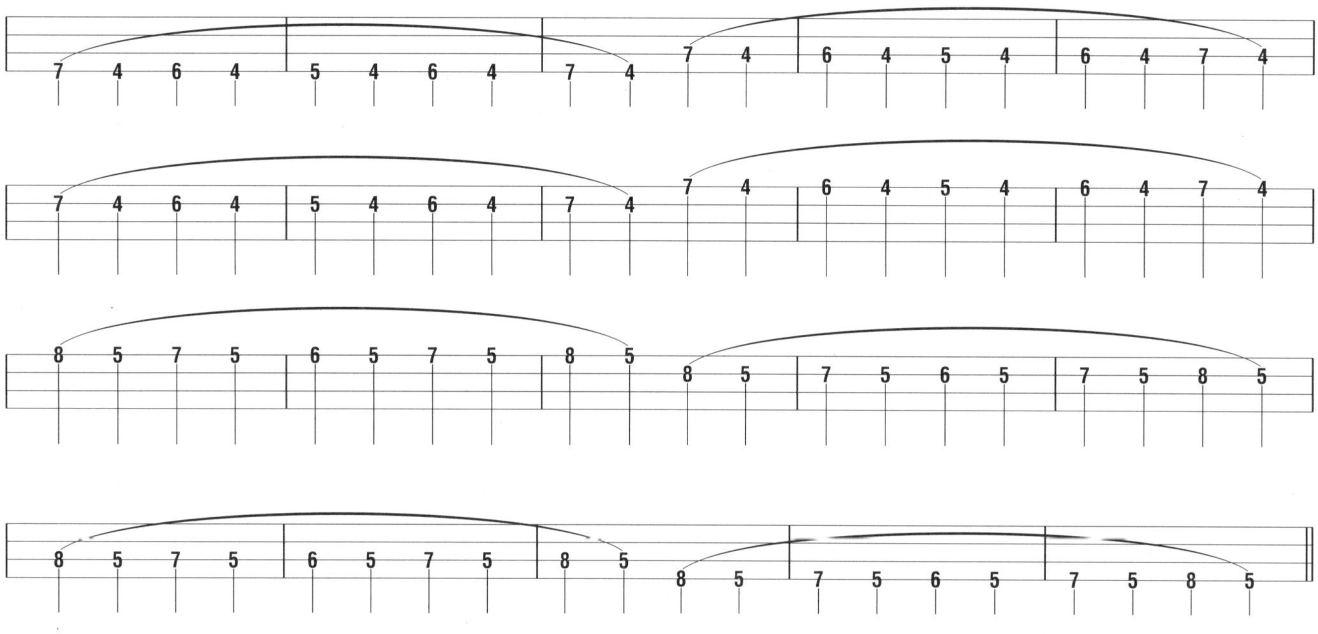

Here is a song that utilizes slurs and arpeggiated power chords in its bass line.

"CAN'T STOP THE FEELING!"

from TROLLS

Words and Music by Justin Timberlake, Max Martin and Shellback

Track 51

Sliding on Bass

Sliding (which we covered earlier in Chapter 8) is a technique that is defined by gliding across multiple pitches. On stringed instruments, this can be done by pressing down on one note and keeping your finger pressed while sliding to the next one. Aside from the sliding octaves that we covered previously, there are several ways to utilize slides on the bass.

Note-to-Note Slides

These slides, from one note to another, are probably the most common. You can slide up to a note (ascending) or down to a note (descending). These types of slides can be very long or very short, depending on where you're going. There are several different notes you can slide to, but here are some beginning ways to get you started.

Octave Slides

We've already covered this, but this is where you slide from one note to its octave, above or below, on the same string. The example that we used to introduce slides is an example of an octave slide. Let's try a different note, this time on G:

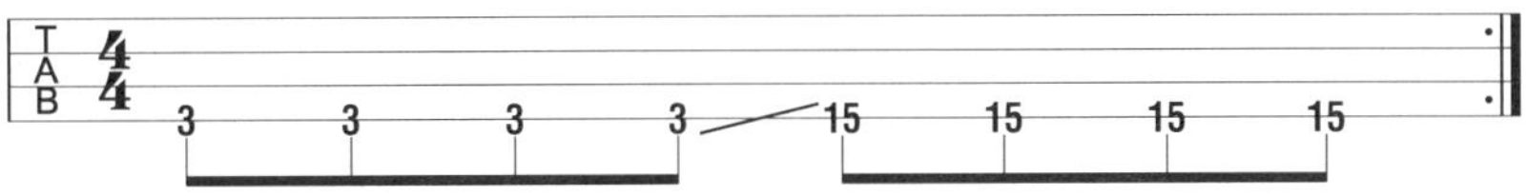

5th Slides

This is where you slide from one note to a *5th* above. To find the 5th above a given note, all you need to do is go up two frets and down one string.

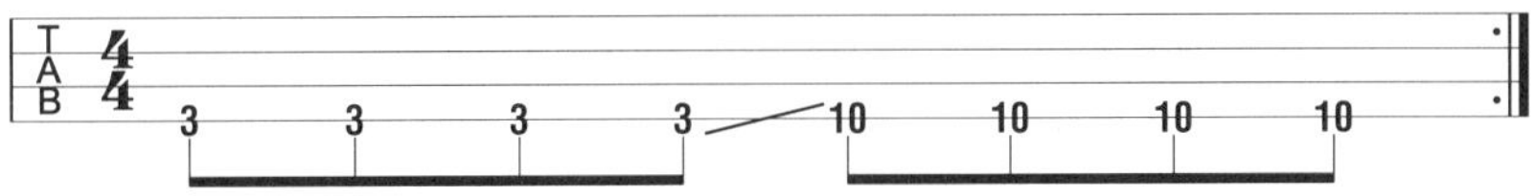

Slide-Ins and Slide-Outs

Slide-ins and *slide-outs* are ways that bass players slide in or out of notes, either in a bass line or groove to create more dramatic movement and interest. To make this dramatic effect work well, start from the lowest register of the string and make a big slide into your target note. Then, descend the same way when you slide out, making sure to cut the note off appropriately. To use this in a practical way, you can slide to each note of a progression to add some interest, like this example below.

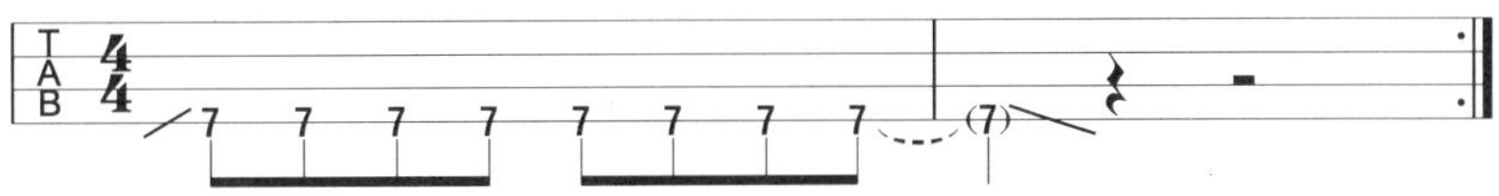

The symbol that you see connecting the last two notes of the exercise is called a *tie*. All this means is that you play the first note of the pair and allow it to ring through to the next note. This is done if we want longer note values to overlap where one bar ends and another bar begins. In this case, you'll pluck the final note of bar 1, let it ring into the first beat of bar 2, and then slide out, making sure to mute the string in time for beat 2.

Grace-Note Slides

Adding *grace-note slides* just adds a little bit of flavor and personality to licks and bass lines that you play. The way this is achieved is by sliding up from one fret or two frets away to the note you are sliding to; this just gives a little flair to your licks and bass lines.

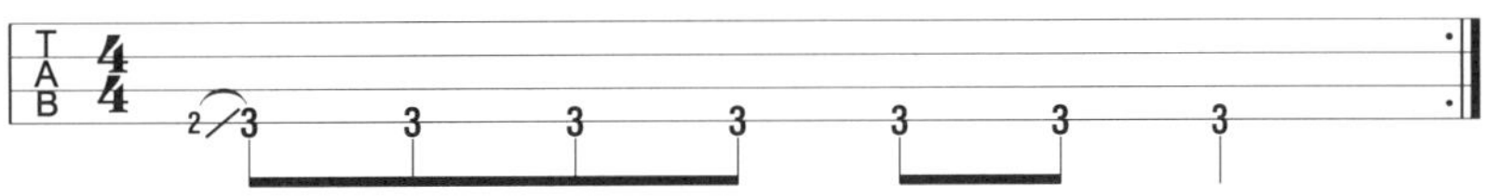

Chapter 10

Slapping and Popping

This technique is probably one of the most popular techniques the bass is known for. *Slapping and popping* was made popular in the funk and disco genres of music, but this combined technique has made its way into a lot of music nowadays, such as gospel, pop, fusion, R&B, soul, and many others. Slapping and popping gives bass players a way of getting a more percussive sound by hitting (slapping) and pulling (popping) with your right hand.

Slapping

A great way to start using this technique is by slapping open strings on the bass. When slapping, you want to use your knuckle joint on the side of your right thumb to strike the string. Make sure to work slowly through the exercise below before speeding up the tempo. (In the tab, slaps are shown with a "T" below the fret number.)

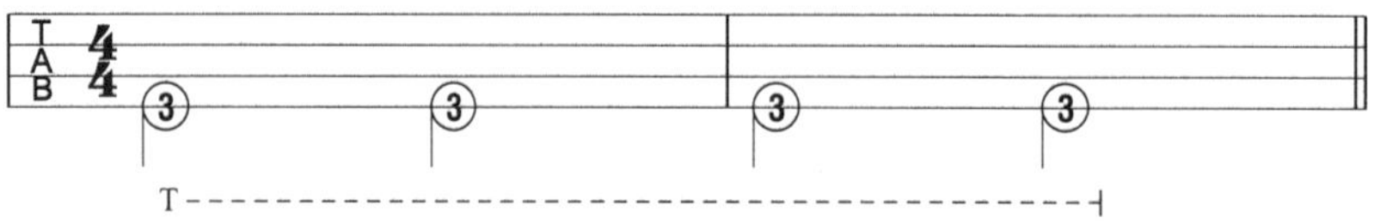

TOOLBOX

Pro tip: To achieve a cleaner slap tone, slap closer to the neck of the bass (away from the bridge).

Now, a way to achieve even more accuracy and clarity with slapping is dampening the strings with your left hand. Basically, you'll mute unwanted strings with your left hand when slapping so you only hear the notes you are going for. Play the same exercise from above, but this time, slap closer to the neck and mute the other strings with your left hand. Work through it slowly, just like the slapping exercise.

Popping

The other essential side of this technique is popping. This is usually done by putting the tip of your index finger up under the string and pulling upwards and away from the bass. This allows the string to slap back on the bass, producing a popping sound. (Pops are indicated with a "P" in the tab.)

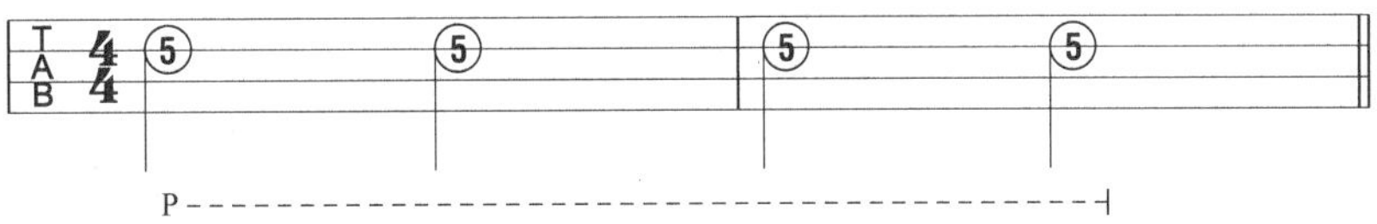

The best way to practice this two-fold technique is to slap on the E string then pop on the D string. Then, do the same thing on the A string and G string. The exercises that follow will help you do just that, so let's move to some more variations of slapping and popping that you can put into your playing.

Octave Slapping

This method of slapping is created by slapping one note and then popping the octave of that note. (Remember the 2x2 rule when finding octaves.)

Track 52

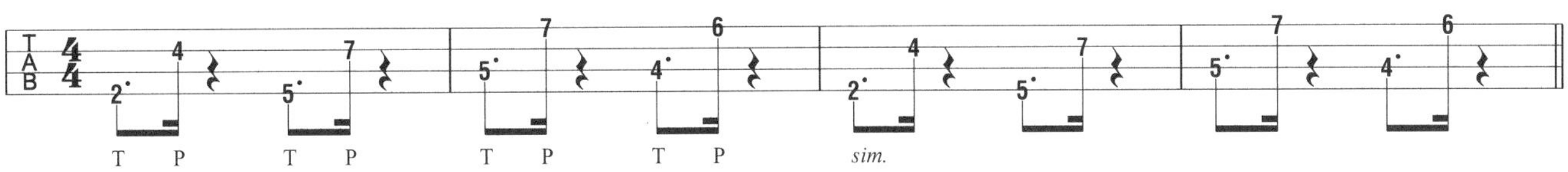

Track 53

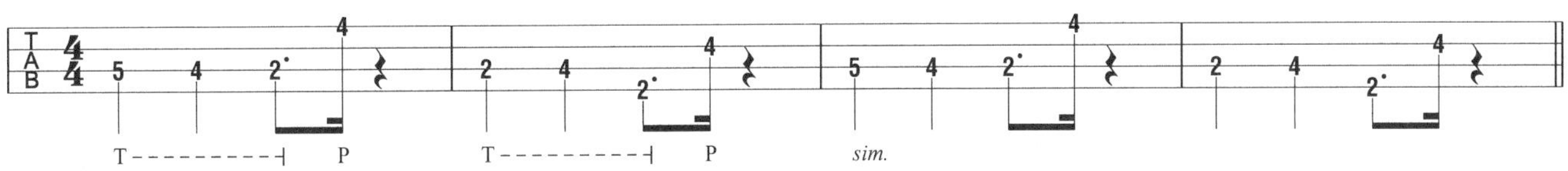

Track 54

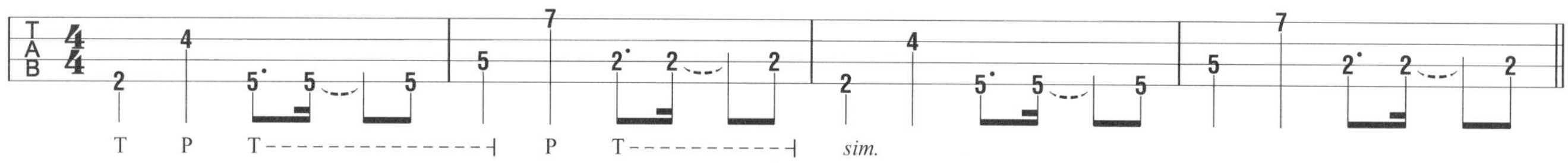

Track 55

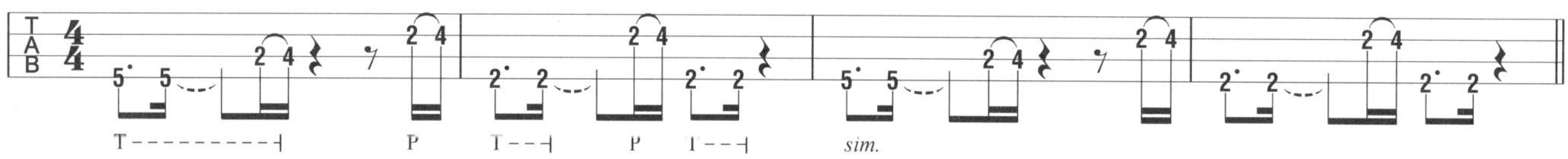

Track 56

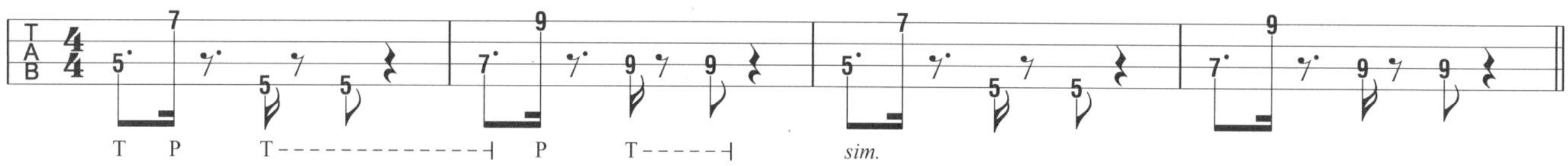

3rd Slapping

This method of slapping is created by slapping the root note and popping the 3rd of that note. (Remember that 3rds on the bass sound best when they're displaced by an octave.)

Track 57

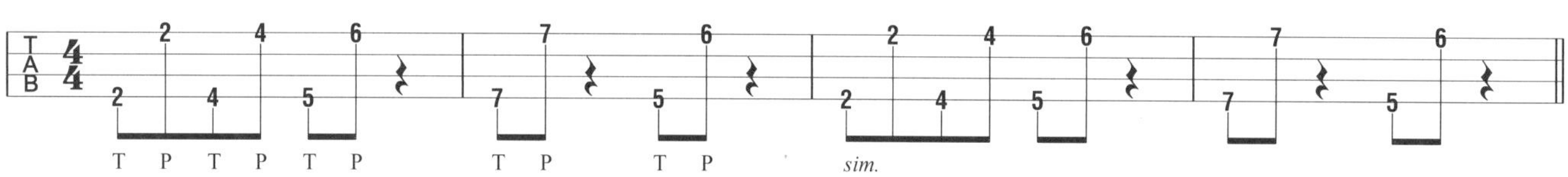

Track 58

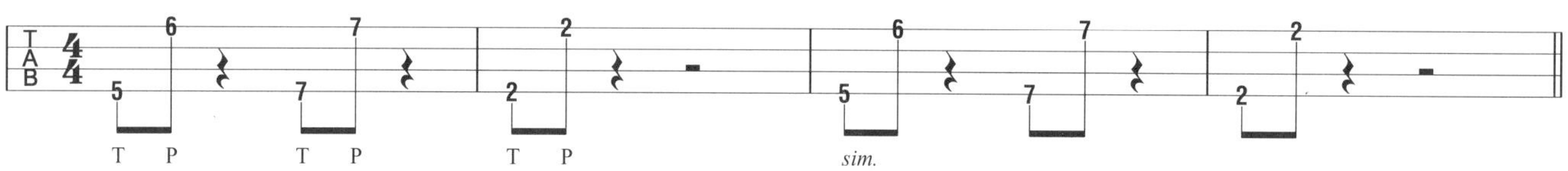

Track 59

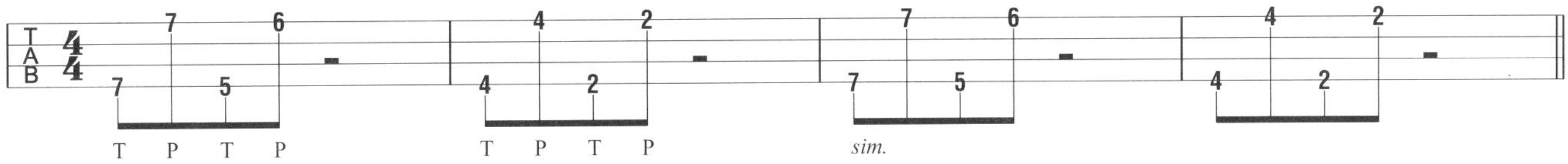

Track 60

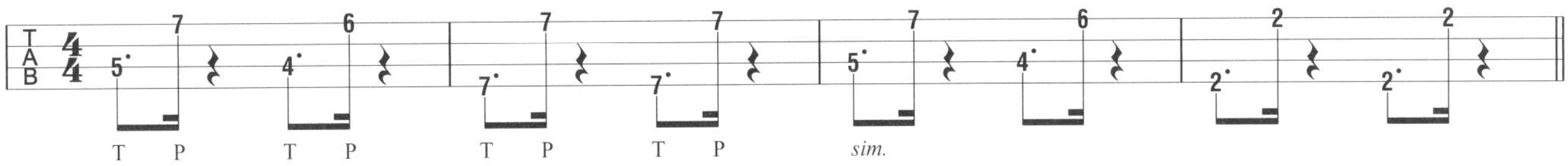

Track 61

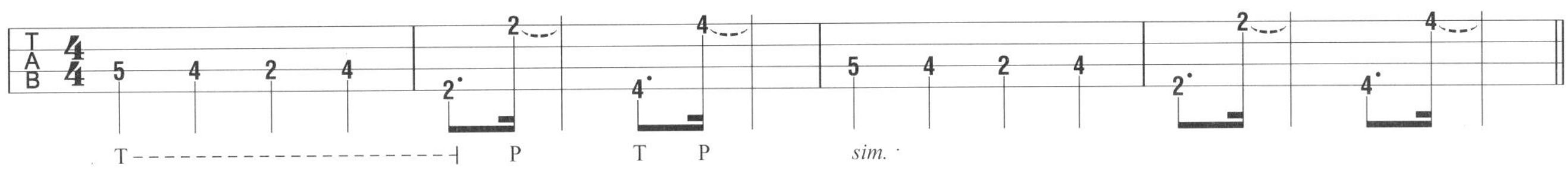

5th Slapping

This method of slapping is created by slapping the root note and popping the 5th of that note. (Remember that 5ths are two frets up and one string down.)

Track 62

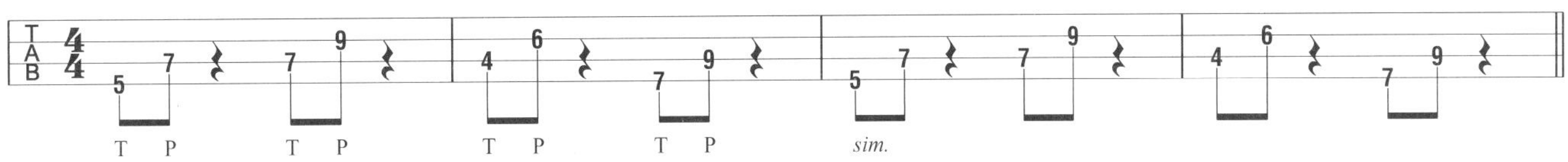

Track 63

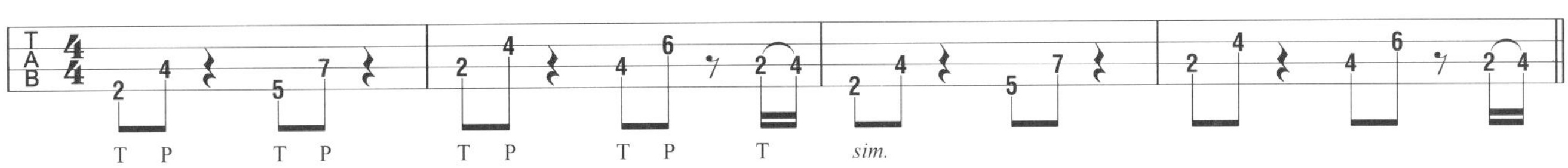

Track 64

Track 65

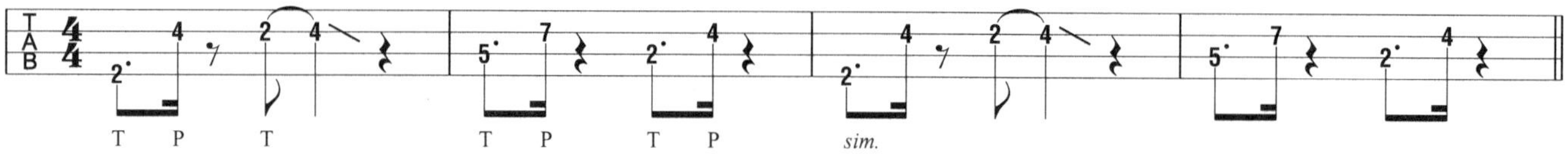

Track 66

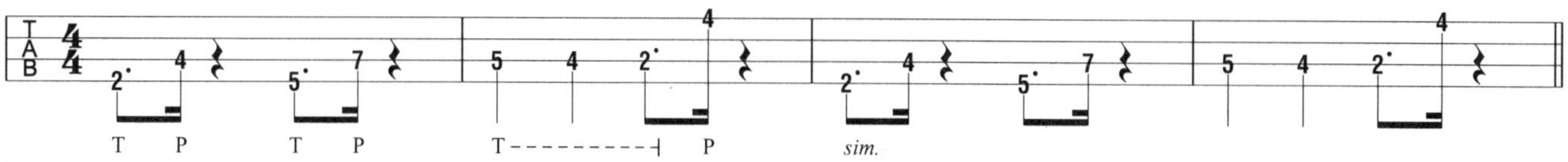

Song Examples

Here are two songs that utilize slapping and popping. Again, the rhythms may look tough, but listen to the audio tracks to understand the phrasing.

"BRICK HOUSE"

Words and Music by Lionel Richie, Ronald LaPread, Walter Orange, Milan Williams, Thomas McClary and William King

Track 67

"GET ON THE FLOOR"

Words and Music by Michael Jackson and Louis Johnson

Track 68

Chorus

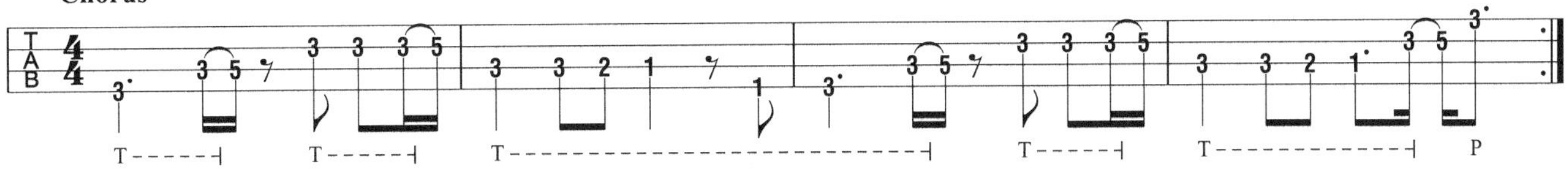

Verse

Play 2 times

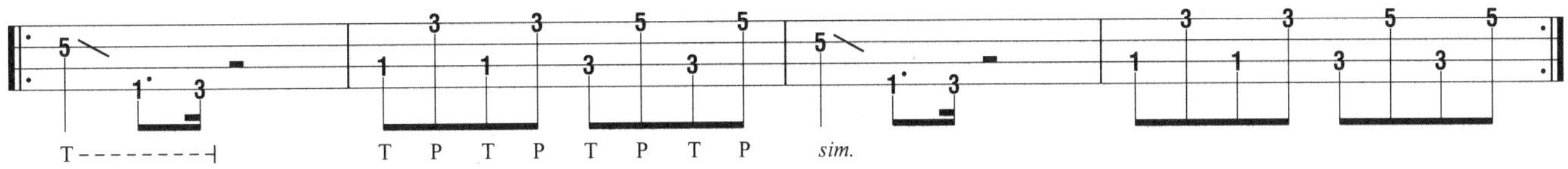

Chorus

Play 2 times

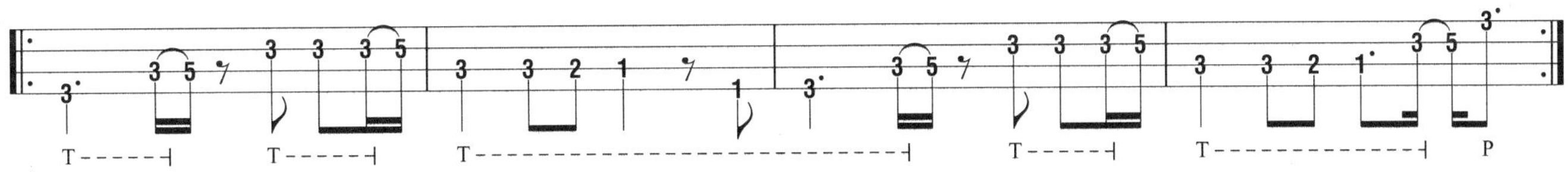

Chapter 11
Exploring More Scales

Relative Minors and Majors

In every family, there are some type of relatives, like an uncle, an aunt, a cousin, etc. In music, there are relatives as well, but between major and minor scales. To make this simple, there is a minor scale in every major scale and a major scale in every minor scale. Since we've been focused on the major scale, to find a relative minor, all you do is play up the major scale, counting each note until you get to the sixth note. That note will be what the relative minor scale is based on. Here is a chart of all the relative minors and majors for every key.

G Major Scale

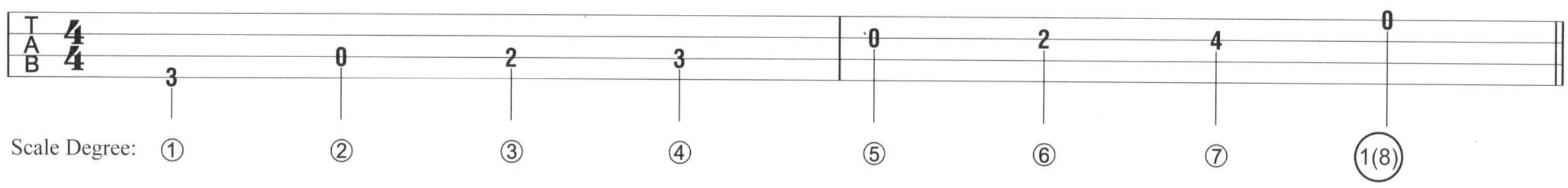

E Minor Scale

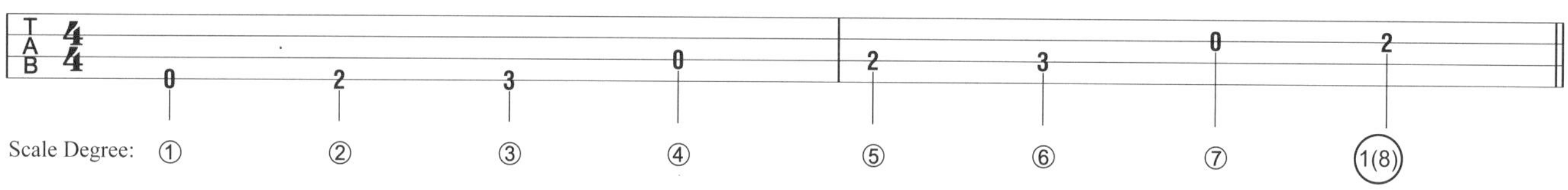

Major and Minor Scale Relatives	
C Major Scale	A Minor Scale
C♯/D♭ Major Scale	A♯/ B♭ Minor Scale
D Major Scale	B Minor Scale
D♯/E♭ Major Scale	C Minor Scale
E Major Scale	C♯/D♭ Minor Scale
F Major Scale	D Minor Scale
F♯/G♭ Major Scale	D♯/E♭ Minor Scale
G Major Scale	E Minor Scale
G♯/A♭ Major Scale	F Minor Scale
A Major Scale	F♯/G♭ Minor Scale
B♭/A♯ Major Scale	G Minor Scale
B Major Scale	G♯/A♭ Minor Scale

The reason that this knowledge is important to learn is because it speeds up the process of learning scales. When you understand this, you only have to learn one type of scale to play both kinds of qualities.

Key of A Major with F♯/G♭ Minor Scale

Track 69

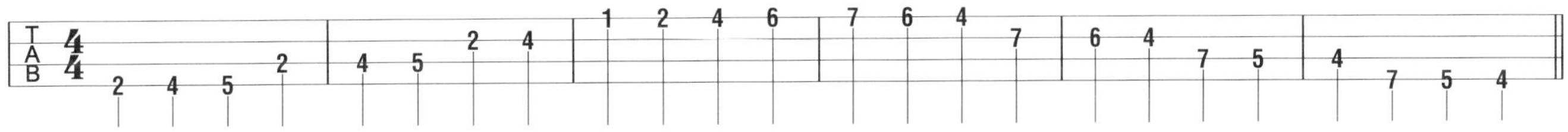

This concept can be applied beyond regular major and minor scales. In the next chapter, we'll learn all about one of the most widely used scales in music: the *pentatonic scale*. As a way to prepare, play through this brief exercise below.

Key of A Major Pentatonic with F♯/G♭ Minor Scale

Track 70

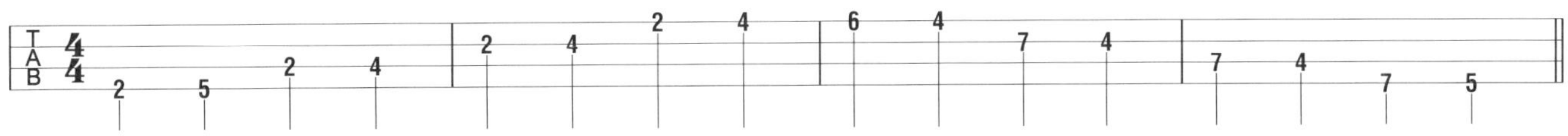

Chapter 12
The Pentatonic Scale

The pentatonic scale is used in almost every genre of music that's been released. The words "penta," which means "five," and "tonic," which means "tone" or "note," tell us exactly what this scale is: a five-note scale. It's particularly versatile and fun to play. An easy way to create a pentatonic scale is by removing the fourth and seventh notes from the major scale.

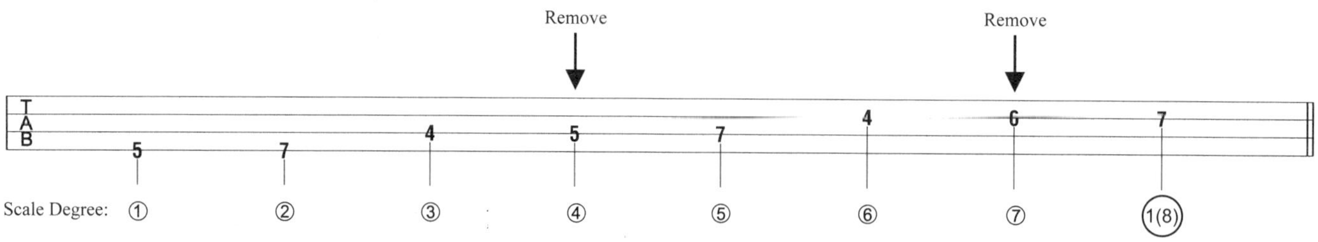

Major Pentatonic Scale

Here's a diagram of the major pentatonic scale pattern in the key of A:

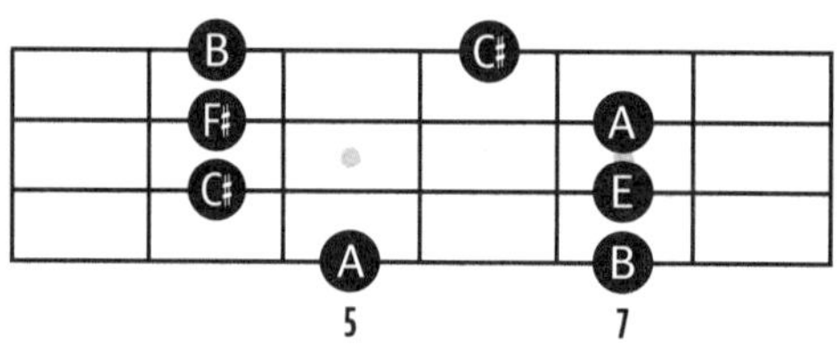

Let's explore some exercises to help you memorize the pattern in the key of A.

Track 71

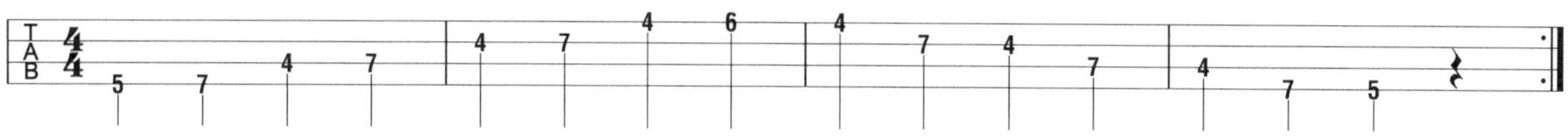

Track 72

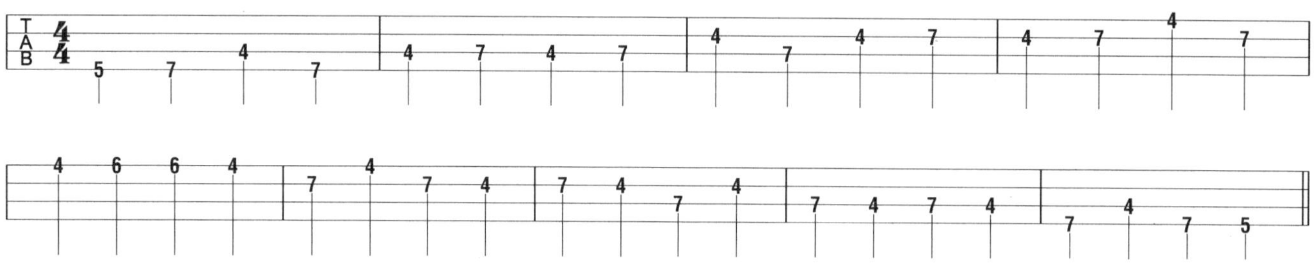

Track 73

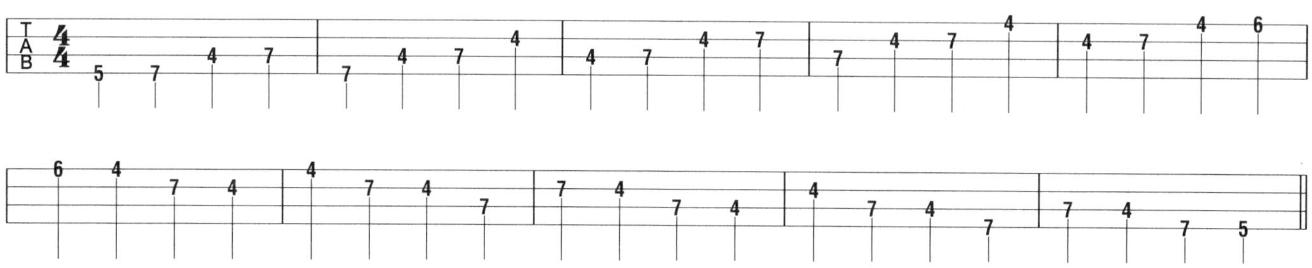

After practicing the basic pattern on one area of the fingerboard, let's move to other areas. This will make it easier for you to create bass lines and licks when we start using the pentatonic scale in songs. Before we learn all the pentatonic scale patterns up the neck of the bass, we need to start with just the E string.

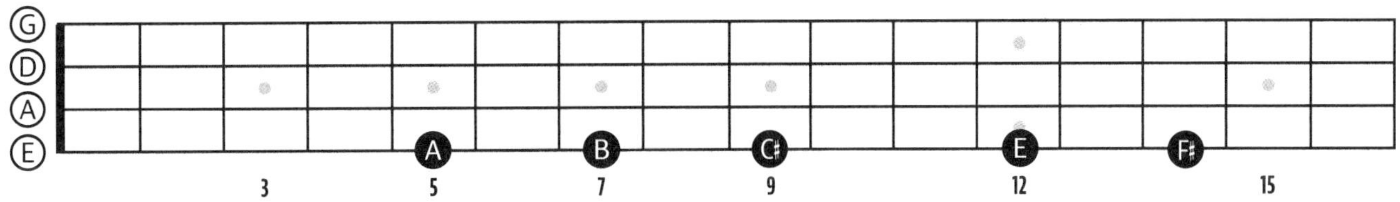

Each of these notes on the E string will be a starting note for the positions we'll learn. Every position uses the same five notes that we learned on the initial major pentatonic scale pattern, the only difference is the patterns change when you start on different notes. Since each position starts at a different note of the scale, there are five total. Here are the five positions, shown here in the key of A:

Major Pentatonic Position 1

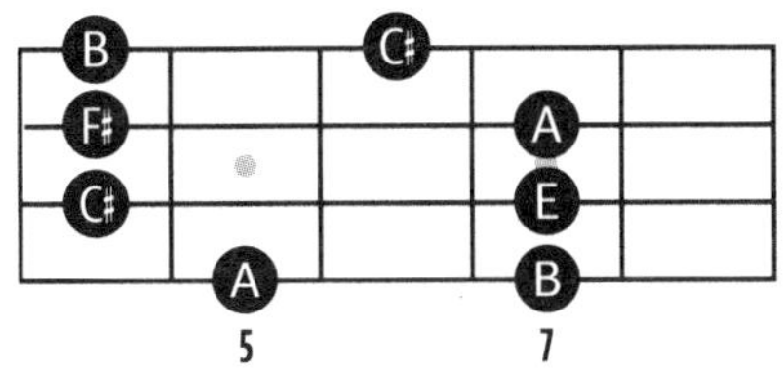

Major Pentatonic Position 2

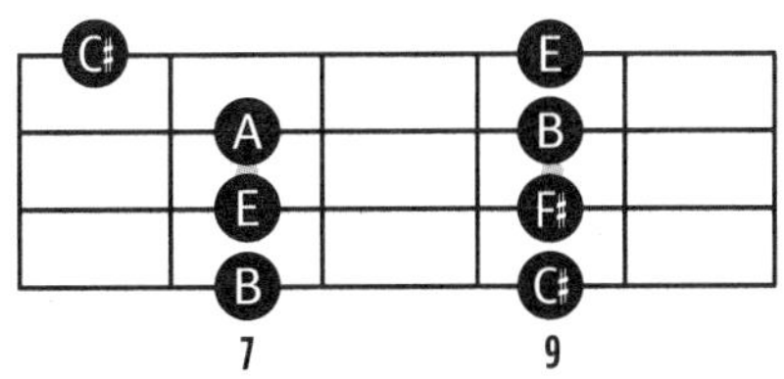

Major Pentatonic Position 3

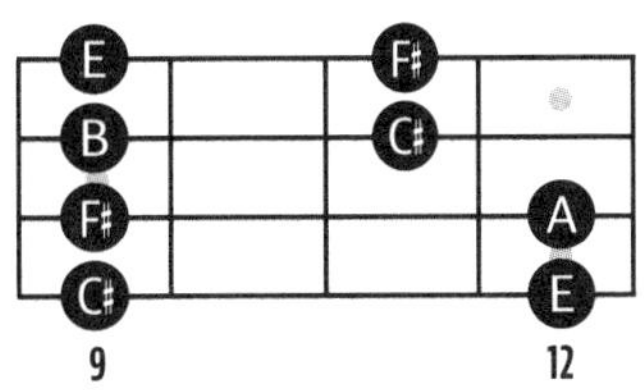

Major Pentatonic Position 4

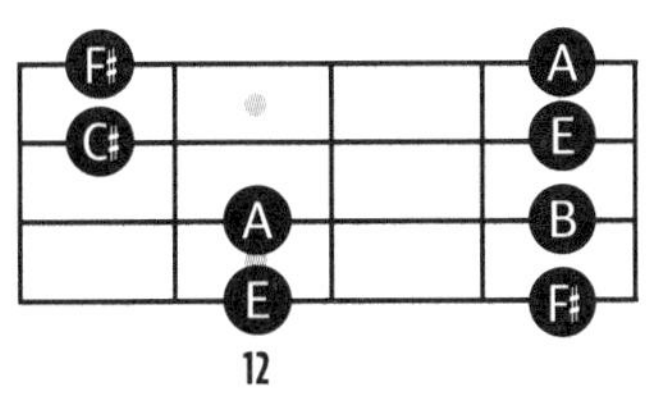

Major Pentatonic Position 5

(The fifth position of the major pentatonic scale is also known as the *minor pentatonic scale*. More on this later.)

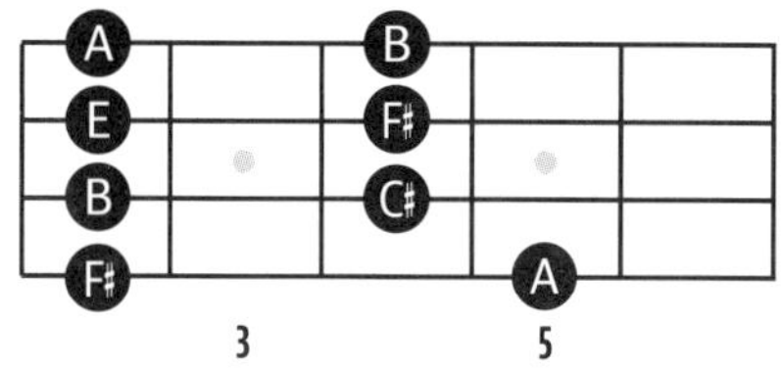

Here are all the positions spread over the neck of the bass.

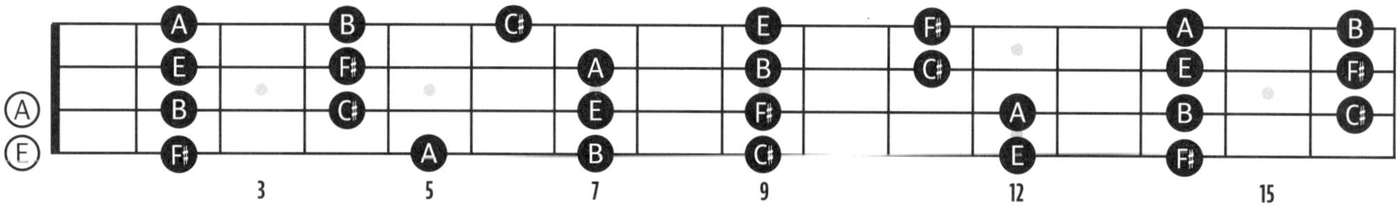

Now that we are semi-familiar with the patterns, let's really lock them into memory with these exercises.

Track 74

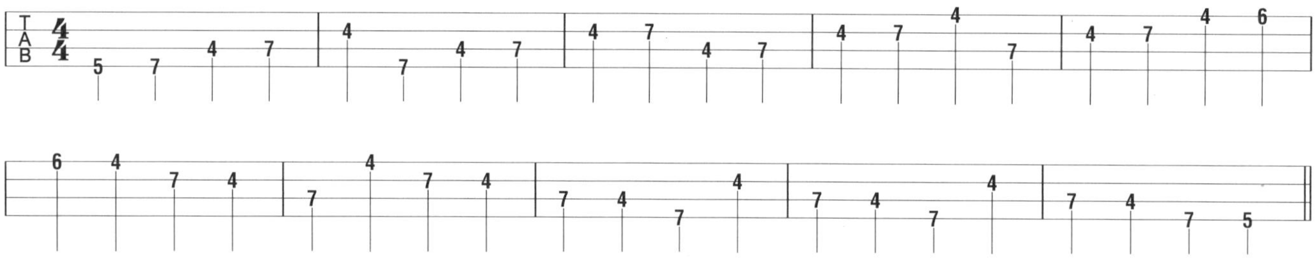

When practicing each of these exercises, make sure you move them around to different keys so you can properly memorize the entire pentatonic scale up the neck of the bass. (We'll put this into practice in Chapter 14.)

How to Use the Pentatonic Scale

Creating your own bass licks and lines is really simple; you just have to use these scales as a map to find notes that will work in your song or bass line. Basically, you need to find where the good notes are as well as the bad notes. Here are a few ways that you can start using it to create licks and spice up bass lines.

Breaking Down Pentatonic Scales with String Groupings

The trick to mastering any technique is to take a big concept and make it small. By using string groupings, you are shrinking down the pentatonic scale to only playing it on two strings at a time. So first, let's practice going up and down the neck, using only the G and D strings.

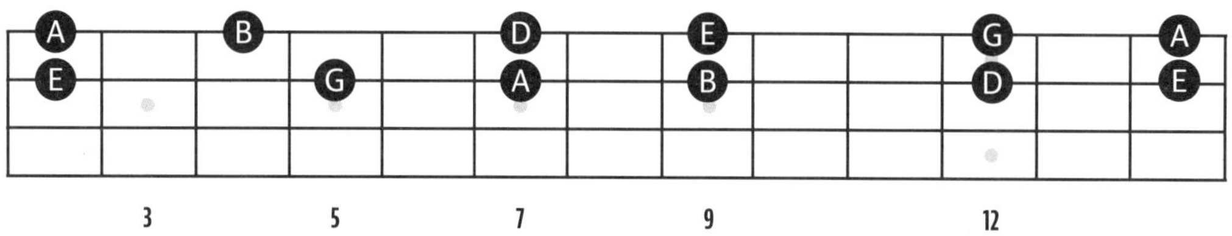

Track 75

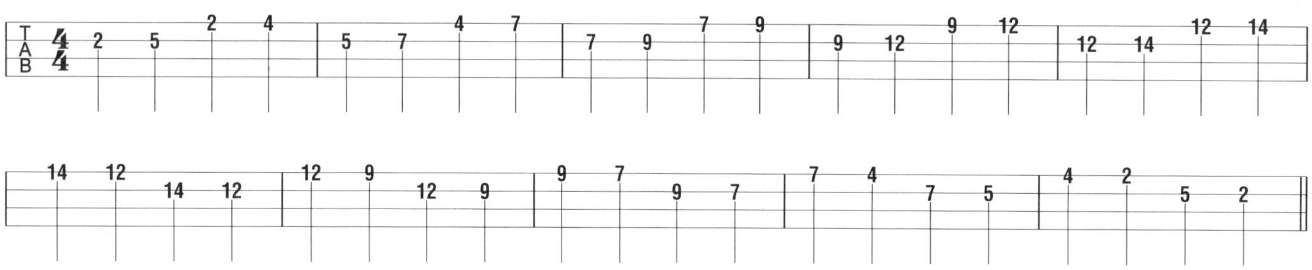

Perfect! Now that we got that one down, let's do the same thing on the E and A strings.

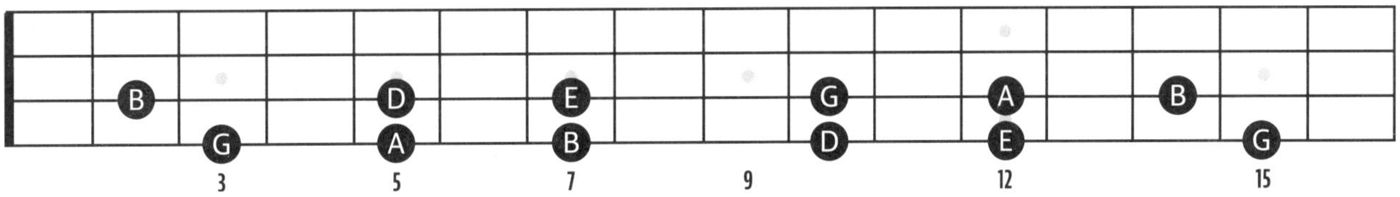

Track 76

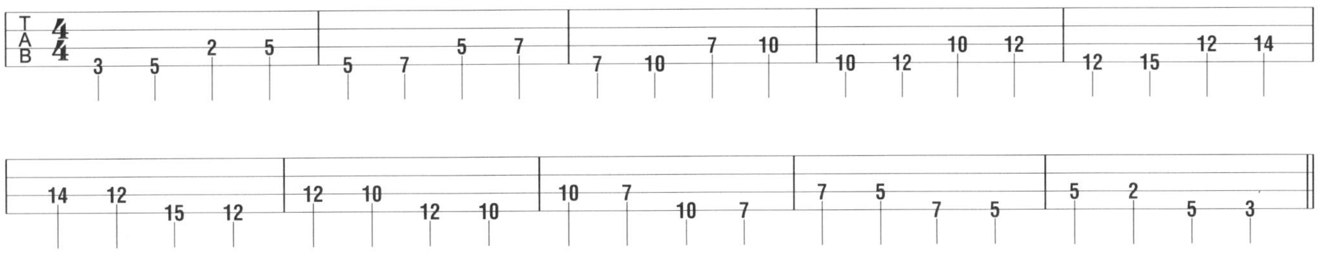

So now, when we go to practice and create bass lines, we can use these groupings to create short licks that enhance our bass lines and songs.

Using the Pentatonic Scale to Create Dyads (Two-Note Chords)

We've talked about dyads before when talking about using 3rds and 5ths in previous chapters. Now, let's take it a little step further by creating dyads, using the pentatonic scale. The way these are found are by going to the G and D strings and identifying which notes are in the pentatonic scale.

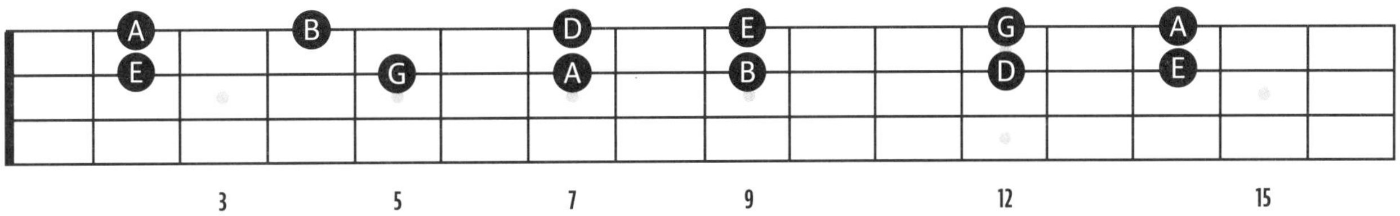

Then, pair notes that are closest together, using one note from the D string and one note from the G string.

G and B

A and D

B and E

D and G

E and A

You can also use your index finger to *barre* across the strings when you encounter two notes at the same fret, holding the notes down together as you pluck them with your right hand. (This is shown in the video, and also in the photo above.) Once you find them, use your index and middle finger on your right hand to play these notes simultaneously to create a dyad.

Now, here are some exercises to help you master your pentatonic scale dyads. We've shown them first as sequenced single notes and then as paired dyads.

Pentatonic Scale Dyads (Arpeggiated)

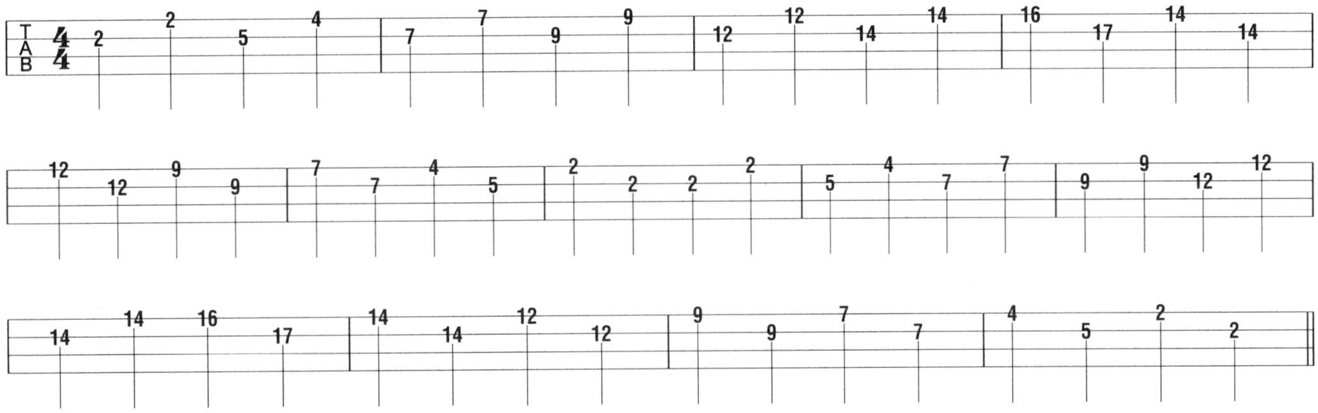

Pentatonic Scale Dyads

Using dyads will immensely increase your groove and lick vocabulary, giving you ways of creating mini-chords to add to your bass lines.

Extended Pentatonic Scales

A big part of mastering the pentatonic scale and getting the most out of it is by connecting the pentatonic positions together. In what I call *extended pentatonic scales*, we literally just connect three pentatonic positions together to create one molded scale. There are two common extended pentatonic scales that will help you connect these positions together.

Extended Pentatonic Scale 1: First, Second, and Third Positions

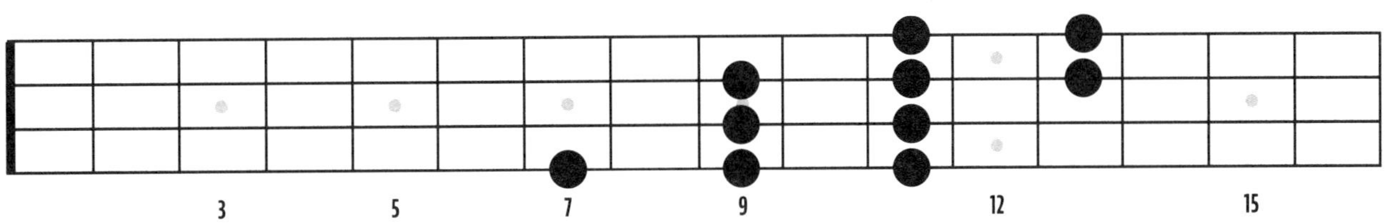

Extended Pentatonic Scale 2: Fourth, Fifth, and First Positions

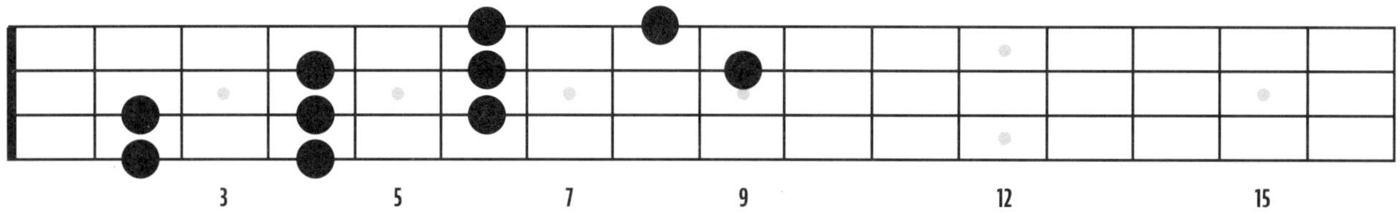

Here are some exercises to help you connect the positions.

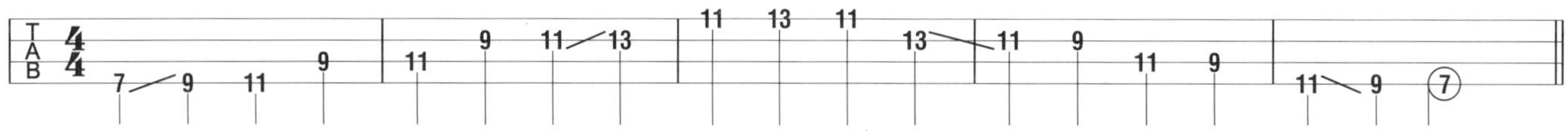

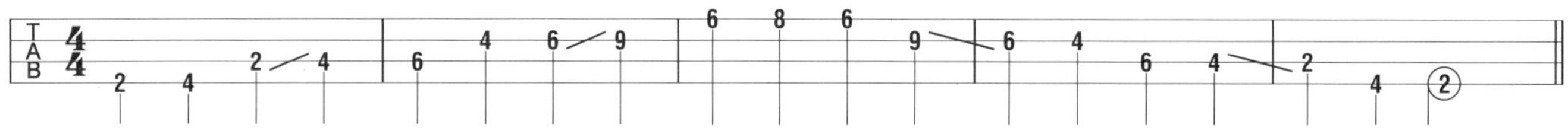

Now, after getting familiar with these exercises, you will instantly have access to all the positions of the pentatonic scale. Extending this scale allows you to create pentatonic licks and lines at the lowest and highest ends of the bass, which will help your ideas stand out.

The Minor Pentatonic Scale

Let's circle back to the minor pentatonic scale. As stated before, it's the fifth position of the major pentatonic scale, but it carries its own distinctive sound, or tonality. Most songs are divided into major or minor keys, and the minor pentatonic scale is used to reinforce minor tonalities in songs. You can think of it just like the relative major and minor scales that we discussed previously. The cool thing that this scale features is a more distinctive "blues" quality. You actually played bass lines that use the minor pentatonic sound in a previous chapter: "Brick House" (A minor pentatonic) and "Get On the Floor" (G minor pentatonic).

Chapter 13

Exploring Arpeggios Further

Up to this point, we have talked about how scales can spice up your licks and bass lines, but we've only explored arpeggios in a very basic sense. The truth is that utilizing an arpeggio is a secret weapon that can make your lines very tasty. Arpeggios open up a whole new dynamic when it comes to creating and performing by shifting our focus to chord tones. Like I have previously mentioned when talking about 3rds, every chord has qualities: major, minor, dominant, etc. To start off learning our basic arpeggios, we need to learn more about triads.

Triads

Like we mentioned earlier, triads are three-note chords. These are what I call the "foundation" of chords; you build other chord types from them by stacking other notes on top of the basic, three-note structure. We will start with learning basic triads, and then we'll add a color note to them to make them stand out.

Major Triad

The *major triad* is made up of a root, major 3rd, and a 5th (to be specific, it's a *perfect 5th*). You can move this shape around the various string pairs as long as they are located next to each other. In the key of G, the notes are G, B, and D.

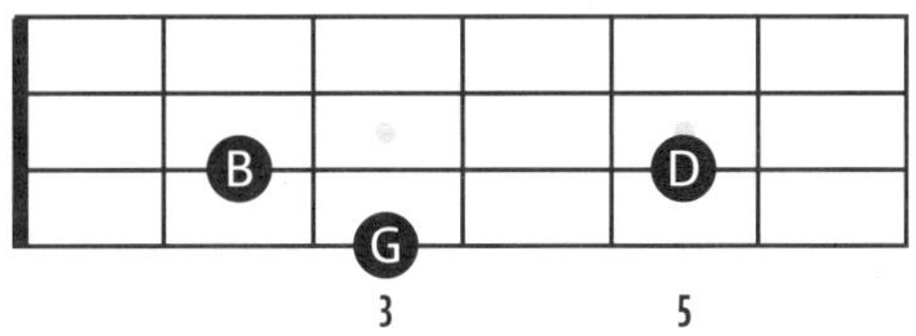

Minor Triad

The *minor triad* is made up of a root, minor 3rd, and a perfect 5th. The same movability of the major triads can also apply here. In the key of G, the notes are G, B♭, and D.

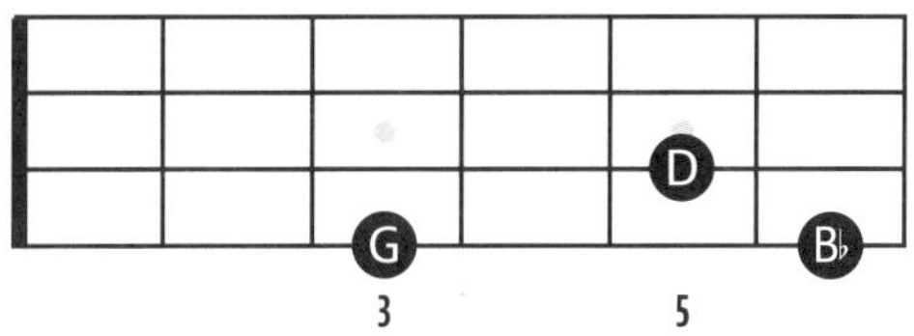

Here are some exercises that will help familiarize you with basic major and minor arpeggios.

Track 77

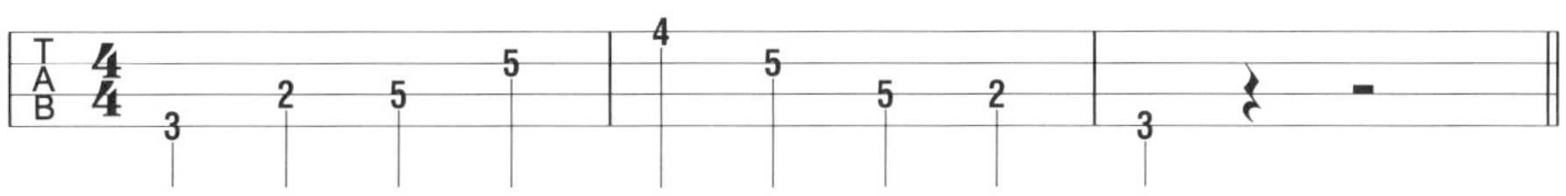

Track 78

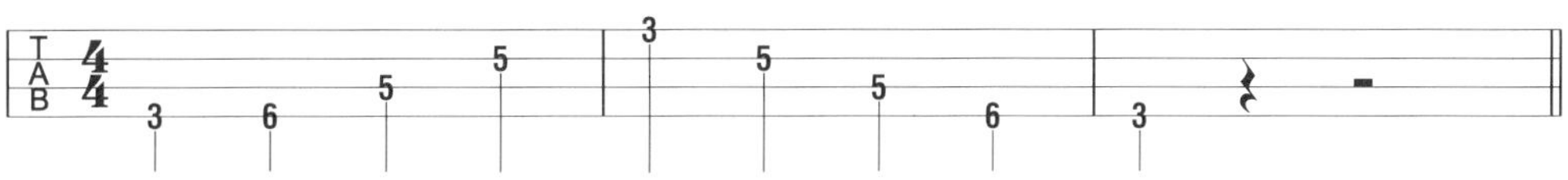

Track 79

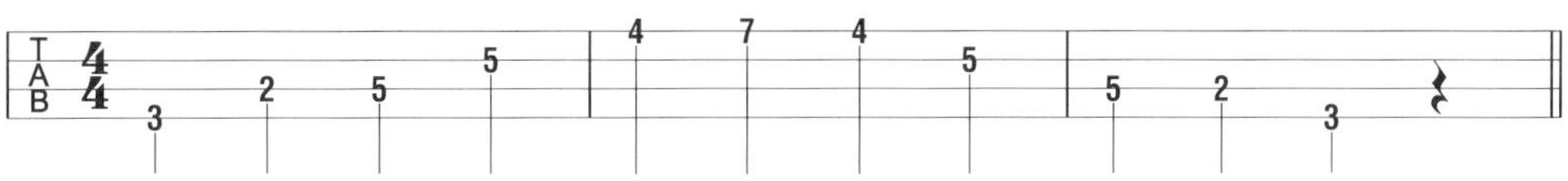

Track 80

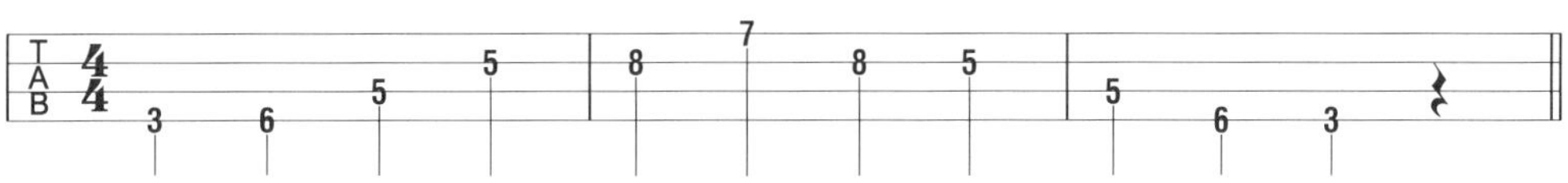

Track 81

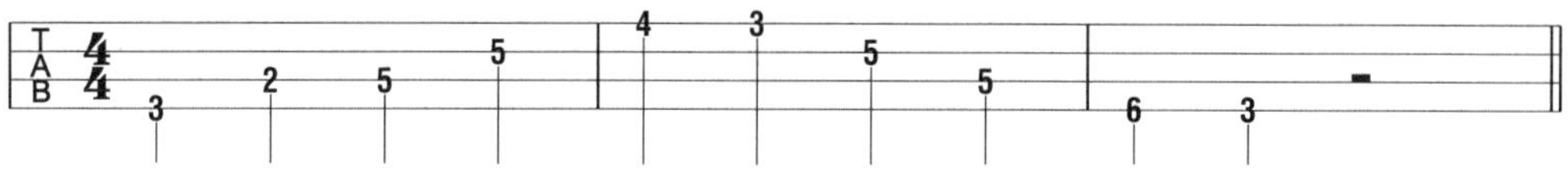

Track 82

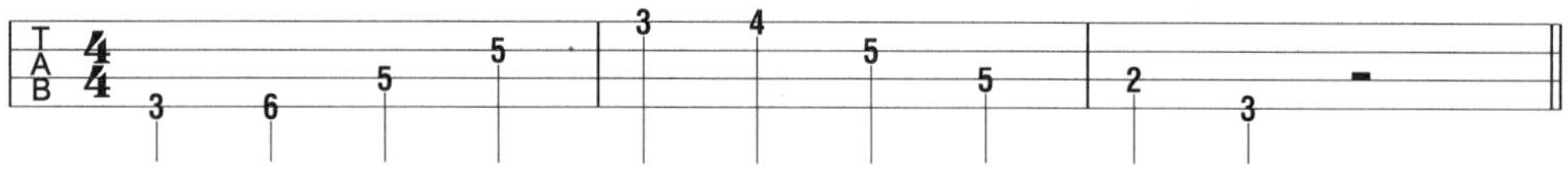

Four-Note Chords (Extensions Beyond the Triad)

So now after you've locked these shapes into memory, let's now add a *color note* (*color tone*) that technically works as an *extension*. (Note: Not all color tones are extensions.) This is a note that is added to chords and scales to add "color" that makes them sound more interesting. The way this works is that once you have learned the foundations of these arpeggios, you can add a fourth note above them, which gives their sound quality a certain "color." The most common color notes/extensions are the *major 7th*, *minor 7th*, and *dominant 7th*.

Major 7th Arpeggio

The major 7th chord is made up of a root, major 3rd, perfect 5th, and a *major 7th* (F♯ in the key of G).

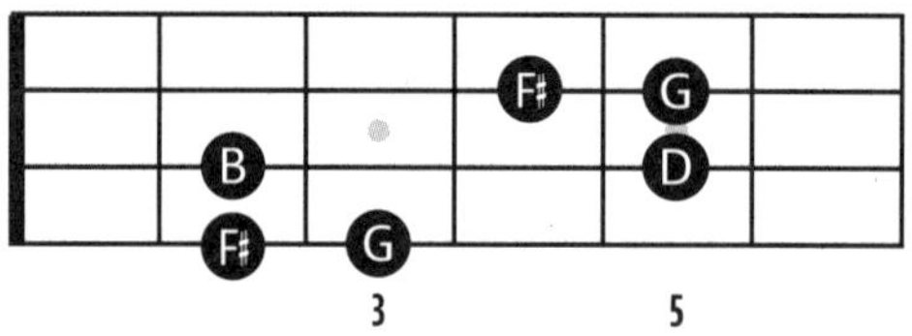

Minor 7th Arpeggio

The minor 7th chord is made up of a root, minor 3rd, perfect 5th, and a *minor 7th* (F♮ in the key of G).

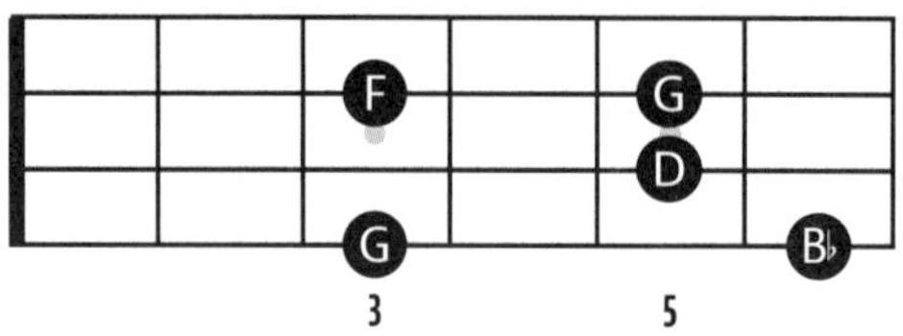

Dominant 7th Arpeggio

The dominant 7th chord is made up of a root, major 3rd, perfect 5th, and a minor 7th (G, B, D, and F).

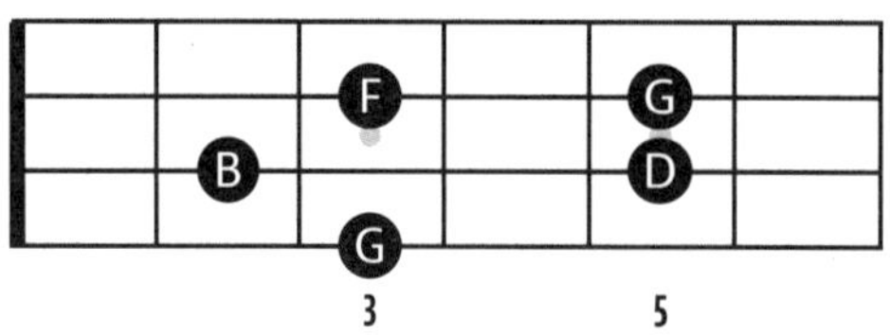

The way you use these is by identifying the chords of each of the notes you are playing in any section of a song. Then, choose which arpeggio would work best with the melody or vibe of that section of the song. Without getting into the nuts and bolts of music theory, most minor triads can be turned into minor 7th chords, whereas the context of the song will determine whether a major triad becomes a major 7th or dominant 7th chord. Usually, chords like the *5 chord* (you'll learn about this in the next chapter) will only have a dominant 7th quality, not a major 7th, but other chords like the *1 chord* or the *4 chord* can have either a dominant or major 7th sound. Mastering these arpeggios are important to adding flavor to your bass lines and songs.

Chapter 14

The Nashville Number System

Just like we discussed before, music is a language and can be written and learned in a variety of different ways. The *Nashville Number System* is the way most professional musicians communicate and learn songs with ease while being able to create and add their own flavor to songs. The way this works is through using the major scale. Basically, we assign a number to each note of the major scale (there are seven in total). For example, here's the C major scale.

C	D	E	F	G	A	B	C

Note that the scale starts over after the seventh note and begins again, this time an octave above where it originally started. Next, let's add numbers to each note:

C	D	E	F	G	A	B	C
1	2	3	4	5	6	7	1

You can apply this concept to every single key (there are 12 in total). By doing this, it allows for songs to be easily learned through patterns rather than just randomized notes. The way we learn this on bass is by learning the patterns on the fretboard and not just the notes. Once you learn the first pattern on the fretboard, you can use it in other keys by shifting the entire pattern up or down, depending on which key you're in. Let's use this pattern that shows the C major scale:

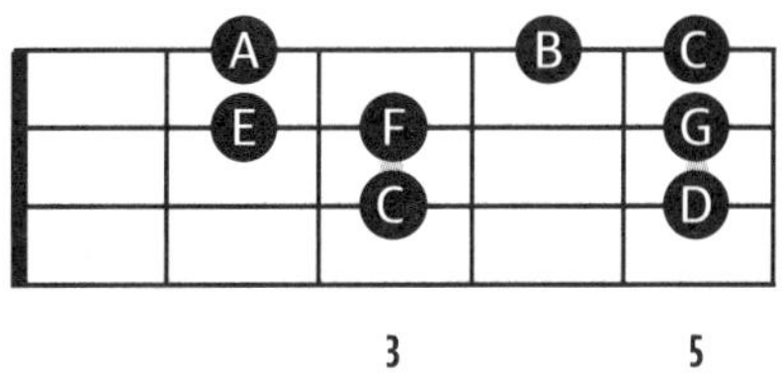

Now, let's replace each letter name with its corresponding number:

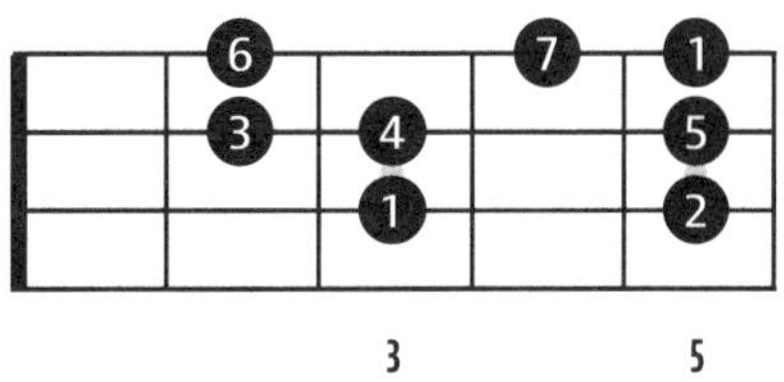

Once you have learned this pattern, you can start using these numbers to identify notes for songs and bass lines. For example, the song "Say" by John Mayer is in the key of B♭, and the chorus section consists of B♭–E♭–G–F. Using the number system, it would be written as 1–4–6–5 in the key of B♭. The reason this is important is because when playing any song, the selection of notes will reference the major scale for the song's progressions. By learning the number system, you shrink down the possibilities of notes to choose from (12 separate keys with all kinds of sharps and flats) to a single, movable system that makes it easier to learn and retain songs. Now, let's take it a step further and use this concept to create charts and learn songs.

What Is a Number Chart?

A *number chart* is basically shorthand writing to identify notes and the rhythms of songs and bass lines—there's no tablature or other kinds of notation on a staff involved. This way of writing out songs makes them easier to learn. Below is an example of a number chart of "Kids" by OneRepublic.

"KIDS"

Words and Music by Ryan Tedder, Brent Kutzle, Brandon Collins and Steve Wilmot

Tempo: 90 Time Sig: 4/4 Key: D

Intro	NO BASS
Verse	5 5 6 4 4 1 :‖
Pre - Chorus	5 5 6 4 4 1 :‖
Chorus	5 5 6 4 4 1 :‖
Verse	5 5 6 4 4 1 :‖
Chorus	5 5 6 4 4 1 :‖
Bridge	1 2 6 4 :‖
Chorus	5 5 6 4 4 1 :‖
Outro	5 5 6 4 4 1 :‖

How to Read a Number Chart

When reading number charts, each number that is written is equal to one bar, which, in the case above, would be four beats. So for example, seeing a number by itself like this would mean that it would be played for the length of four beats:

5

The next thing would be to see two numbers side by side underlined, like this:

5 6

The underline means that this would be a *split bar*. A split bar is basically each number sharing the measure, each having two beats. This can also be indicated by a box, like this:

6^{-} 4

Sometimes, songs with split bars are not equally split between the four beats, but instead, they are unequal. For instance, this example shows that you would stay on the 4 chord for three beats and stay on the 6m chord for one beat:

III I
4 6m

When reading or writing number charts, make sure to pay attention to the time signature because that will determine how long one bar would be within a song. For example, here is a song that's written in 6/8:

Time Sig: 6/8 Key: B

1 1 1 𝄇 PIANO INTRO

So now that we know that the song is in the 6/8, each of those numbers will be equal to six beats rather than four. Knowing this will help you keep accurate timing when reading each chart.

An *anticipation* or *push* is described by an arrow on top of the note that you're pushing before. Below, the 4 chord and the 2 chord are struck on the "and" or upbeat of beat 2 within the measure.

$$\underline{6^{-}\ \overset{<}{4}}\quad \underline{5\ \overset{<}{2}^{-}}$$

If a section or progression repeats once it is indicated by this symbol, called a *repeat sign*:

𝄇

If numbers are indicated with a flat symbol or sharp symbol, this means that the chord is either moved down or up one fret from that number, but it still retains its quality:

$$3^{\flat} \qquad 3^{\sharp}$$

A diamond indicates that you play a note once and let it ring out for the length of the bar. It is indicated by the number either being in the center of the diamond or the diamond being on top of the number.

◇1 $\overset{\diamond}{5}$

Sometimes, you will see diamonds that are connected like this:

$\overset{\diamond}{2}\frown\overset{\diamond}{2}$

When diamonds are connected, this means you play a note and hold for the length of both numbers, which in this case would be two bars.

A *cut-off* or *mute* is when you strike a note for one beat and let the rest of the measure stay silent for the length of the bar. It's shown by a triangle placed over the number, like this:

$\overset{\blacktriangle}{1}$

You may also see split bars and numbers that look like this:

$$\underline{\tfrac{5}{7}\ \ 1}$$

Numbers like this 5/7 just mean there is a chord played over a bass note other than the tonic or root. As a bass player, you would just play whatever note is on the bottom, so for this example, we would play the 7.

Let's take these concepts and explore them in some real songs. Here are a few charts to get you started.

"BAREFOOT BLUE JEAN NIGHT"

Words and Music by Dylan Altman, Eric Paslay and Terry Sawchuk

Tempo: 86bpm   Time Sig: 4/4   Key: G

Intro	1 5 4 5 1 5 4 5
V1	1 5 4 5 1 5 4 5 BASS IN ON V1 part 2
	1 5 4 5 1 5 4 5
CH	1 5 4 5 1 5 4 5 :]
Inst	1 5 4 5
V2	1 5 4 5 1 5 4 5 :]
CH	1 5 4 5 1 5 4 5 :]
CH	HALF DOWN, Hits (4, 5) BACK IN
Turn	4 5 4 5 4 5 4 5
CH	SAME UNTIL END

"USE SOMEBODY"

Words and Music by Caleb Followill, Nathan Followill, Jared Followill and Matthew Followill

Tempo: 137bpm Time Sig: 4/4 Key: C

Intro	1 3^- 4 4 (2x)
	6^- 1 4 4 (2x)
V1	1 3^- 4 4 (2x)
	6^- 1 4 4 (2x)
V2	1 3^- 4 4 (2x)
	6^- 1 4 4 (2x)
CH	1 3^- 4 4 (2x)
	6^- 1 4 4 (2x)
V3	(Same as first)
CH	(Same as first)
Br	2^- 2^- $5^\flat$ $5^\flat$ (2x)
Inst	1 3^- 4 4
	6^- 1 4 4 (3x)
	6^- 1 ◇4 ◇4
	END

"HEARTBREAK WARFARE"

Words and Music by John Mayer

Tempo: 97bpm Time Sig: 4/4 Key: A

Section	Chords
Intro	1 1 4 4 :|
Verse	1 1 4 4 1 1 4 4 :|
Chorus	6 1 4 4 :|
Verse	1 1 4 4 1 1 4 4 :|
Chorus	6 1 4 4 :|
Solo	$6^{\flat}$ $3^{\flat}$ $6^{\flat}$ $3^{\flat}$:|
Bridge	$6^{\flat}$ $6^{\flat}$ $7^{\flat}$ $7^{\flat}$:|
Chorus	◇1 ◇1 ◇1 ◇1
Verse	1 1 4 4 1 1 4 4 :|
Outro	1 1 4 4 1 1 4 4 :|

Seeing number charts is a great thing, but it's even better to apply this knowledge to other songs to understand the harmonic structure of other tunes at a deeper level. Let's circle back to "Dear Marie" from Chapter 5. What would it look like as a number chart? Let's start with just the verse to keep things simple.

"DEAR MARIE"

Words and Music by John Mayer

Verse 1

```
A
Dear Marie,

D                                        A
Tell me what it was I was I used to be?

            D
Oh, dear Marie,

                                         A
Tell me what it was I was I used to be?

                 E                          D                      A
And if you're further up the road, can you show me what I still can't see?
```


This song is in the key of A, so using our formula, we get the following numbers that correspond to the note names of the A major scale.

A	B	C#	D	E	F#	G#
1	2	3	4	5	6	7

Using those numbers, fill in the blank chart with the correct chords.

"DEAR MARIE" (Number Chart)

Words and Music by John Mayer

Tempo: 95bpm   Time Sig: 4/4   Key: A

Intro	___ ___ ___ ___	
V1	___ ___ ___ ___	BASS IN
	___ ___ ___ ___	
	___ ___ ___ ___	

Now, compare your answers to the filled-in chart below.

"DEAR MARIE" (Number Chart)

Words and Music by John Mayer

Tempo: 95bpm   Time Sig: 4/4   Key: A

Intro	1 1 1 1	
V1	1 4 1 1	BASS IN
	4 4 1 1	
	5 4 1 1	

Great! Now, go ahead and fill out the rest of the chart and compare your results with the answers at the end of the book.

"DEAR MARIE" (Number Chart)

Words and Music by John Mayer

Tempo: 95bpm Time Sig: 4/4 Key: A

Intro	___ ___ ___ ___
V1	___ ___ ___ ___ BASS IN
	___ ___ ___ ___
	___ ___ ___ ___
V2	___ ___ ___ ___
	___ ___ ___ ___
	___ ___ ___ ___
V3	___ ___ ___ ___
	___ ___ ___ ___
	___ ___ ___ ___
Gtr Solo	___ ___ ___ ___
	___ ___ ___ ___
	___ ___ ___ ___
V1	___ ___ ___ ___
	___ ___ ___ ___
	___ ___ ___ ___
	END

Now, do the same for the rest of the chord charts from Chapter 5. (You can find the answers at the end of the book.)

"AMAZING GRACE" (Number Chart)

Traditional American Melody

Words by John Newton

Tempo: 80bpm   Time Sig: 3/4   Key: C

V1

___ ___ ___ ___

___ ___ ___ ___

___ ___ ___ ___

___ ___ ___ ___

V2

___ ___ ___ ___

___ ___ ___ ___

___ ___ ___ ___

___ ___ ___ ___

V3

___ ___ ___ ___

___ ___ ___ ___

___ ___ ___ ___

___ ___ ___ ___

END

"THINKING OUT LOUD" (Number Chart)

Words and Music by Ed Sheeran and Amy Wadge

Tempo: 79bpm   Time Sig: 4/4   Key: C

V1   ___ ___ ___ ___ ___ ___ ___ ___ :||

Pre   ___ ___ ___ ___ ___ ___ ___ ___ :|| BASS IN

___ ___ ___ ___ ___

___ ___ ___ ___ ___

CH   ___ ___ ___ ___ ___ ___ ___ ___ :||

___ ___ ___ ___ ___ ___ ___

V2   ___ ___ ___ ___ ___ ___ ___ ___ :||

Pre   ___ ___ ___ ___ ___ ___ ___ ___ :||

___ ___ ___ ___ ___

___ ___ ___ ___ ___

CH   ___ ___ ___ ___ ___ ___ ___ ___ :||

___ ___ ___ ___ ___ ___ ___

Outro   ___ ___ ___ ___ ___ ___ ___ :|| (repeat 3x)

"ALL OF ME" (Number Chart)

Words and Music by John Stephens and Toby Gad

Tempo: 120bpm   Time Sig: 4/4   Key: G

Intro	___ ___ ___ ___ :|| PIANO INTRO
V1	___ ___ ___ ___ ___ ___ ___ ___ :||
Pre	___ ___ ___ ___ :|| BASS IN
CH	___ ___ ___ ___ ___ ___ ___ ___ :||
V2	___ ___ ___ ___ :|| ___ ___ ___ ___
Pre	___ ___ ___ ___ :||
CH	___ ___ ___ ___ ___ ___ ___ ___ :||
Pre	___ ___ ___ ___ :||
CH	___ ___ ___ ___ ___ ___ ___ ___ :||
Outro	___ ___ ___ ___ :||

Chapter 15:
Mastering the Fretboard

After getting all these scales and techniques under your belt, something you may notice is that after a while, your playing may start to shrink down to a box that you can't get out of. This is where mastering the fretboard comes in.

When you master the fretboard, the entire bass is unlocked for you, making playing anywhere on the neck of the bass possible. The way you do this is by shifting the starting point of your patterns and scales to other notes on the fretboard from where you initially started. Soon, you'll be able to play your scales from the E string to the G string, making your mastery more complete.

Moving to Different Keys

Part of fretboard mastery is being able to transpose the patterns you've learned to different areas of the neck. Let's start with the A major pentatonic scale.

A Major Pentatonic Scale

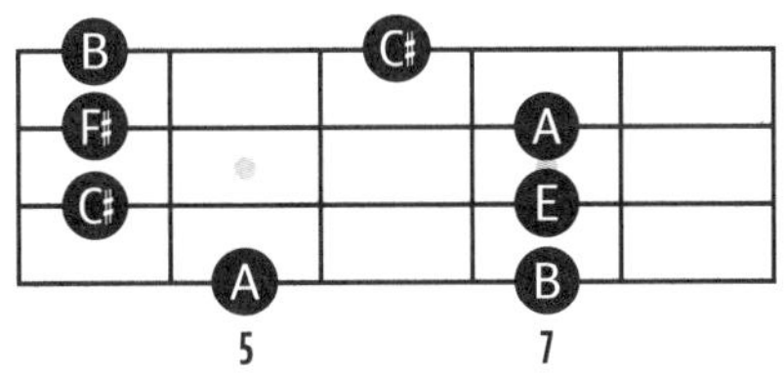

Now, let's move this scale to the key of G. You'll keep the spacing between each feet the same, but you'll just move the overall pattern down two frets.

G Major Pentatonic Scale

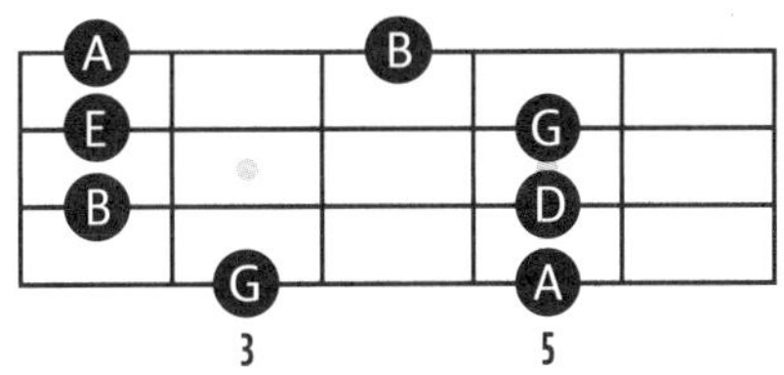

OK, let's figure out where the scale fits on a single string. Here's the A pentatonic scale you learned.

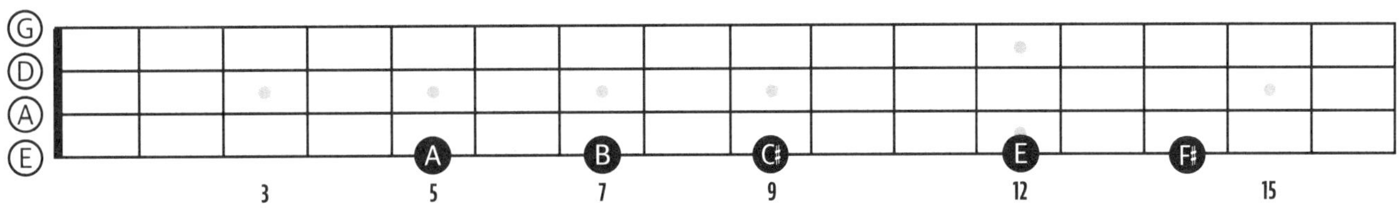

Now, here's the scale transposed to G.

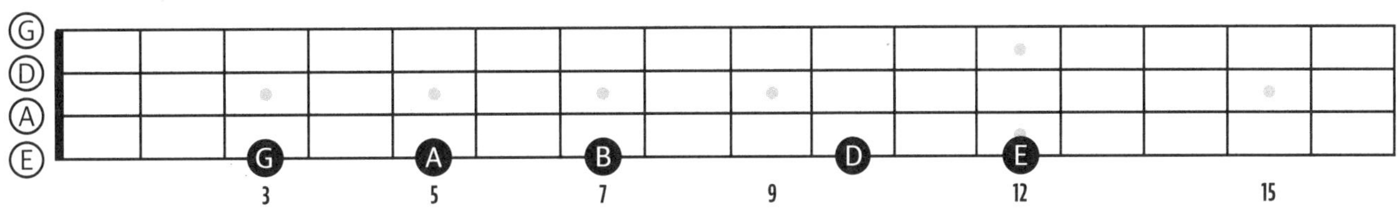

Once you are familiar with the major scale on the E string, we will go to our next step: shifting the starting note to another degree within the scale.

A Major Pentatonic Scale, Second Position

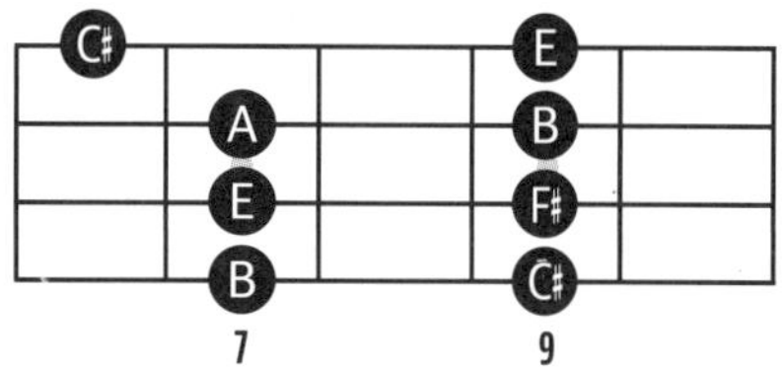

G Major Pentatonic Scale, Second Position

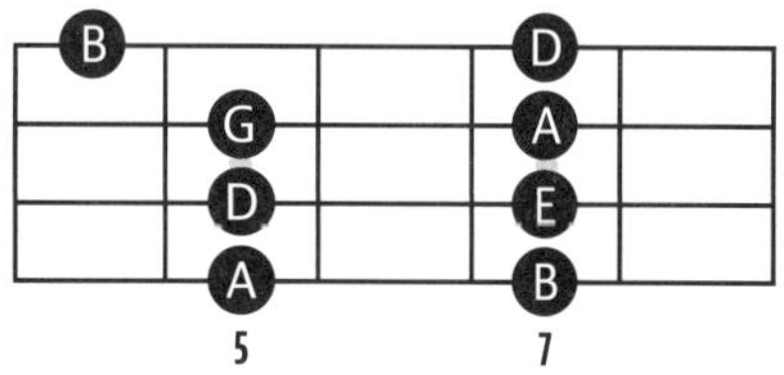

Let's keep moving. Next, we'll move through each note on the 1st string as a starting point and apply the rest of the pentatonic shapes you learned earlier in the book. Here's the third position transposed from A to G:

A Major Pentatonic Scale, Third Position

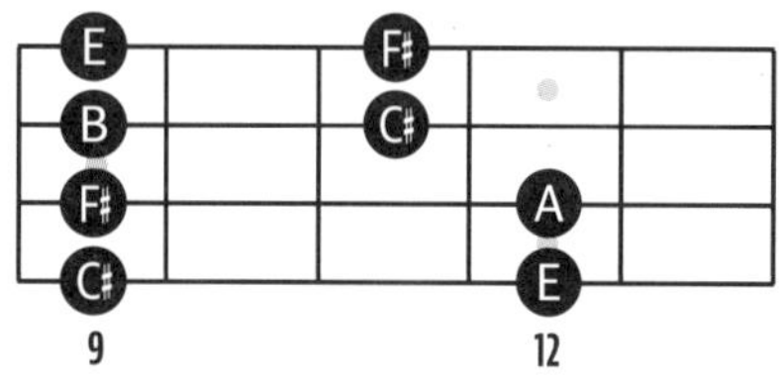

G Major Pentatonic Scale, Third Position

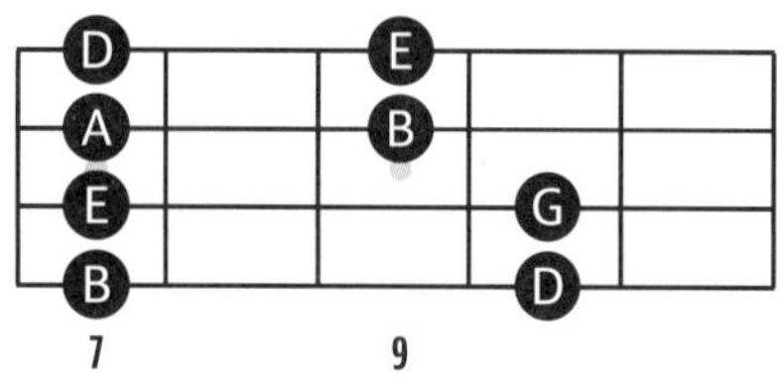

Let's continue up the scale to the next note:

A Major Pentatonic Scale, Fourth Position

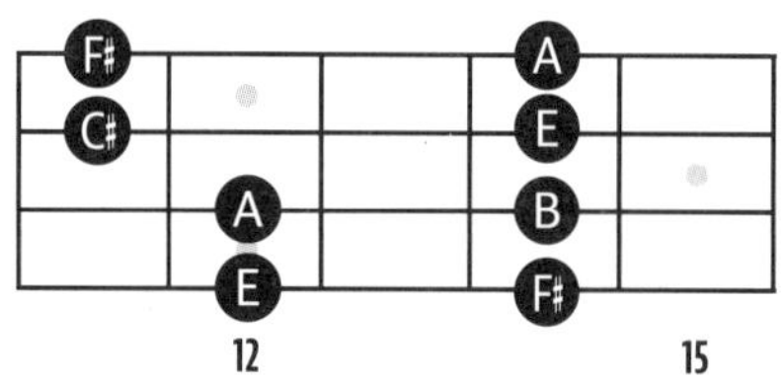

G Major Pentatonic Scale, Fourth Position

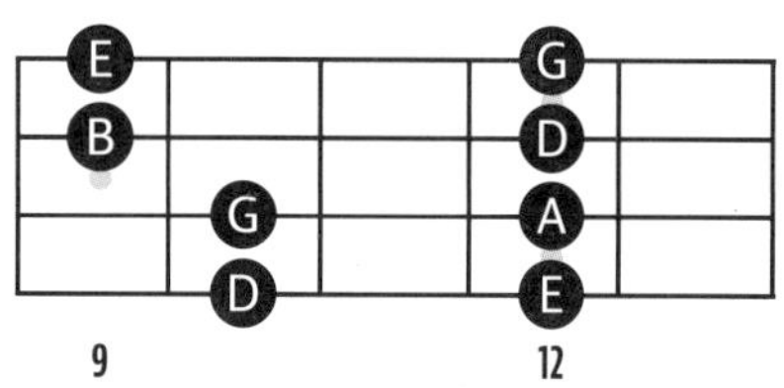

Finally, let's apply this to the last note of the scale (which is also the relative minor—in A it's the F♯ minor pentatonic scale, and in G, it's E minor):

A Major Pentatonic Scale, Fifth Position
(F♯ Minor Pentatonic Scale, Root Position)

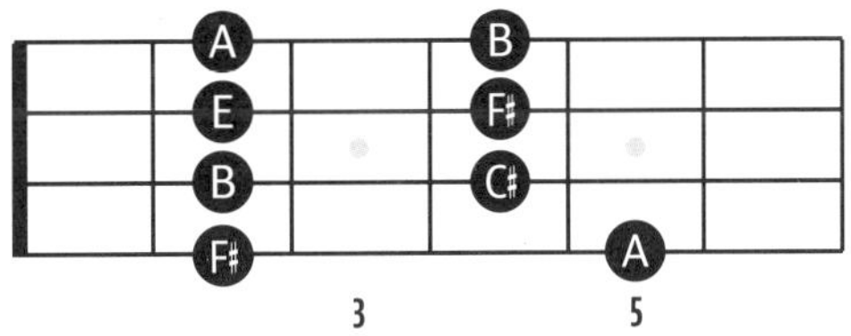

G Major Pentatonic Scale, Fifth Position
(E Minor Pentatonic Scale, Root Position)

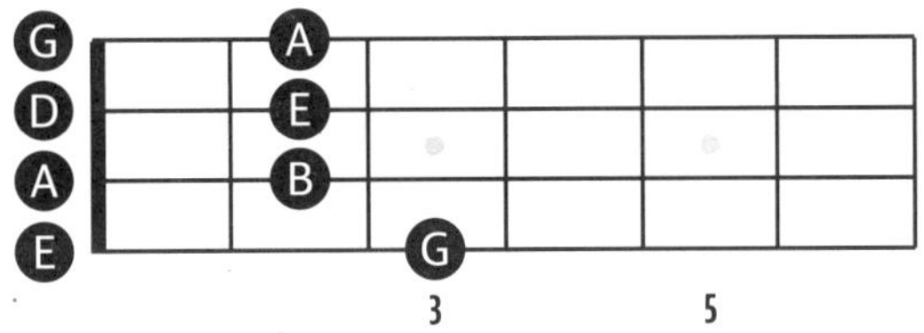

Learning these patterns will start to increase your familiarity with the fretboard so that you are never lost. Now, let's apply this same approach to the major scale.

Using Modes to Master the Fretboard

The major scale and major pentatonic scale have very similar notes to each other; the only difference is there are two notes added to the pentatonic scale to make it a major scale. These notes are the 4th and 7th, which in the key of A would be D and G♯, respectively.

When applying this concept to the major scale, the shifted patterns as they move up positions are called *modes*. The seven modes of the major scale are as follows:

- Ionian (1, the same as the major scale)
- Dorian (2)
- Phrygian (3)
- Lydian (4)
- Mixolydian (5)
- Aeolian (6; also known as the relative minor scale)
- Locrian (7)

These modes utilize three notes per string, using your index, middle, and pinky fingers. It's a little bit of a stretch, but no worries—you'll get it down in no time!

Major Scale, First Position (Ionian Mode/Primary Major Scale)

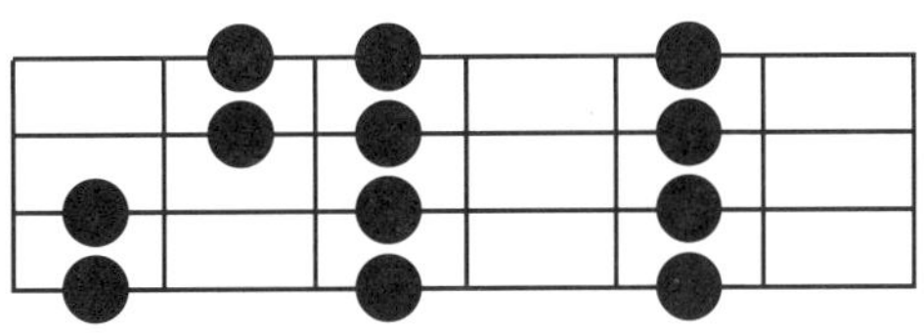

Major Scale, Second Position (Dorian Mode)

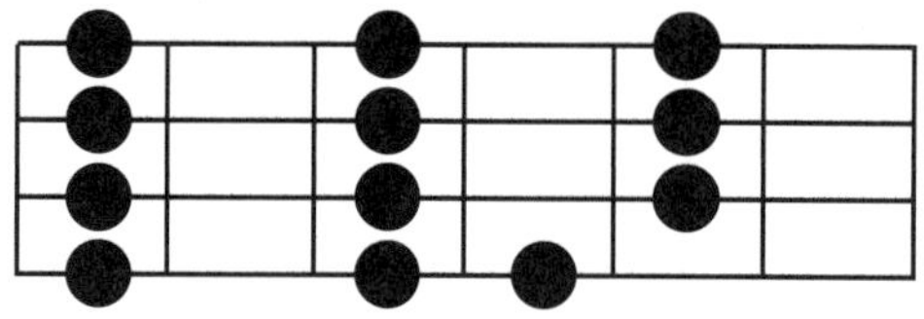

Major Scale, Third Position (Phrygian Mode)

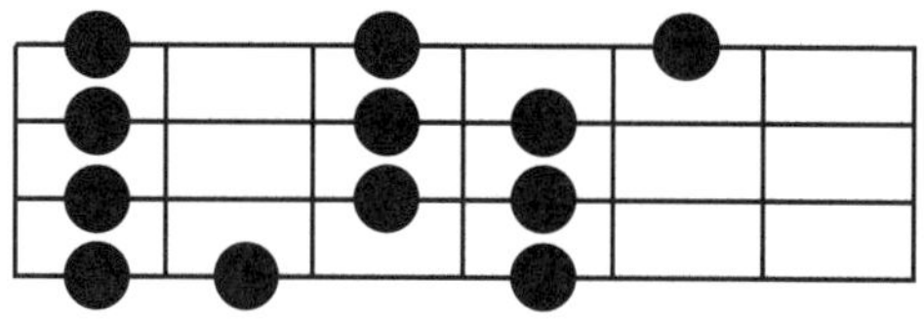

Major Scale, Fourth Position (Lydian Mode)

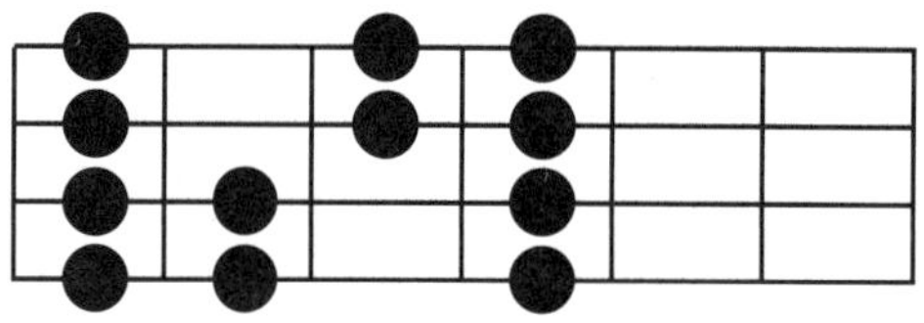

Major Scale, Fifth Position (Mixolydian Mode)

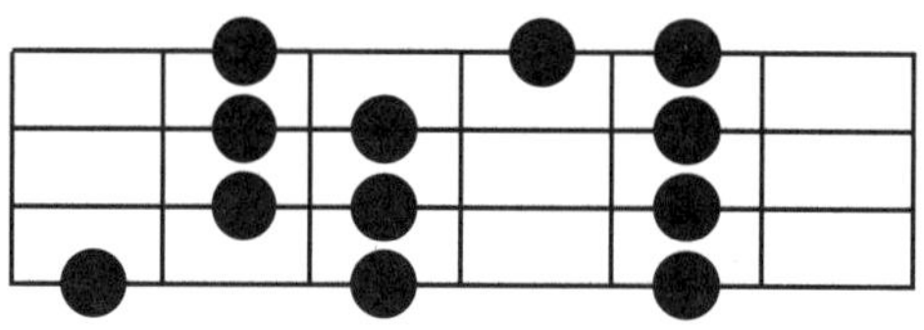

Major Scale, Sixth Position (Aeolian Mode/Relative Minor Scale)

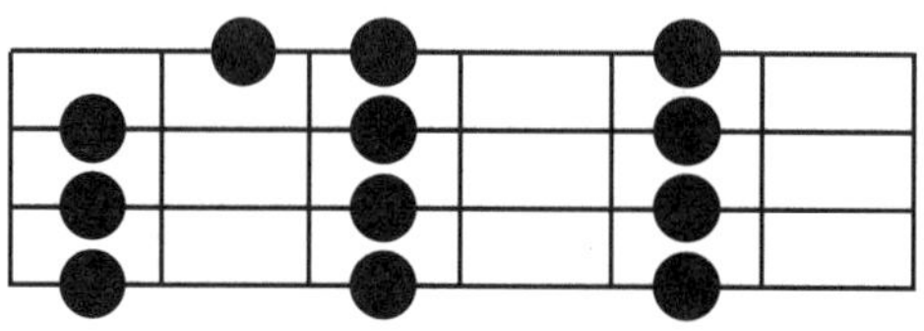

Major Scale, Seventh Position (Locrian Mode)

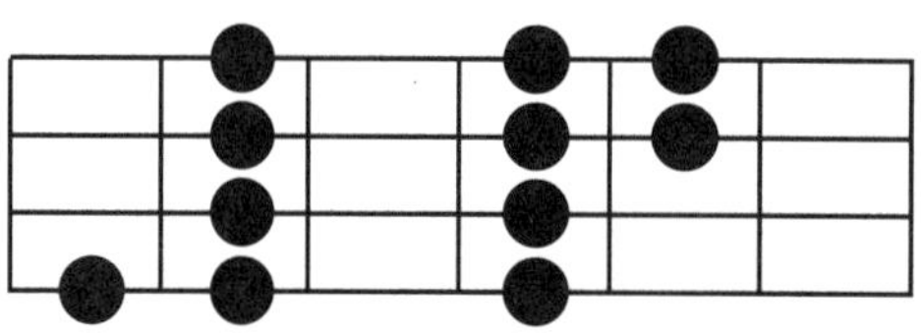

Just like what we did before, let's identify the major scale by going up the E string to know where the starting notes are.

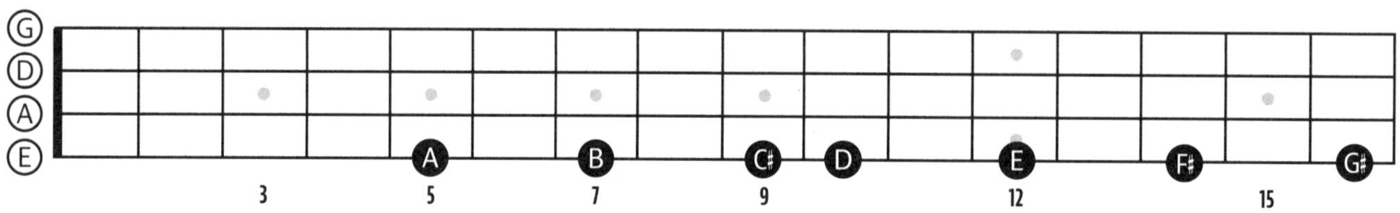

Now let's apply this to the A major scale.

A Major Scale

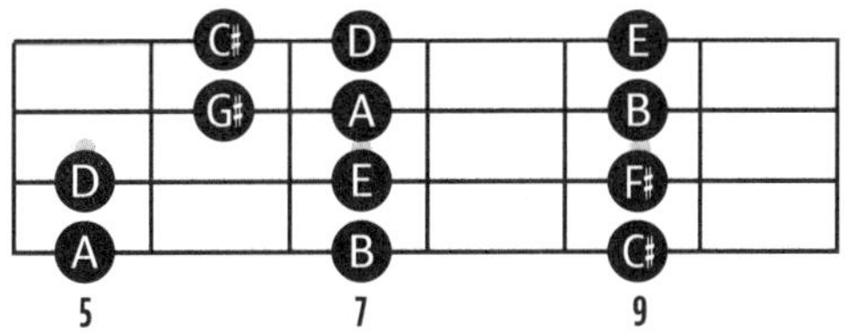

Next, we'll assign each shape to its respective starting note, starting with A:

A Ionian

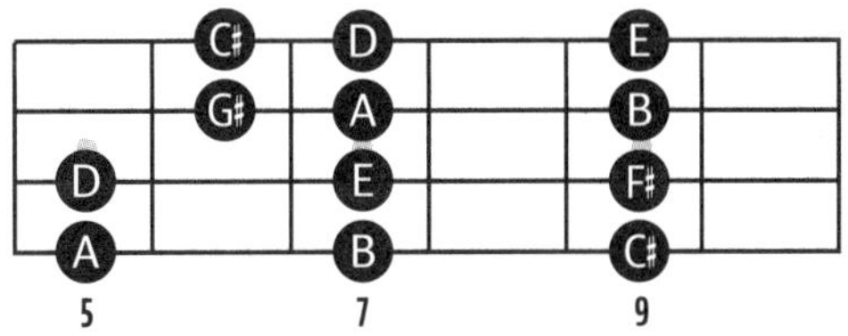

B Dorian

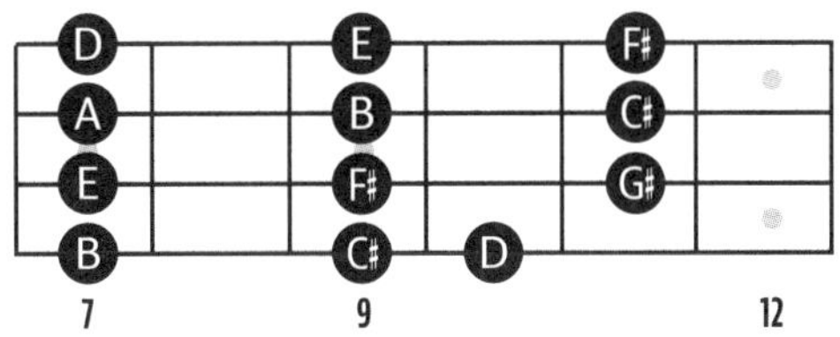

C♯ Phrygian

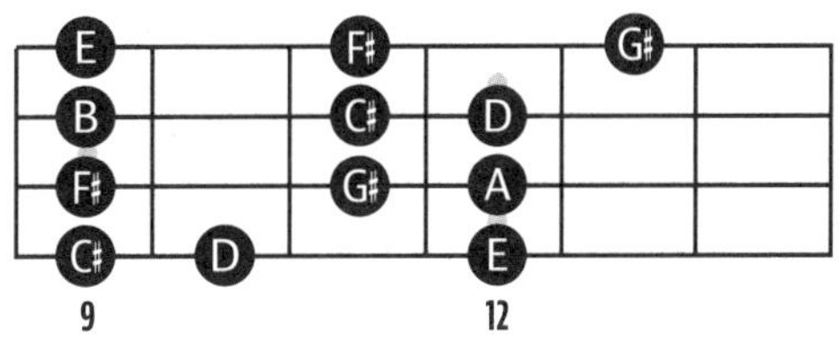

D Lydian

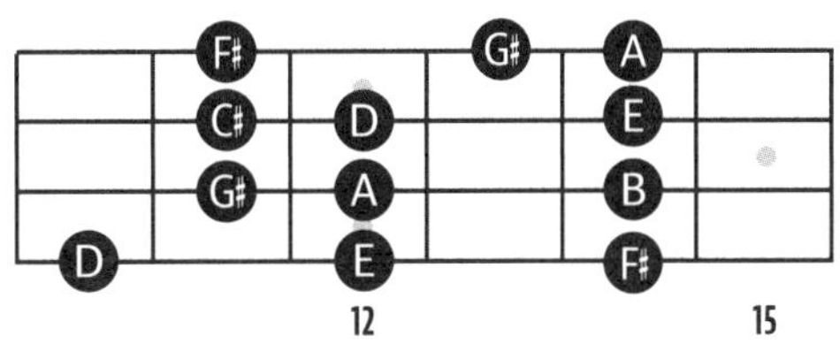

E Mixolydian

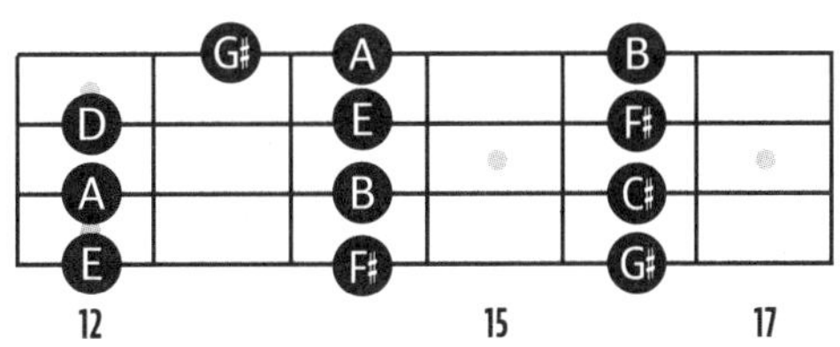

F♯ Aeolian

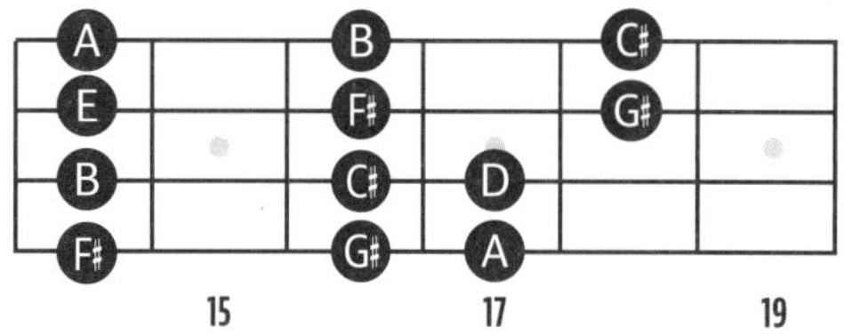

G♯ Locrian

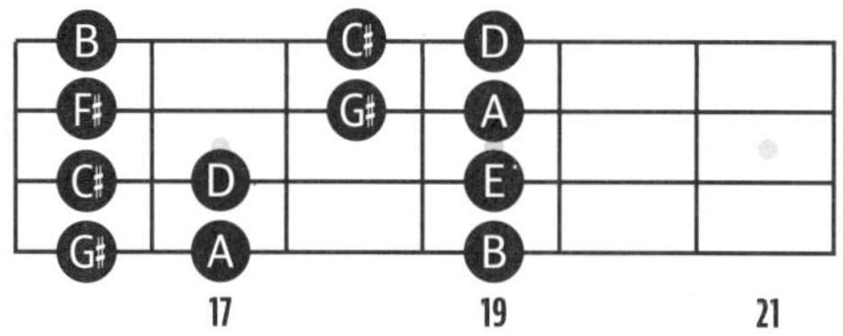

Learning these modes and positions will speed up the process of mastering the fretboard. For an even greater challenge, we've moved to the key of G.

G Ionian

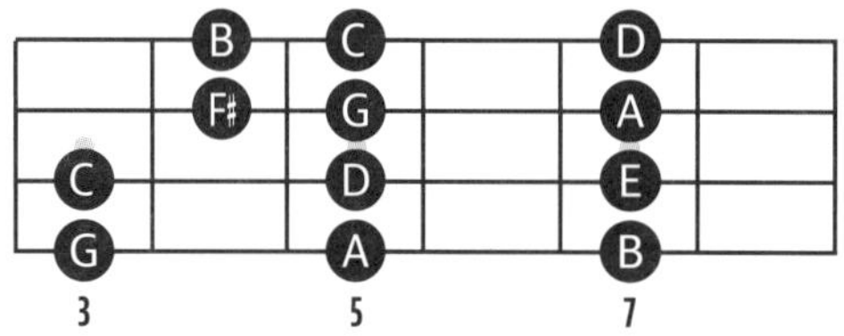

A Dorian

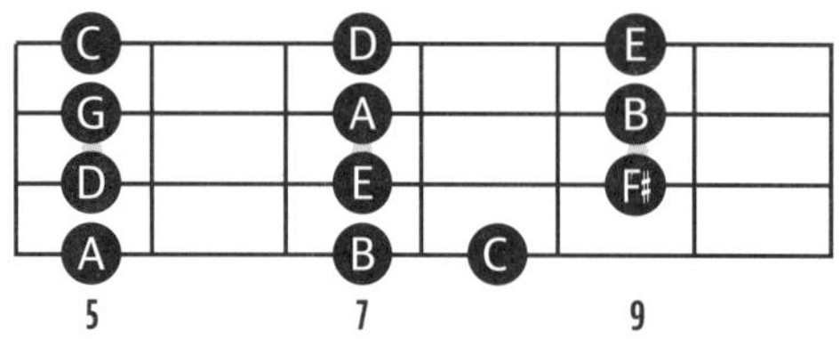

B Phrygian

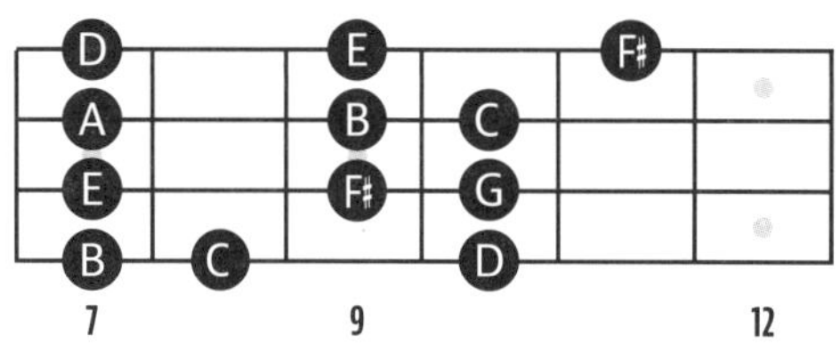

C Lydian

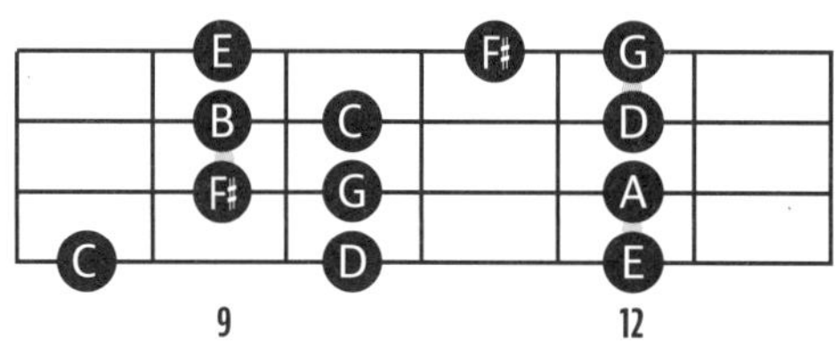

D Mixolydian

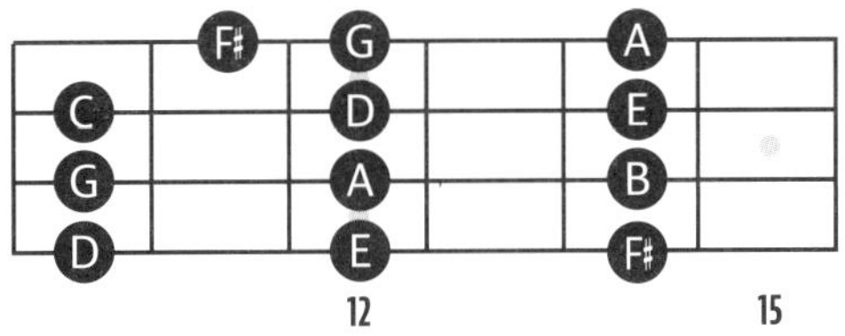

E Aeolian

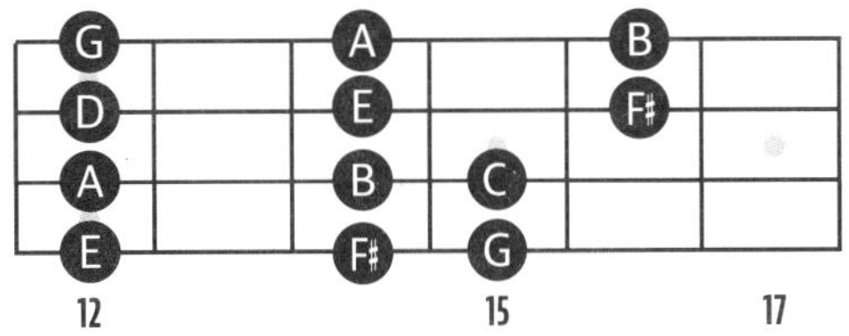

F♯ Locrian

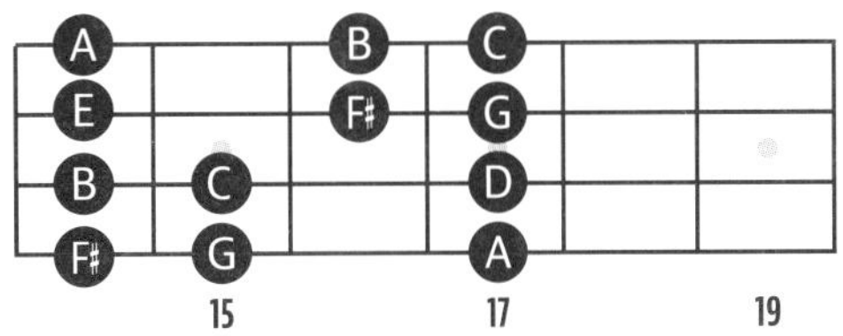

Chapter 16
Scale Exercises

Now that you've familiarized yourself with the modes in the key of G, tackle the next set of exercises. The first set of exercises work with the pentatonic scale. (Refer back to pages 79 through 81 for a refresher on the positions.)

Pentatonic Scale Exercises (Key of G)

Track 83

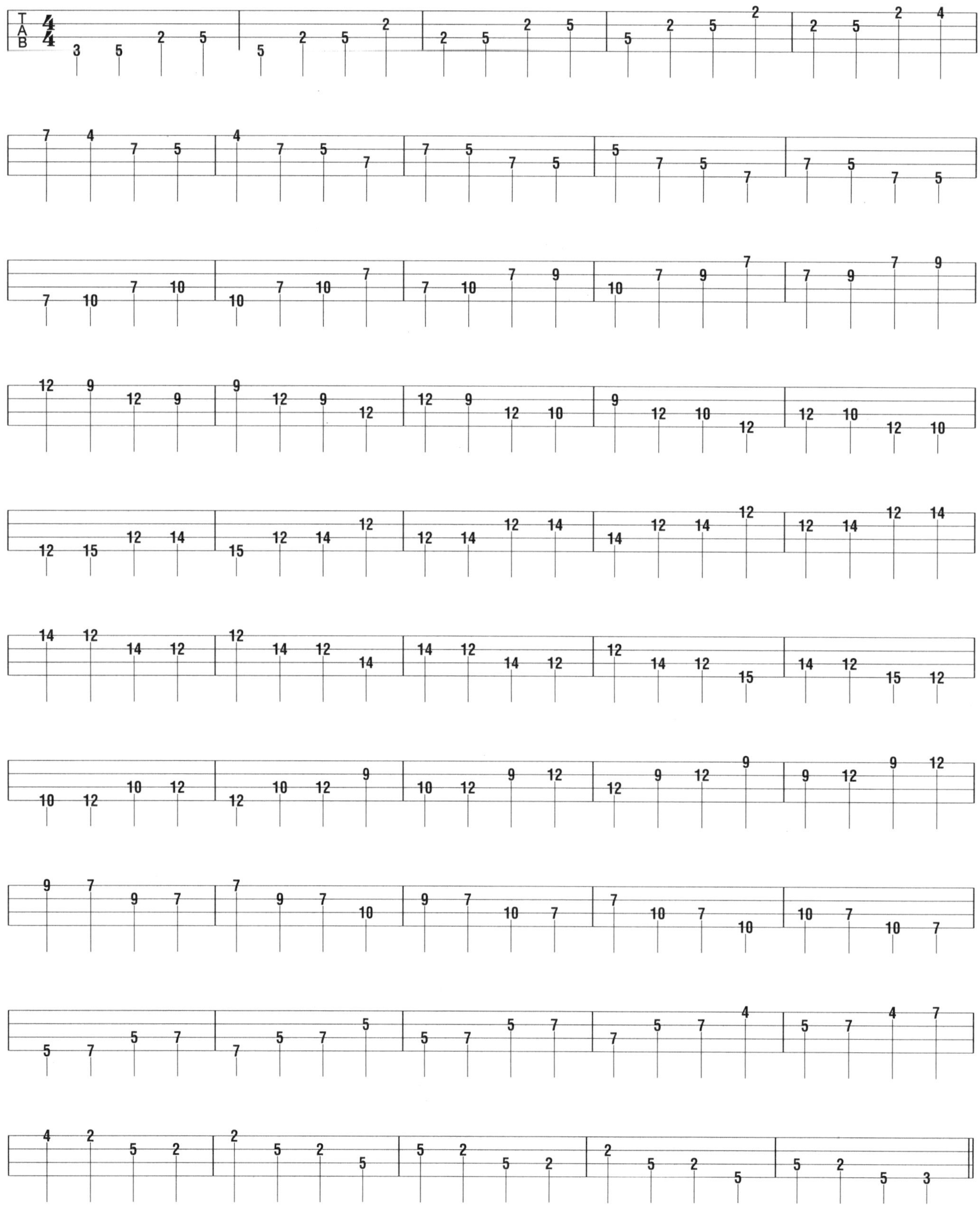

Track 84

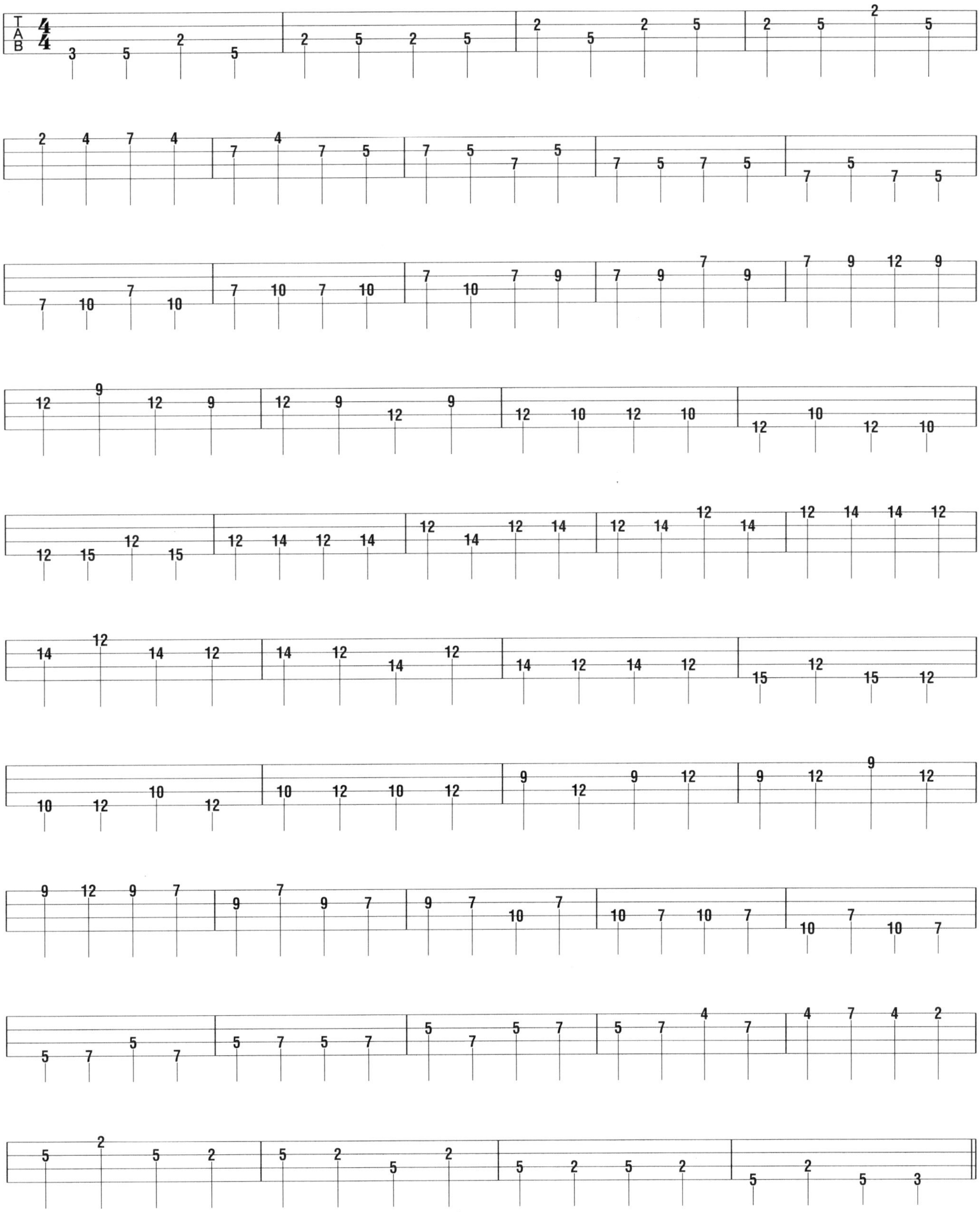

Track 85

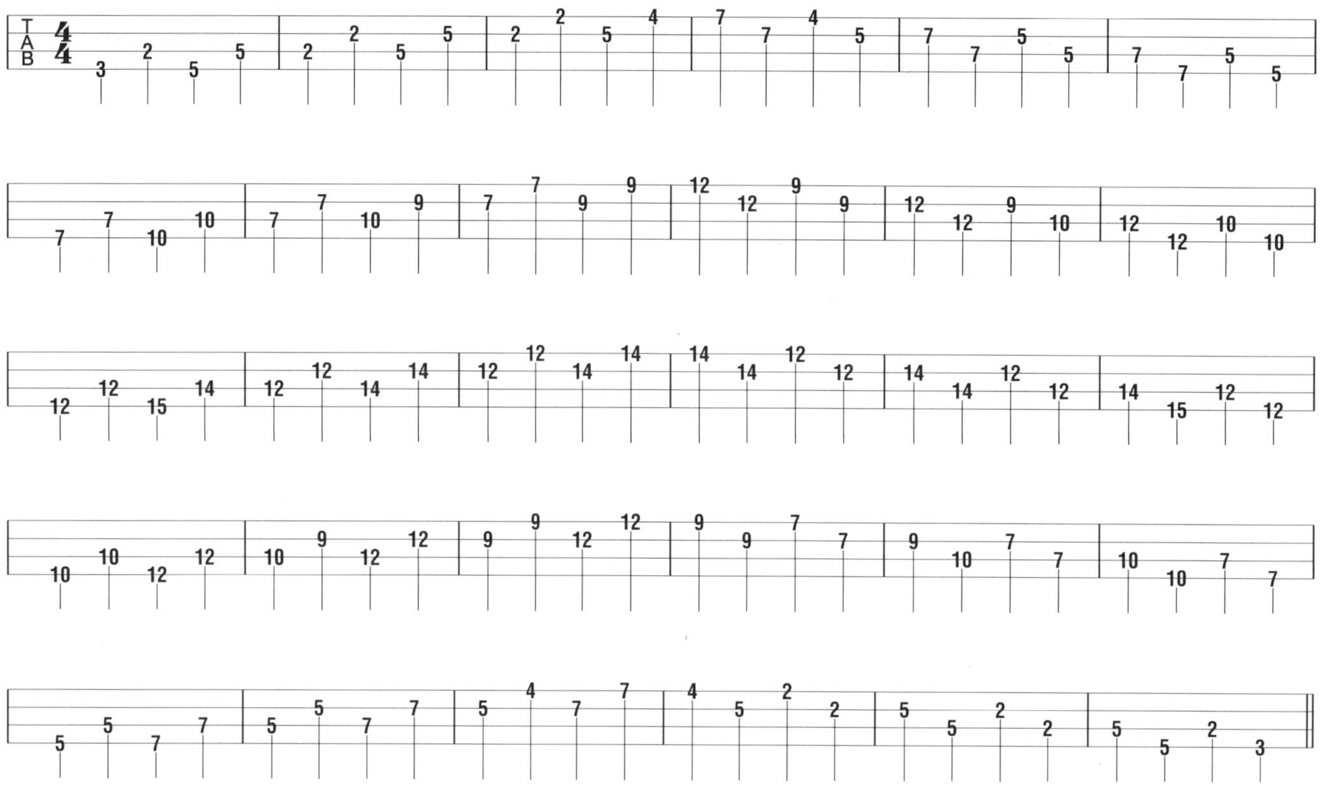

Next, play through these major scale exercises.

Major Scale Exercises (Key of G)

Track 86

Track 87

Track 88

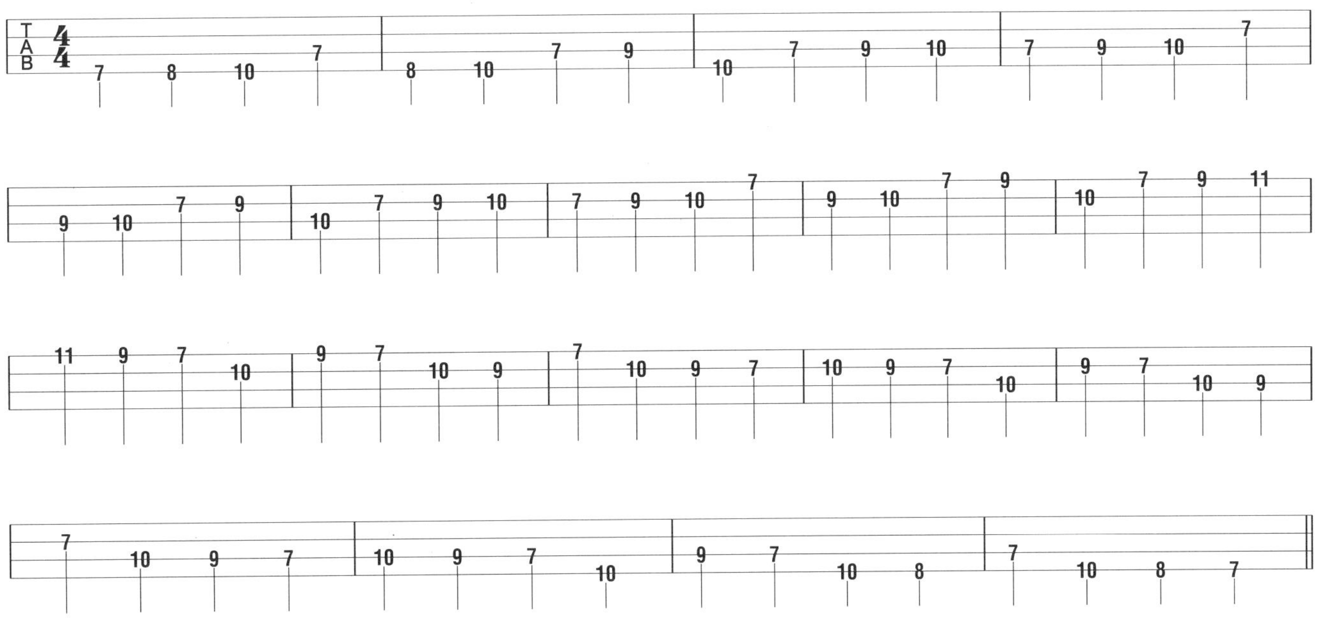

Track 89

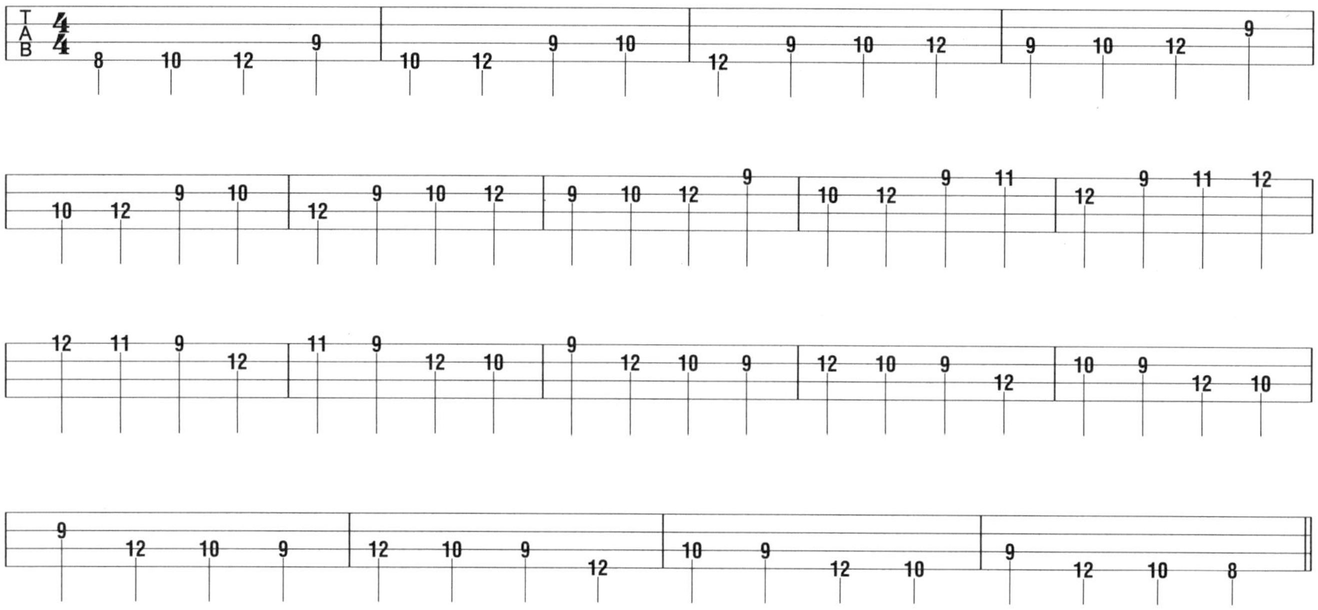

Track 90

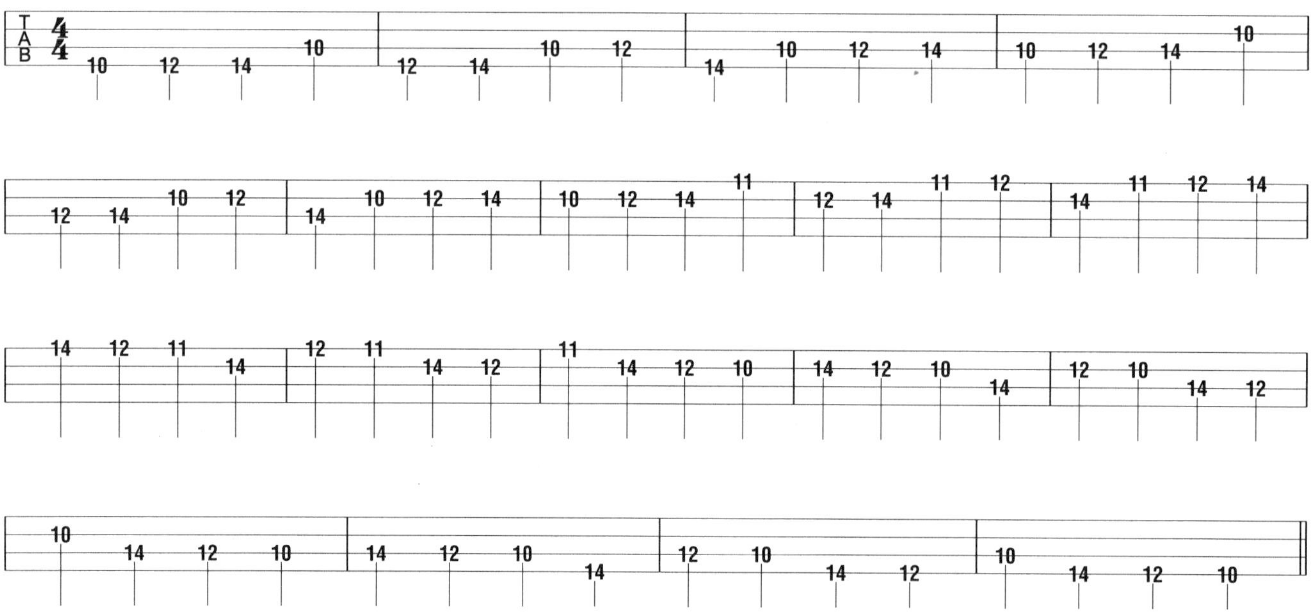

Track 91

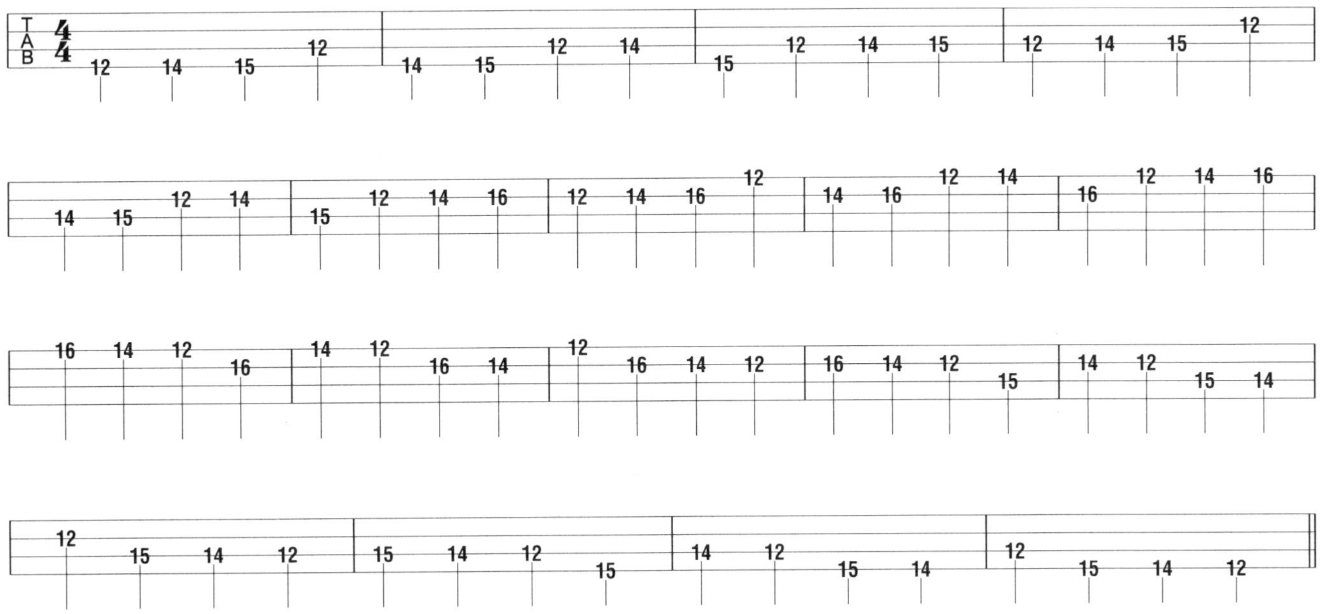

Track 92

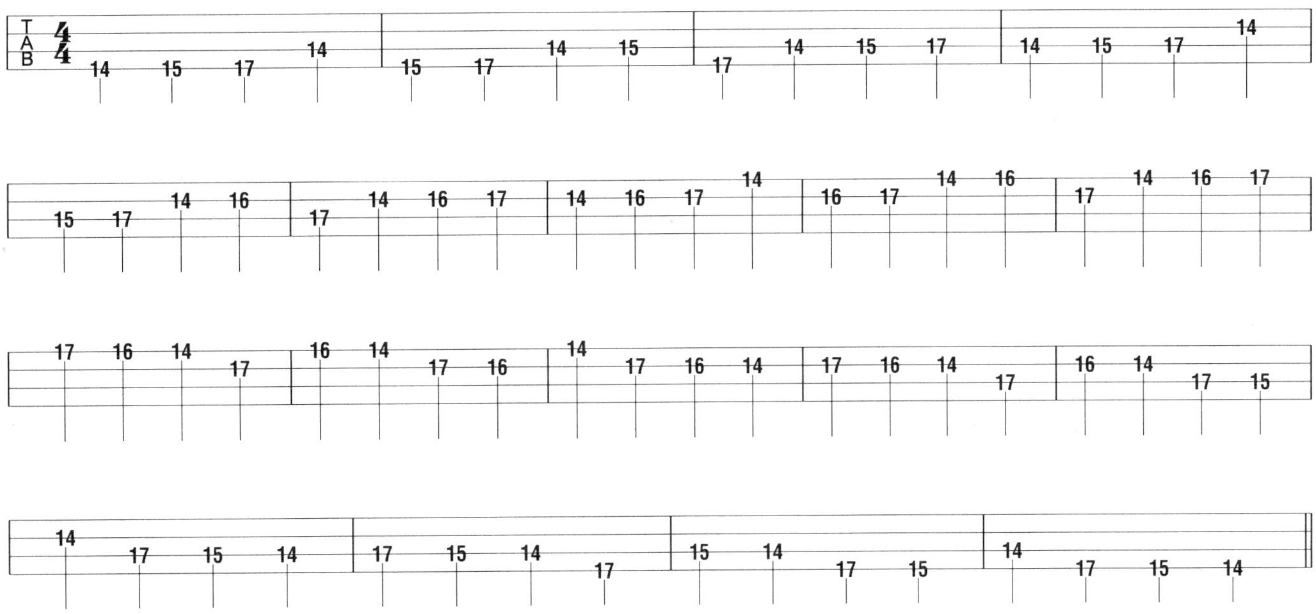

Track 93

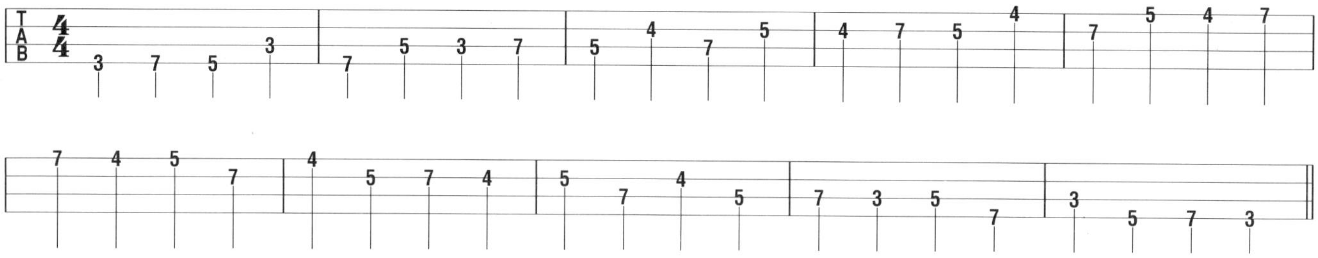

Track 94

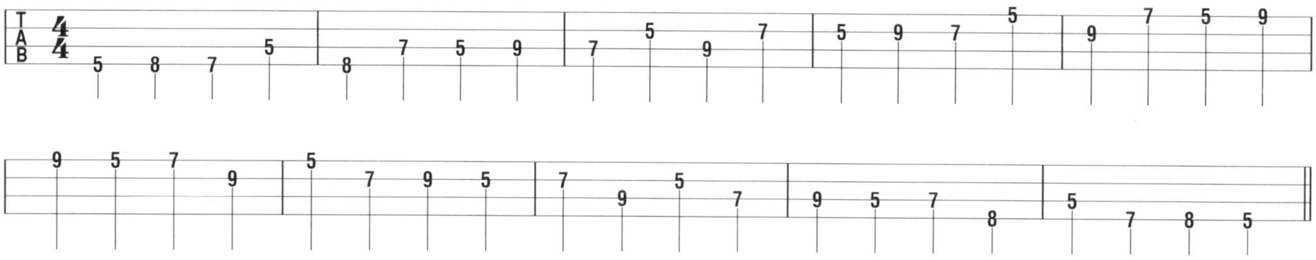

Track 95

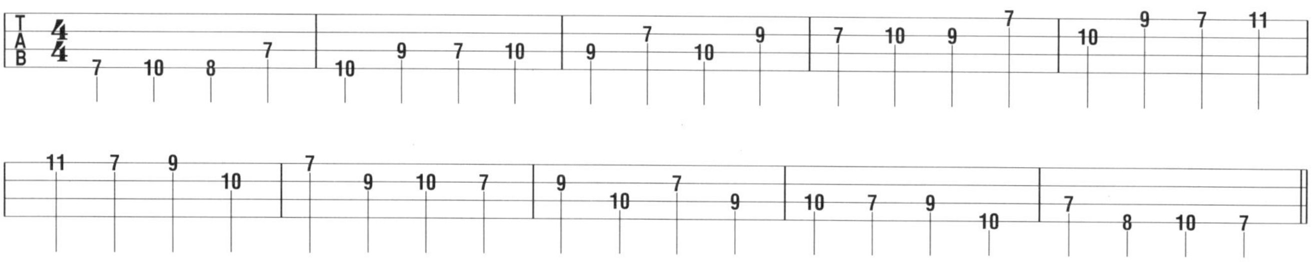

Track 96

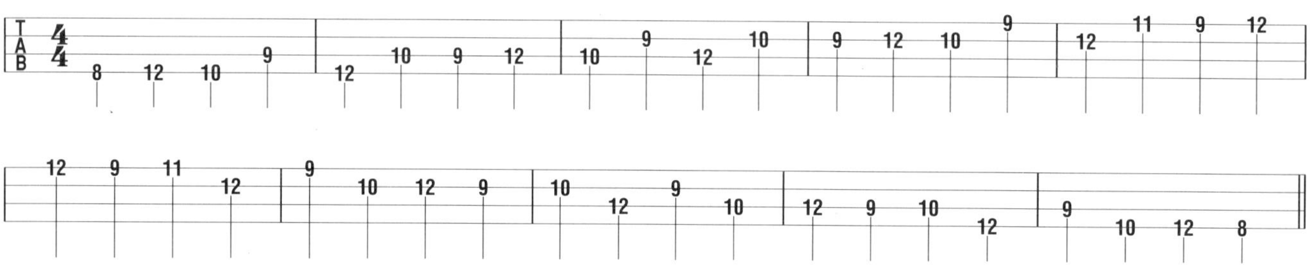

Track 97

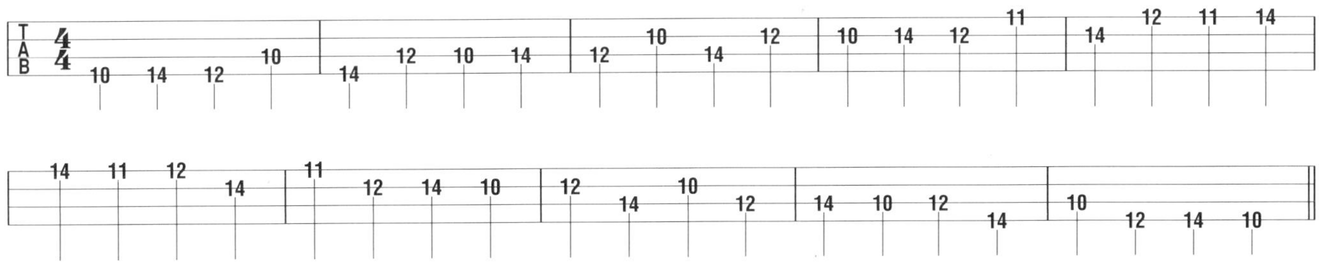

Track 98

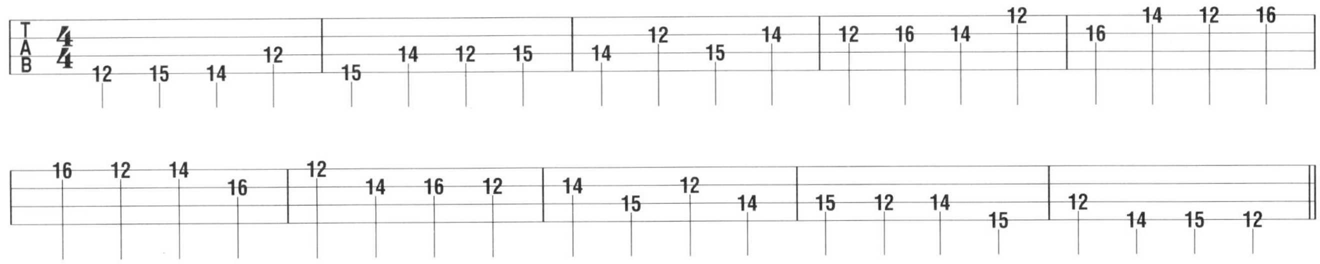

Track 99

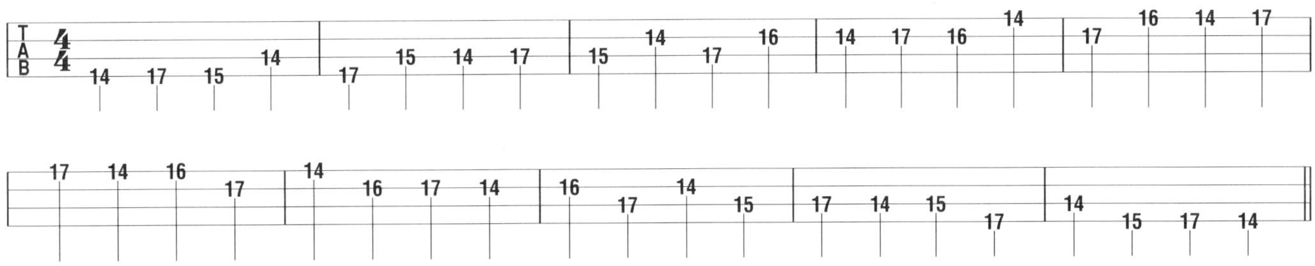

Combining Major Pentatonic Positions and Major Scale Modes

Track 100

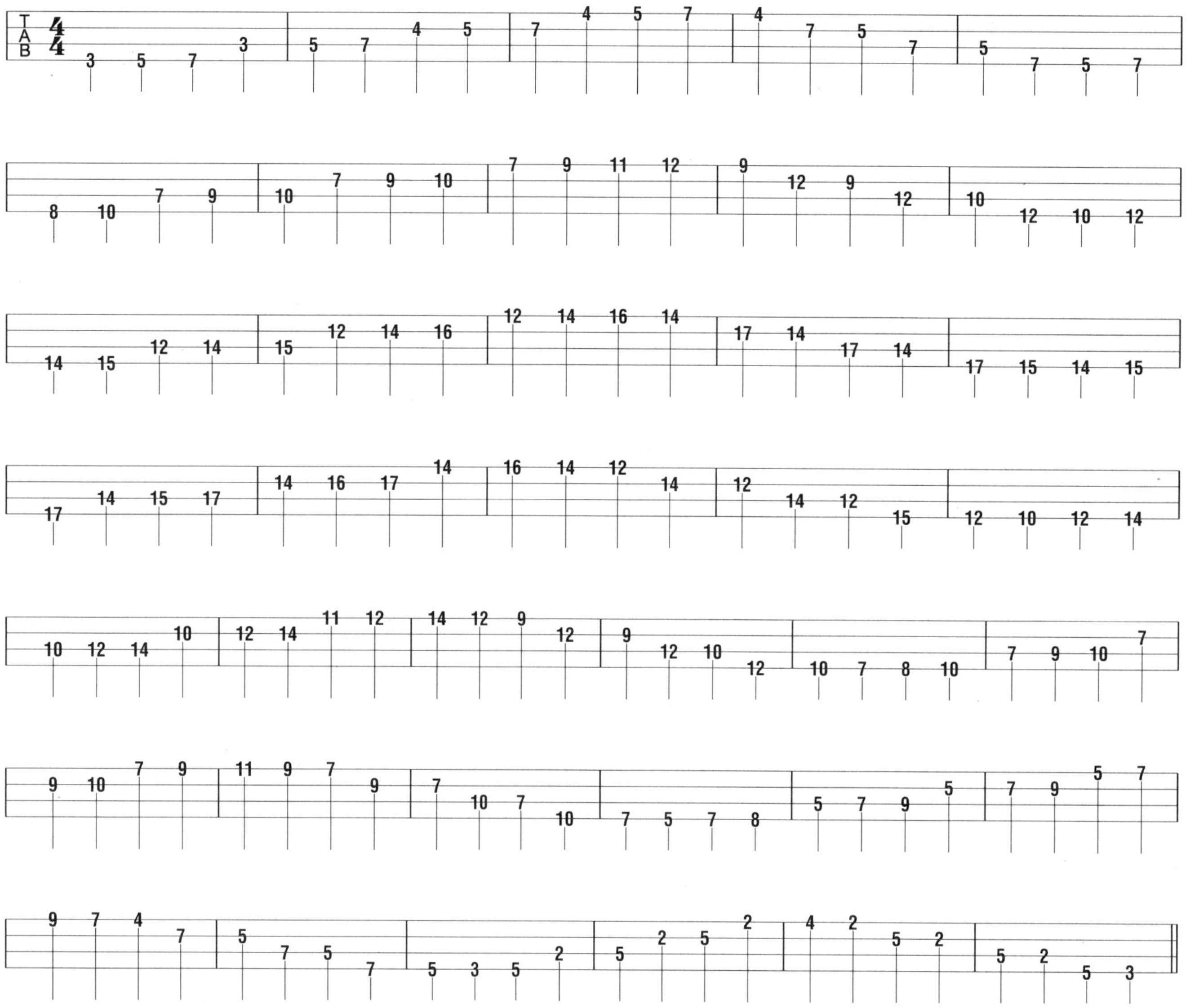

Index of Scales

Major Scale Modes

C Ionian

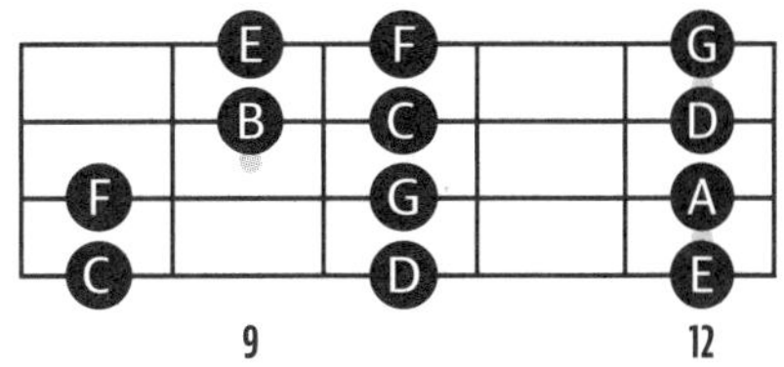

C♯/D♭ Ionian

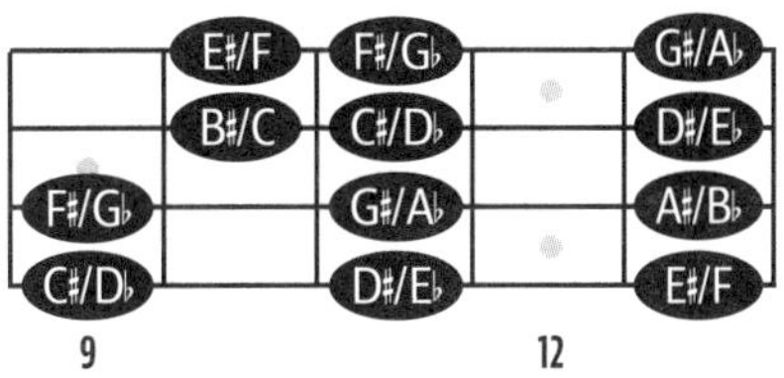

D Ionian

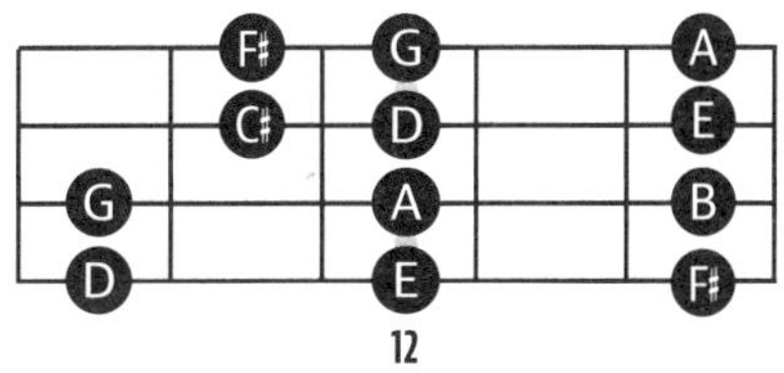

E♭ Ionian

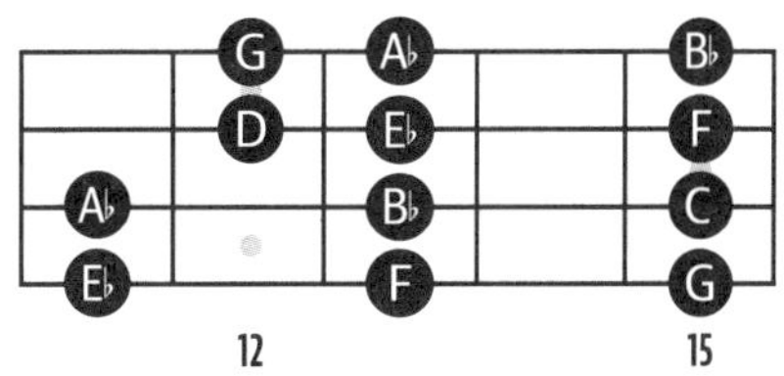

E Ionian

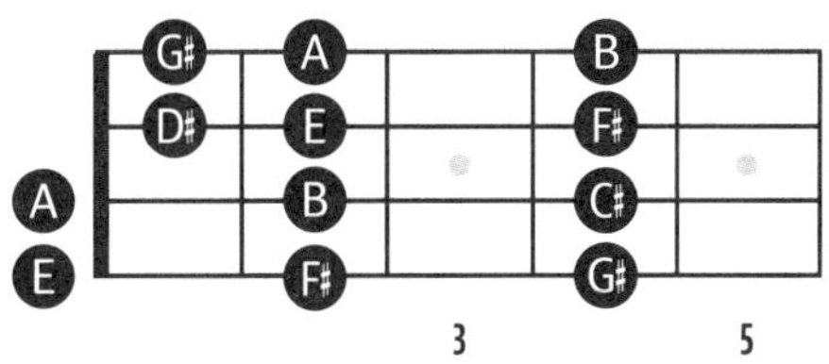

F Ionian

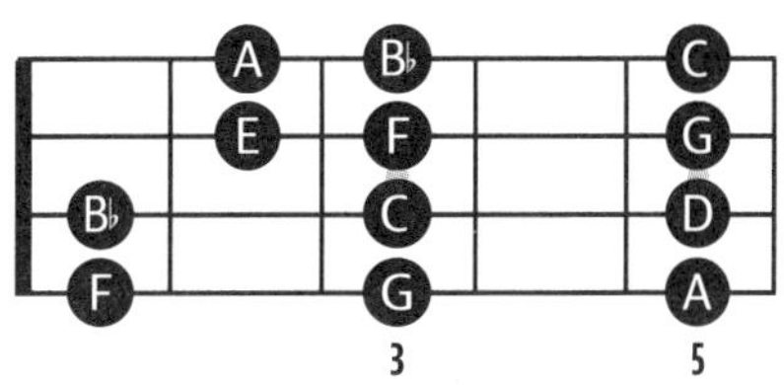

F♯/G♭ Ionian

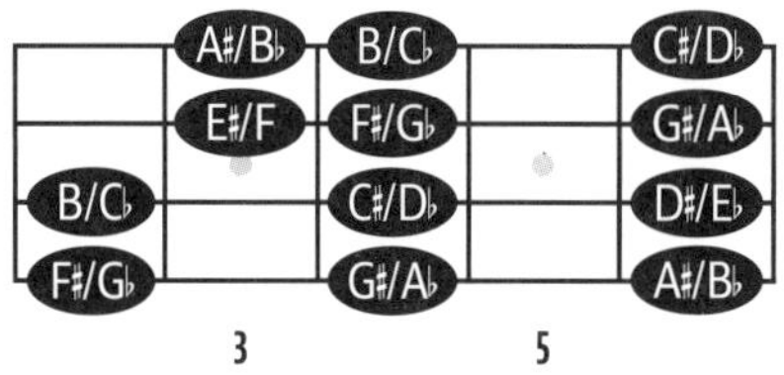

G Ionian

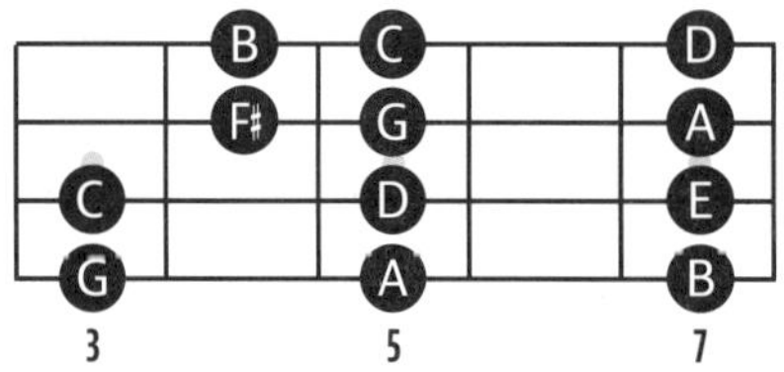

A♭ Ionian

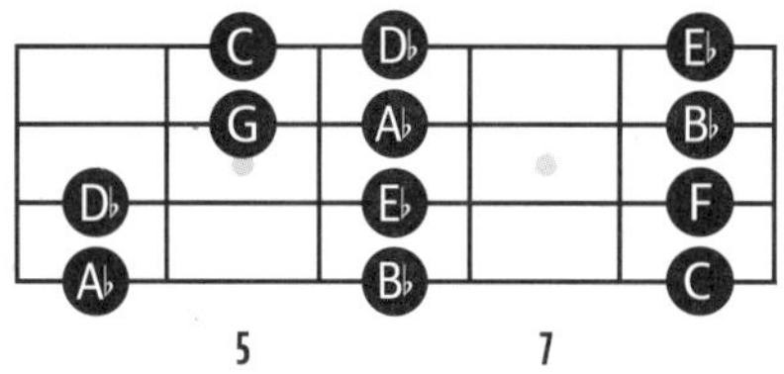

A Ionian

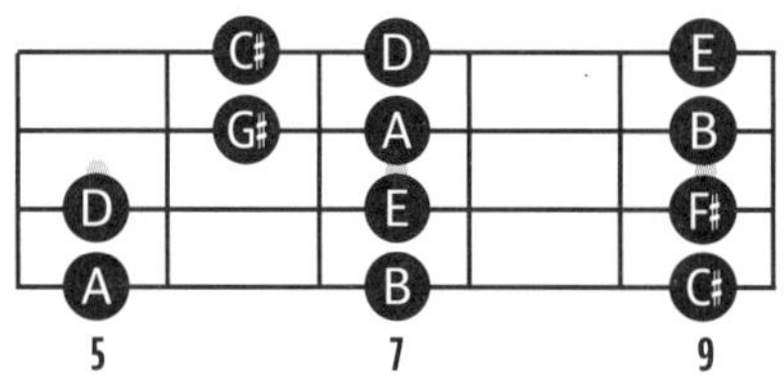

B♭ Ionian

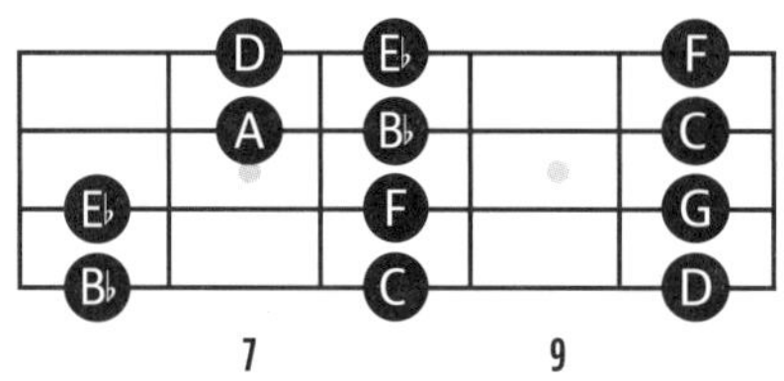

B Ionian

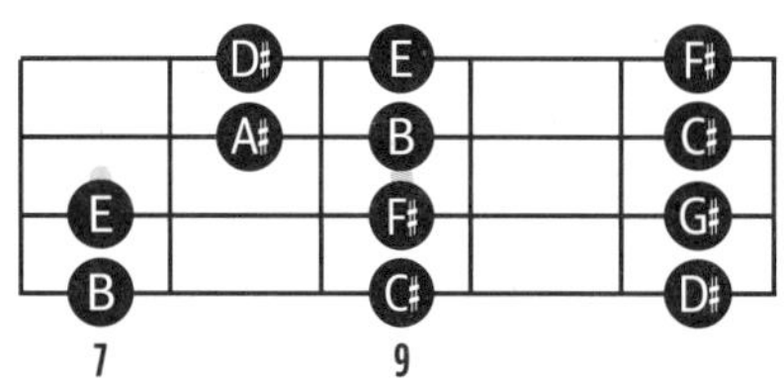

C Dorian

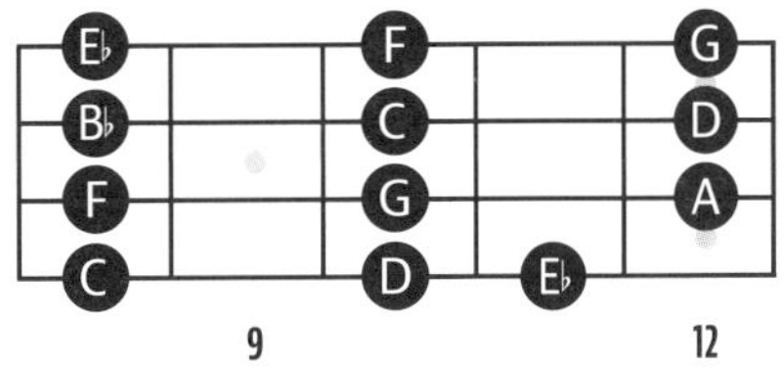

C♯ Dorian

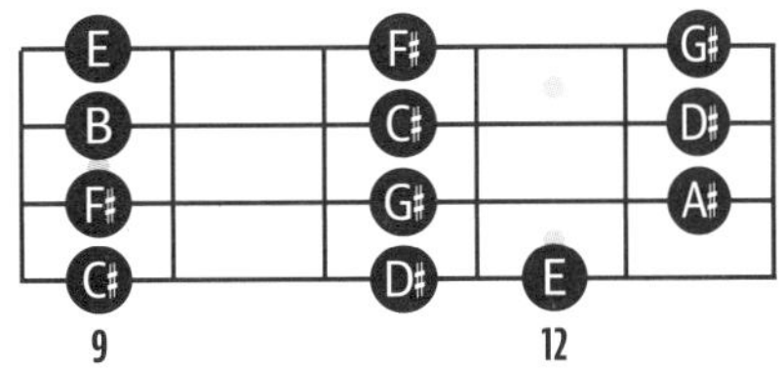

D Dorian

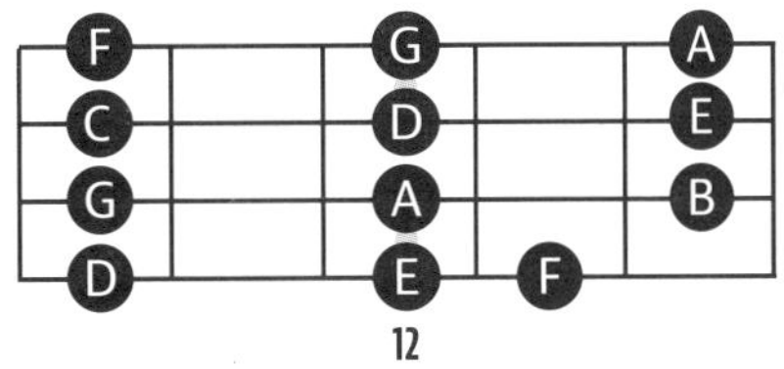

E♭ Dorian

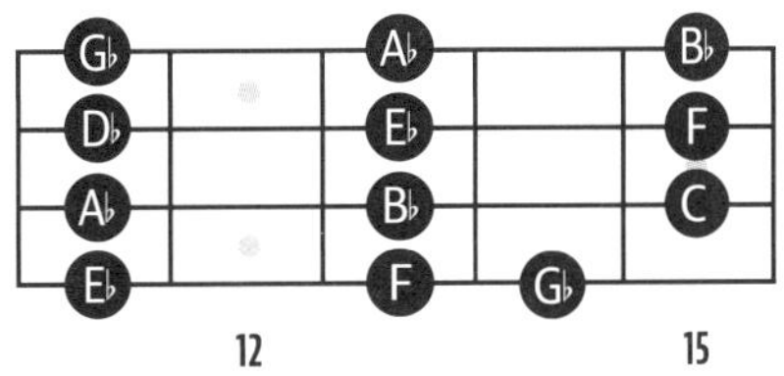

E Dorian

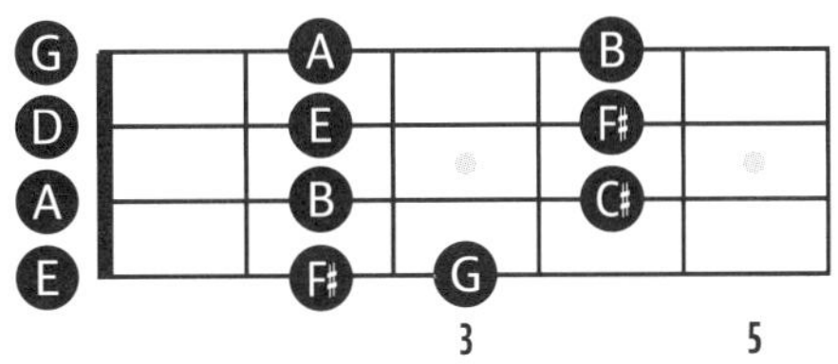

F Dorian

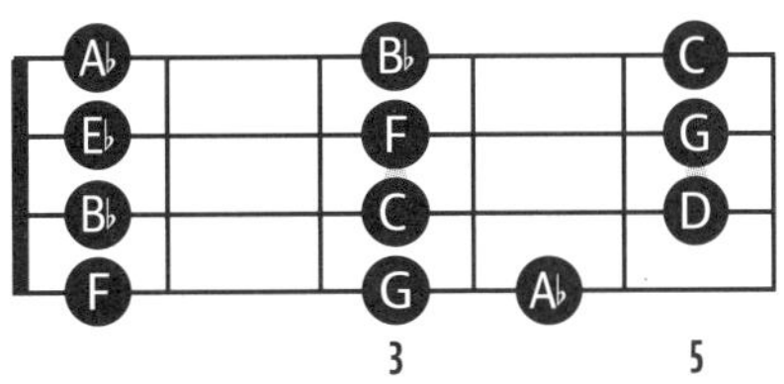

F♯ Dorian

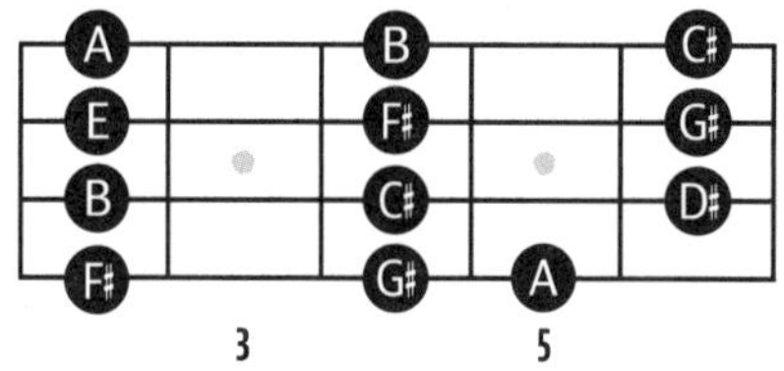

G Dorian

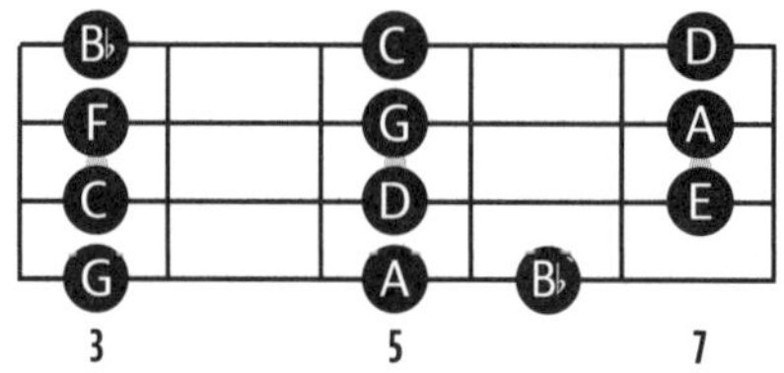

A♭ Dorian

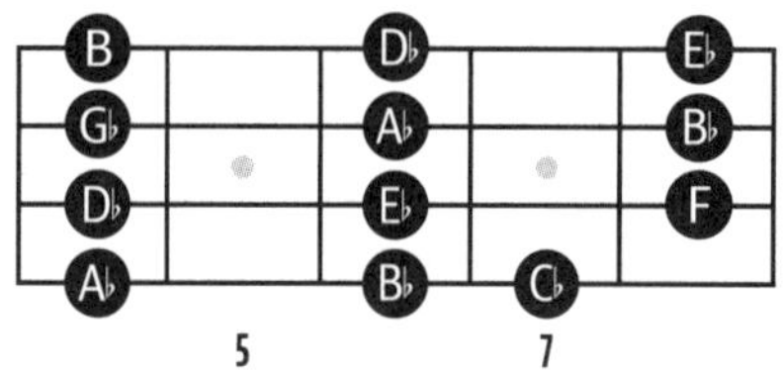

A Dorian

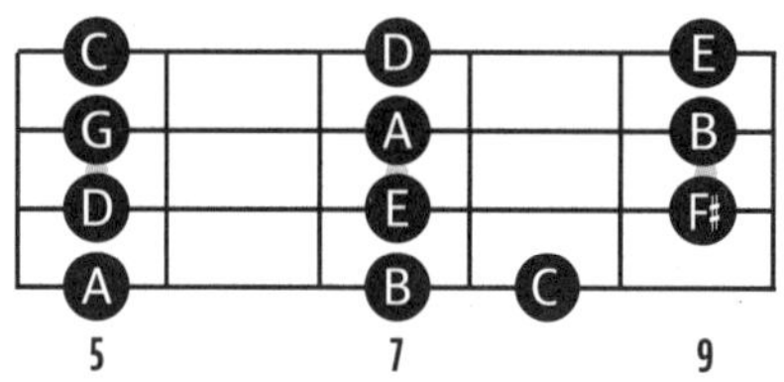

B♭ Dorian

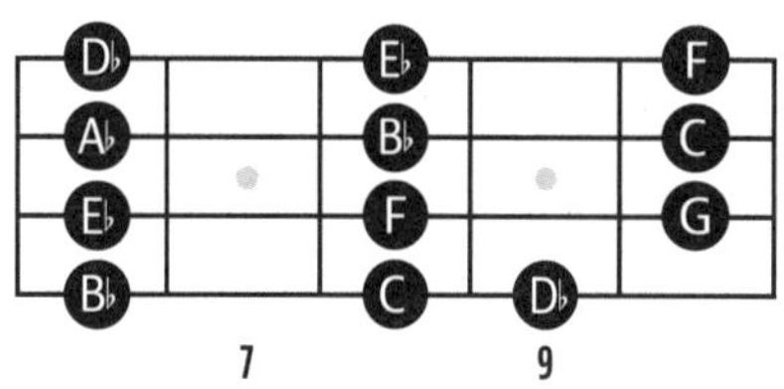

B Dorian

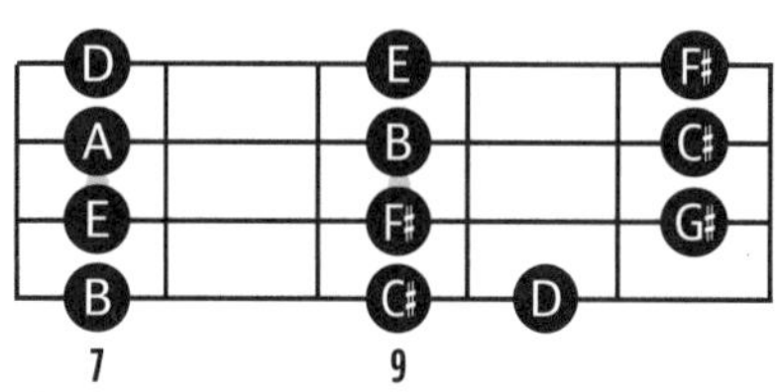

C Phrygian

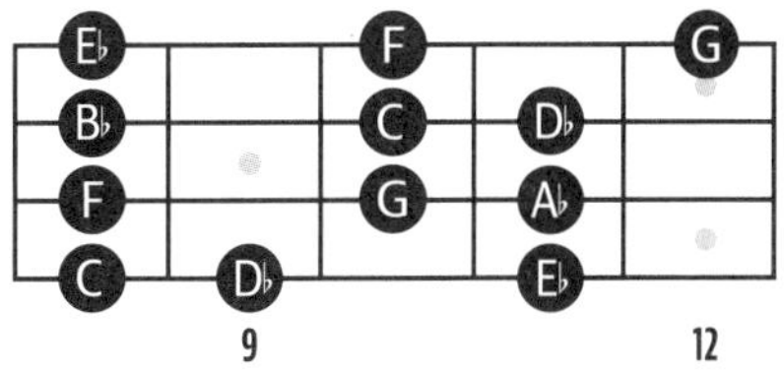

C♯ Phrygian

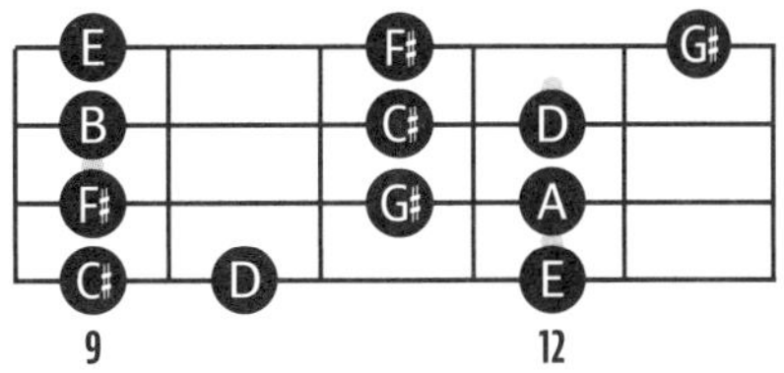

D Phrygian

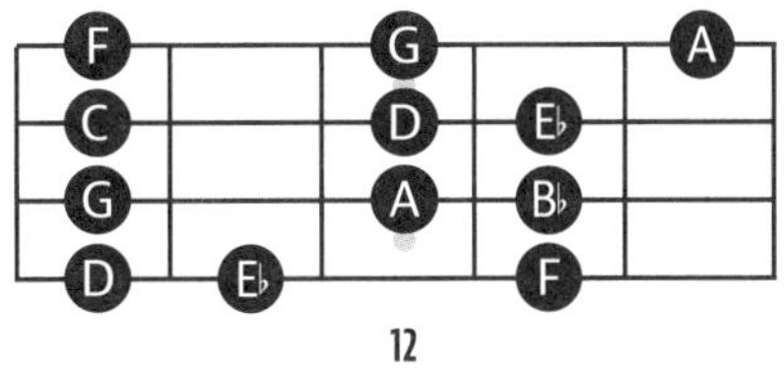

D♯ Phrygian

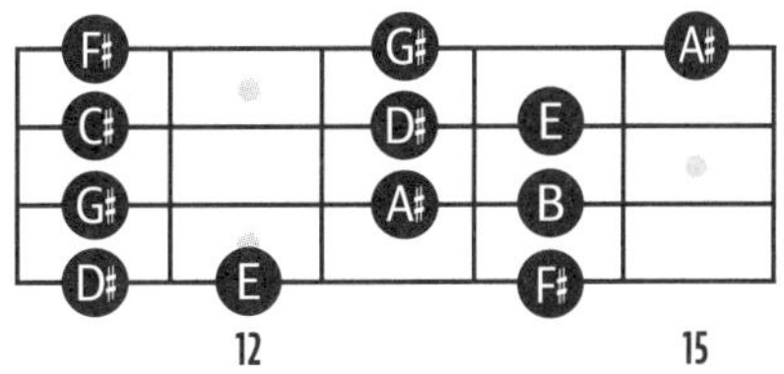

E Phrygian

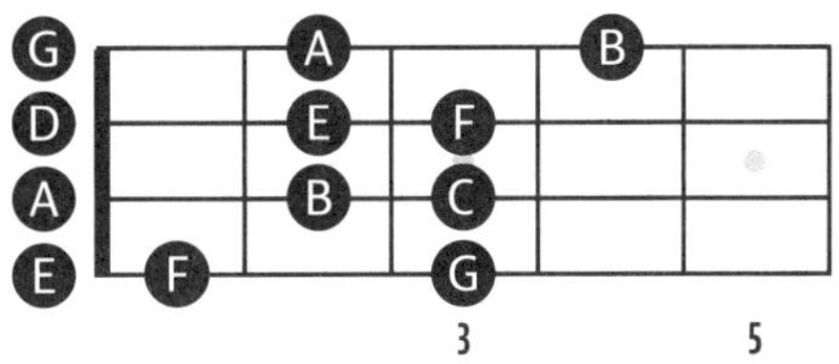

F Phrygian

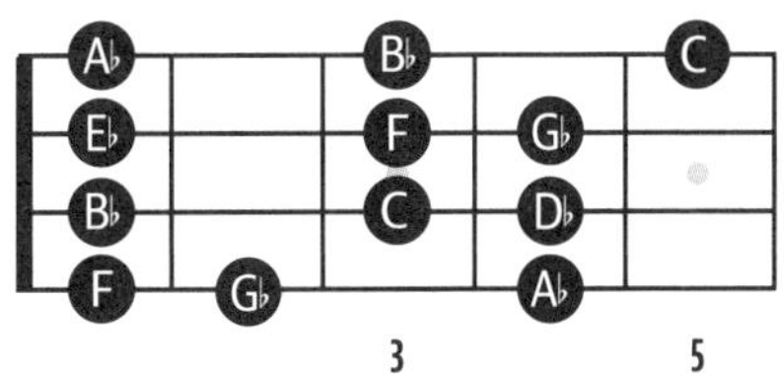

F♯ Phrygian

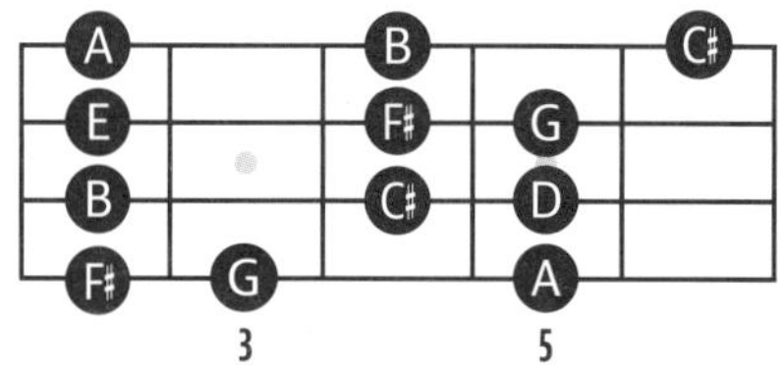

G Phrygian

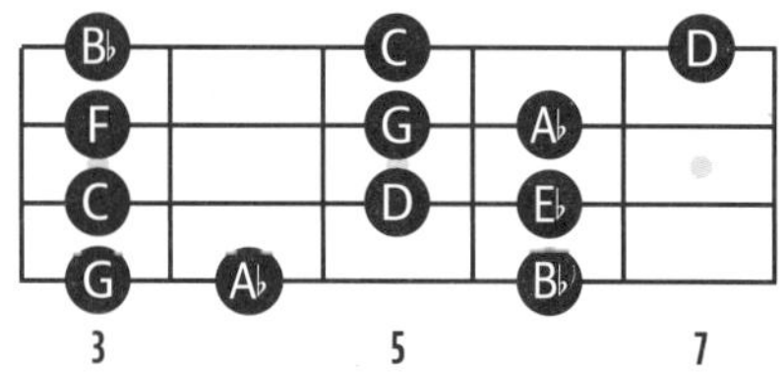

G♯ Phrygian

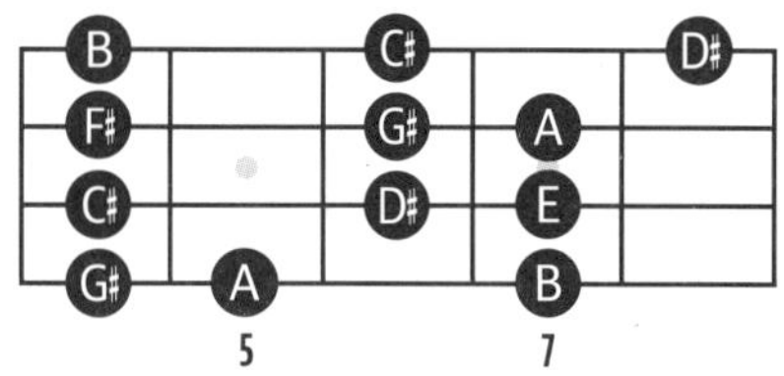

A Phrygian

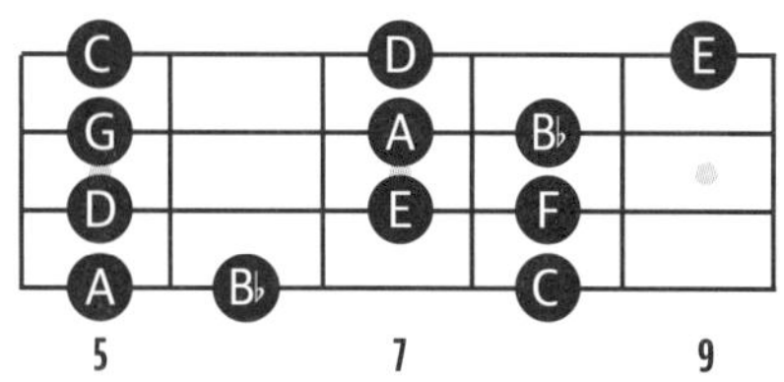

B♭ Phrygian

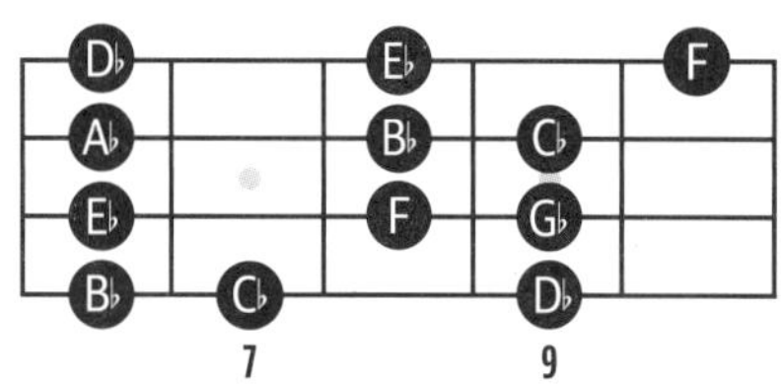

B Phrygian

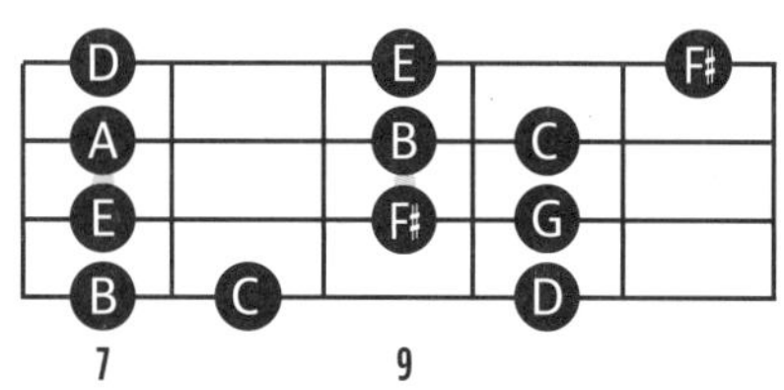

C Lydian

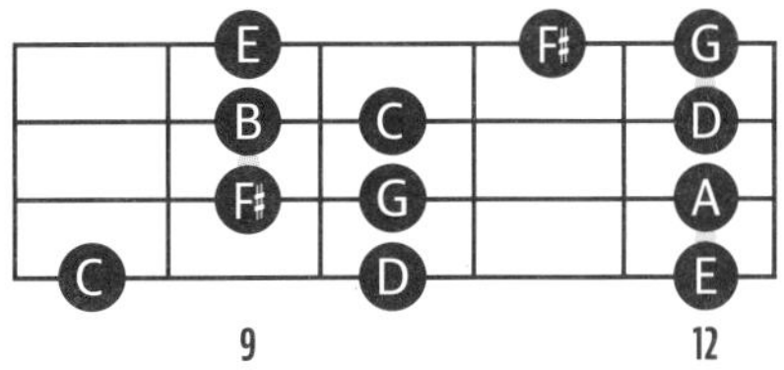

D♭ Lydian

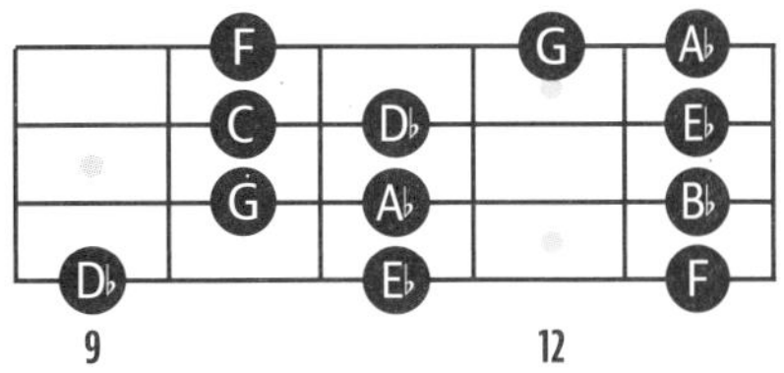

D Lydian

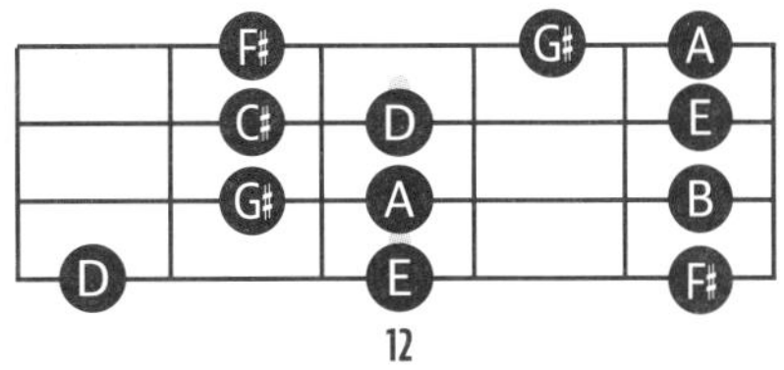

E♭ Lydian

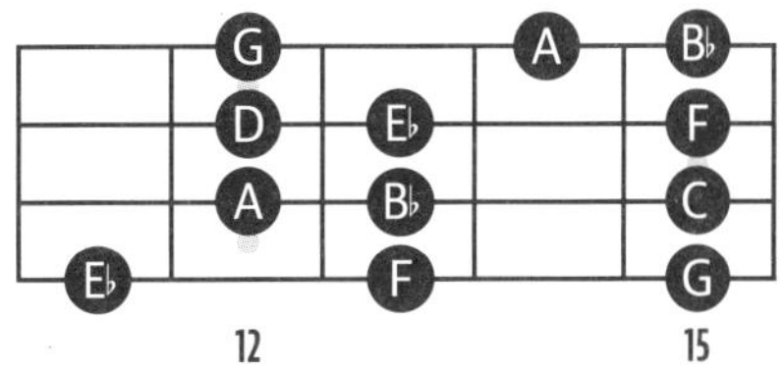

E Lydian

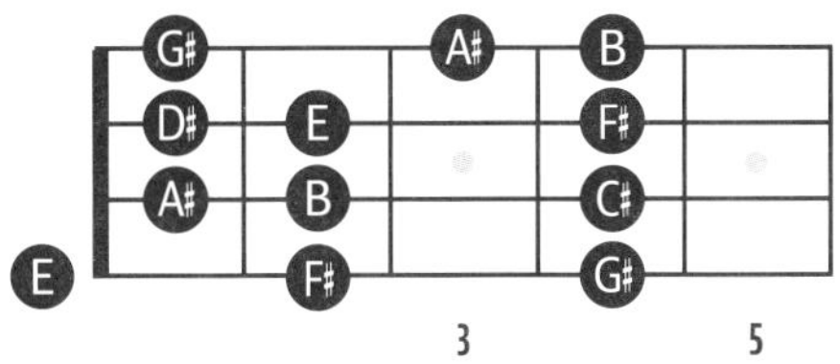

F Lydian

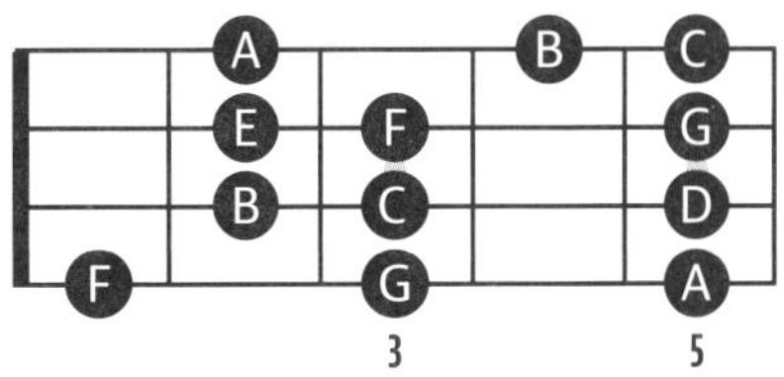

F♯/G♭ Lydian

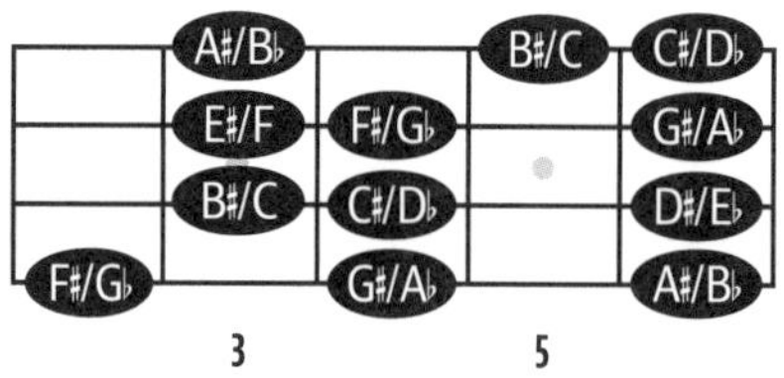

G Lydian

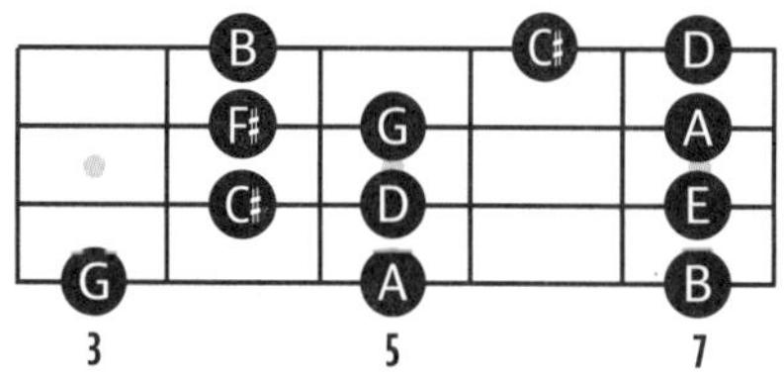

A♭ Lydian

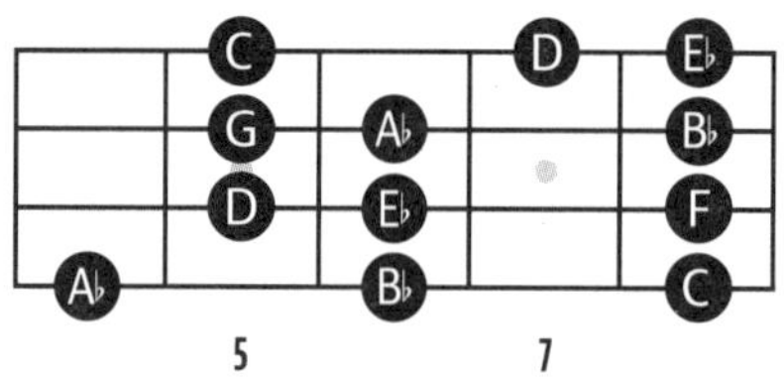

A Lydian

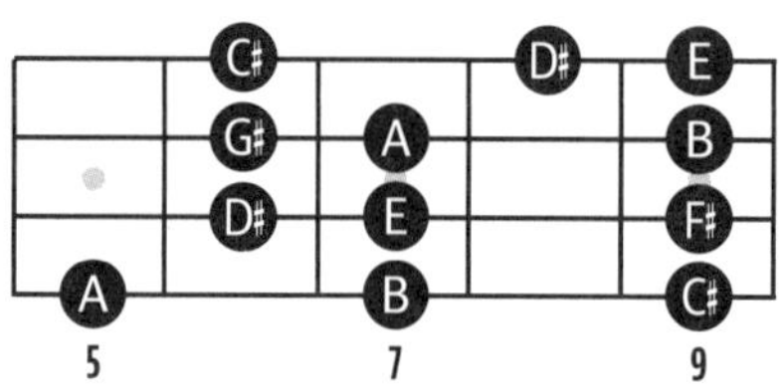

B♭ Lydian

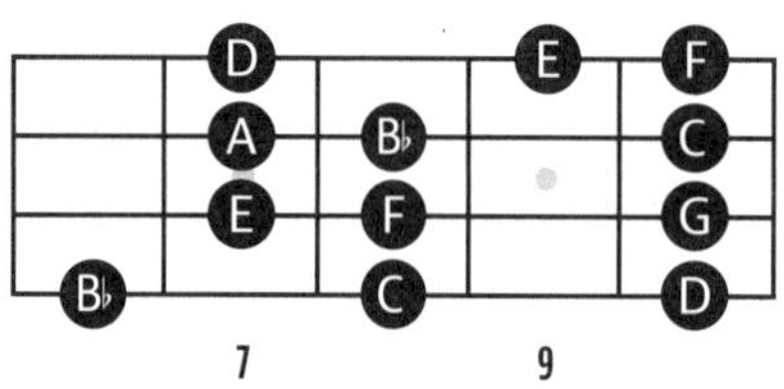

B Lydian

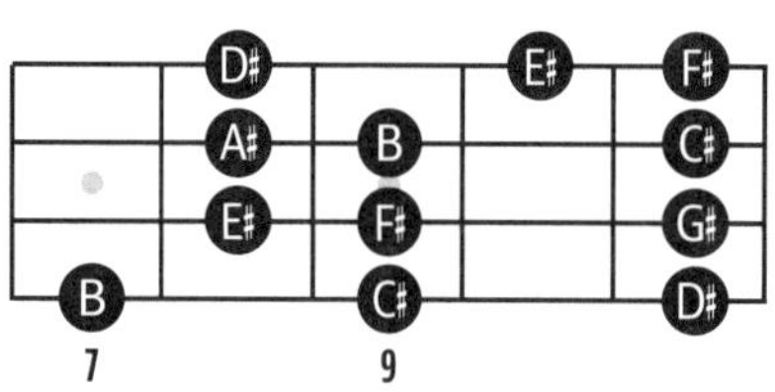

C Mixolydian

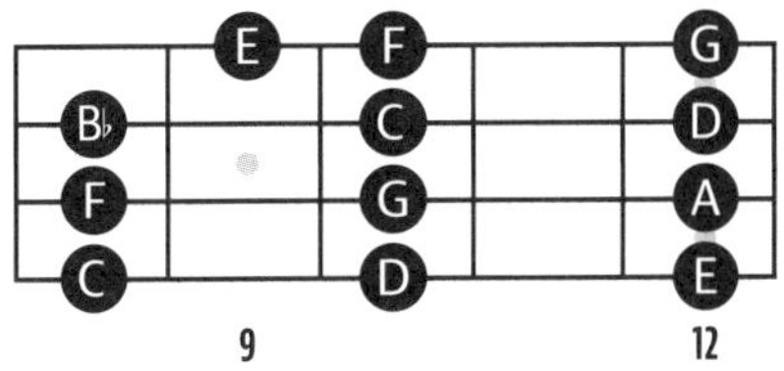

C♯/D♭ Mixolydian

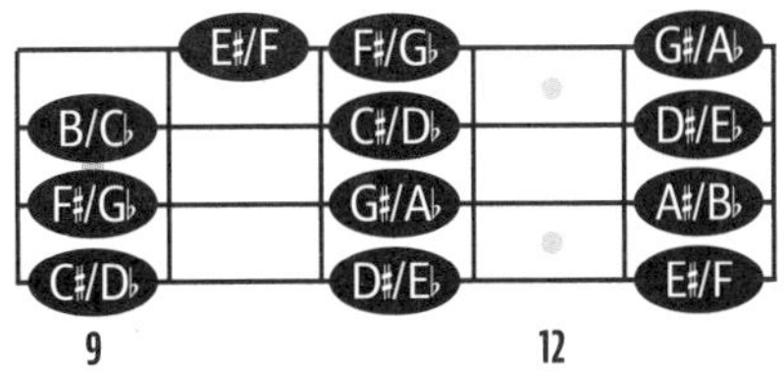

D Mixolydian

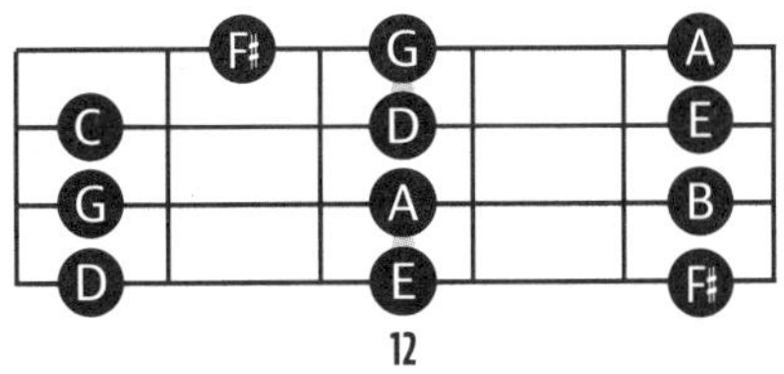

E♭ Mixolydian

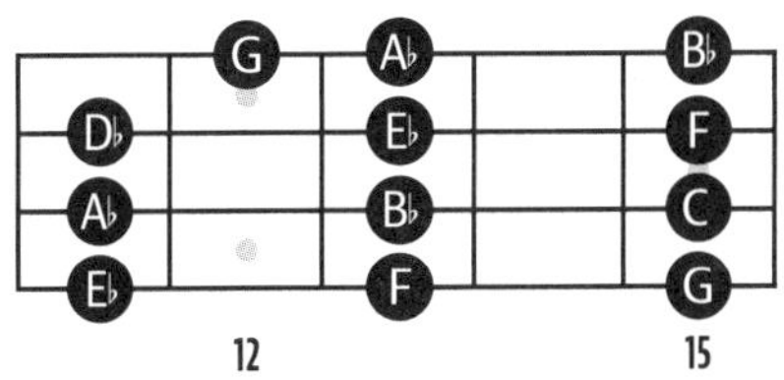

E Mixolydian

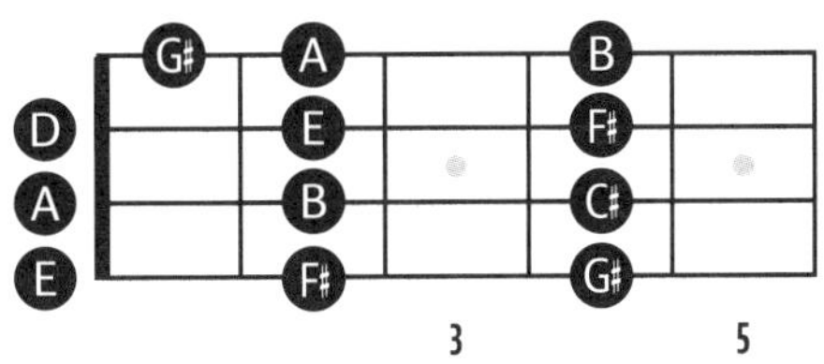

F Mixolydian

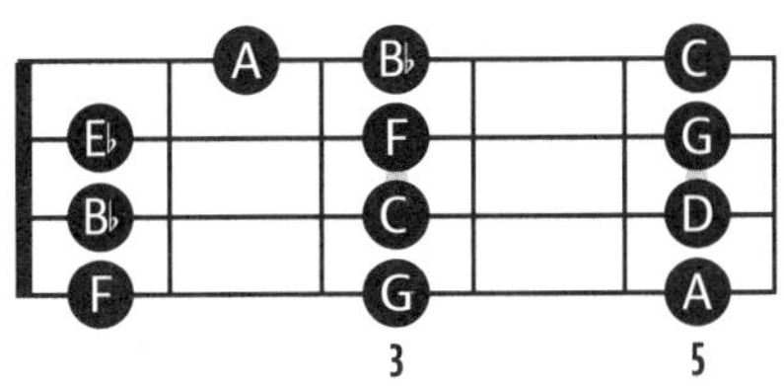

F♯/G♭ Mixolydian

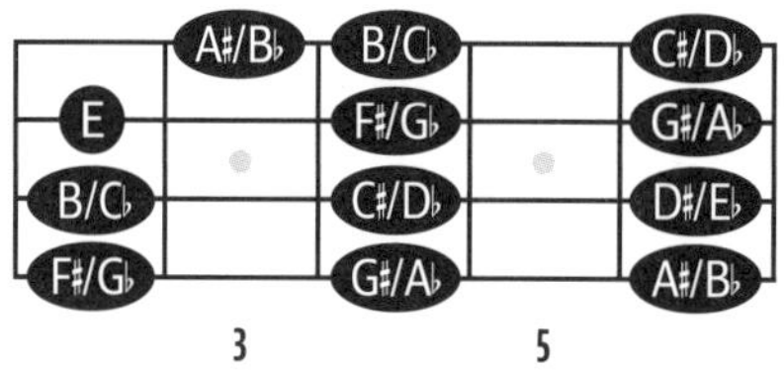

G Mixolydian

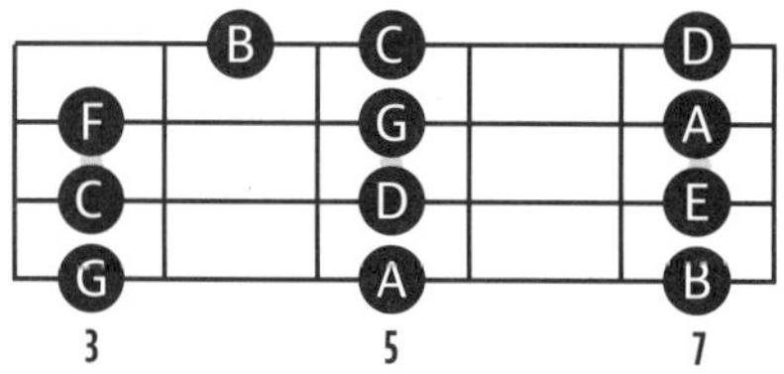

A♭ Mixolydian

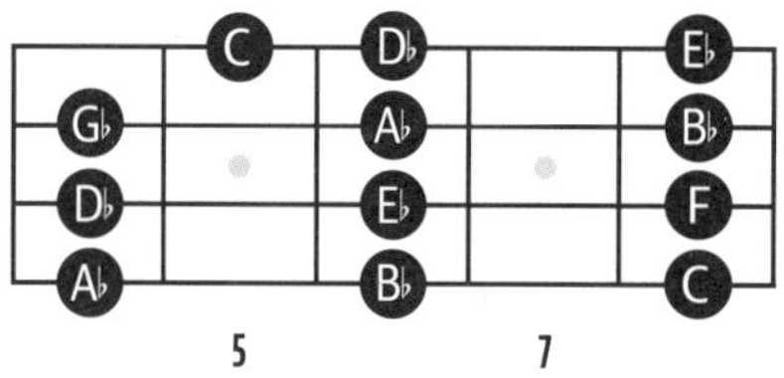

A Mixolydian

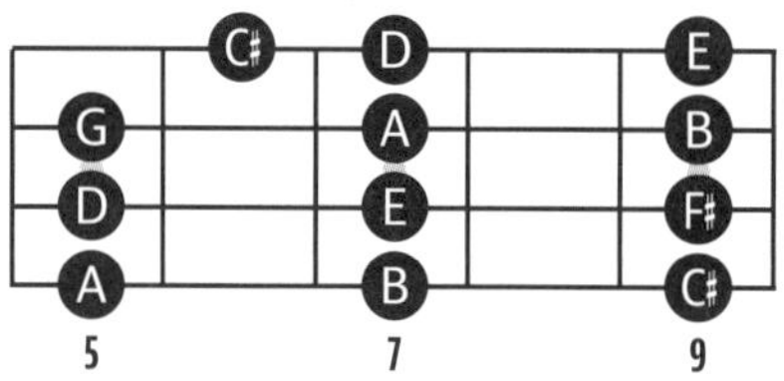

B♭ Mixolydian

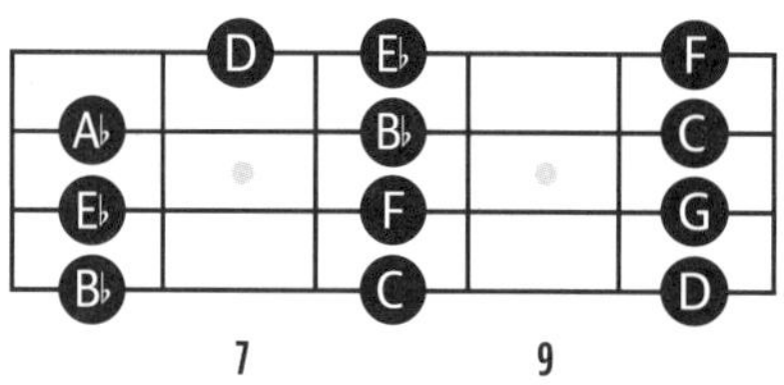

B Mixolydian

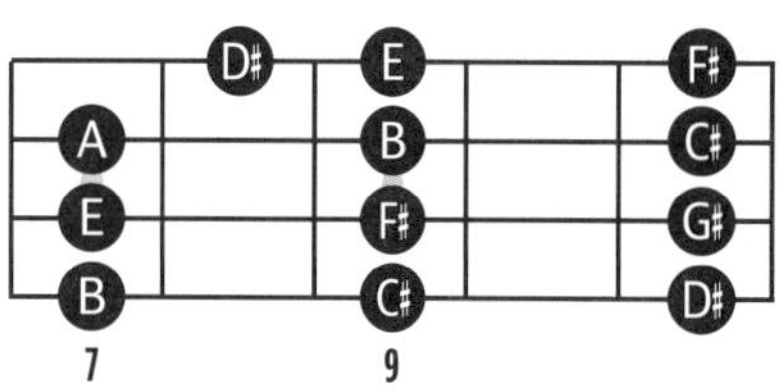

C Aeolian

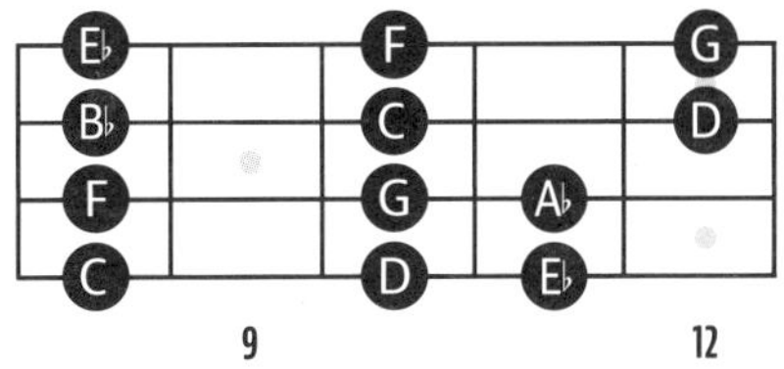

C♯ Aeolian

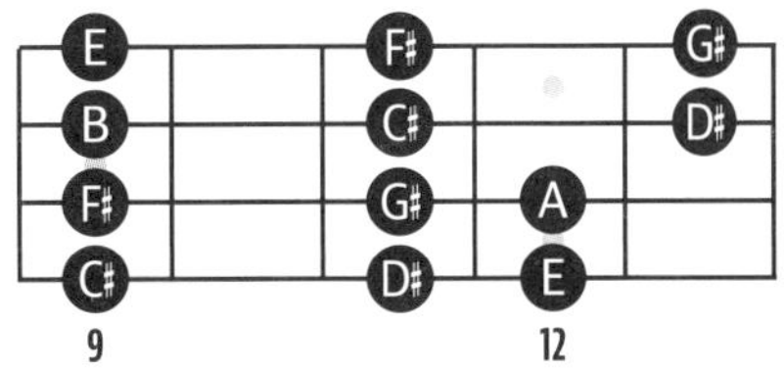

D Aeolian

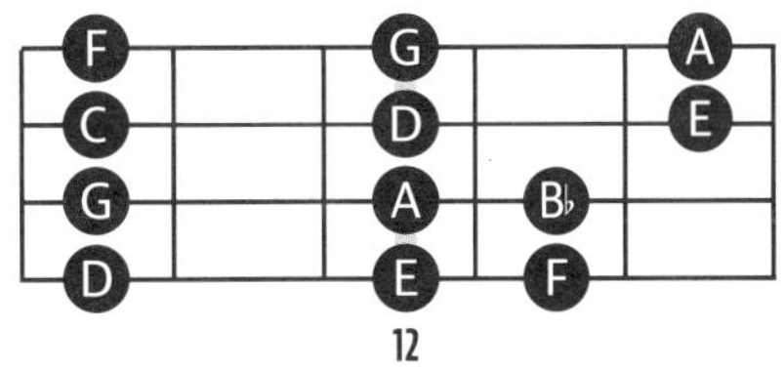

D♯/E♭ Aeolian

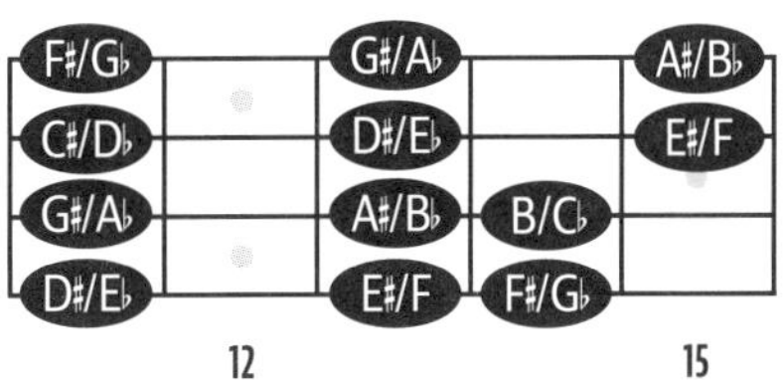

E Aeolian

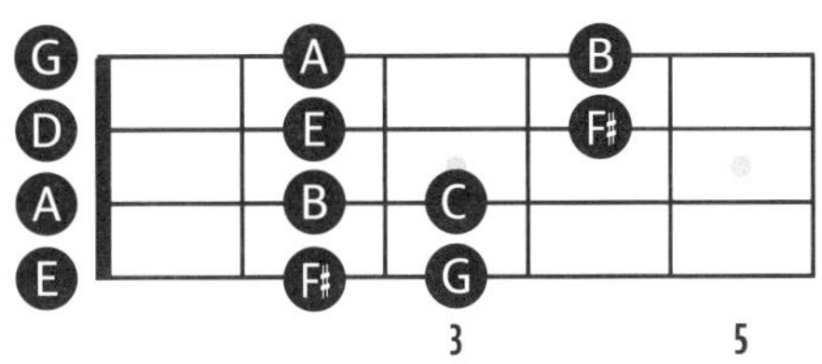

F Aeolian

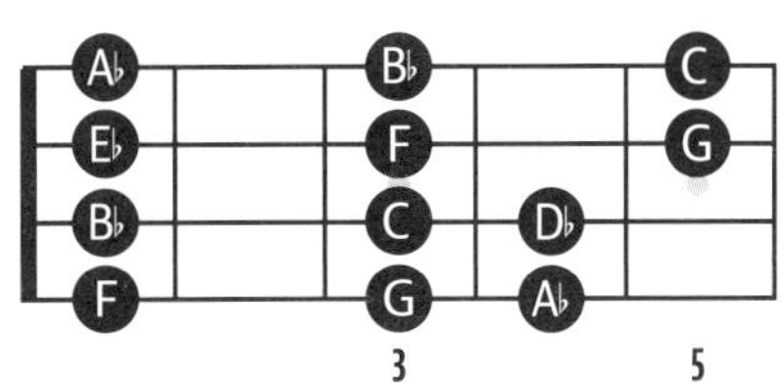

F♯ Aeolian

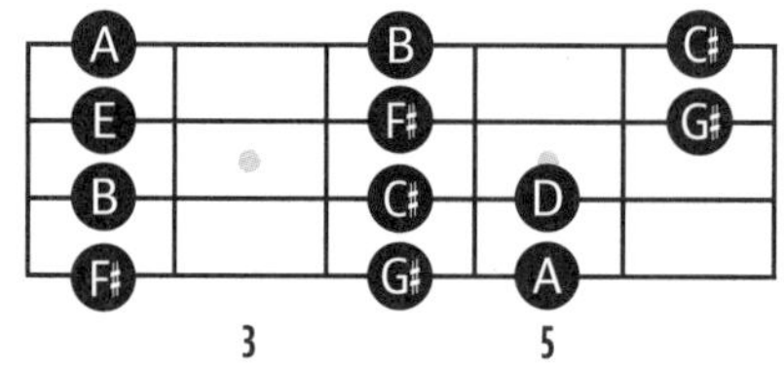

G Aeolian

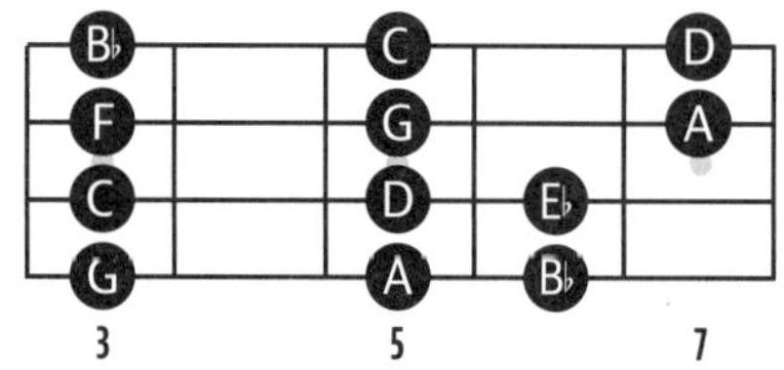

A♭ Aeolian

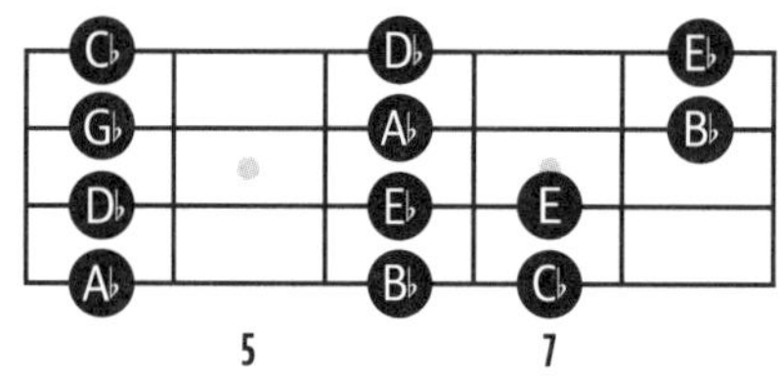

A Aeolian

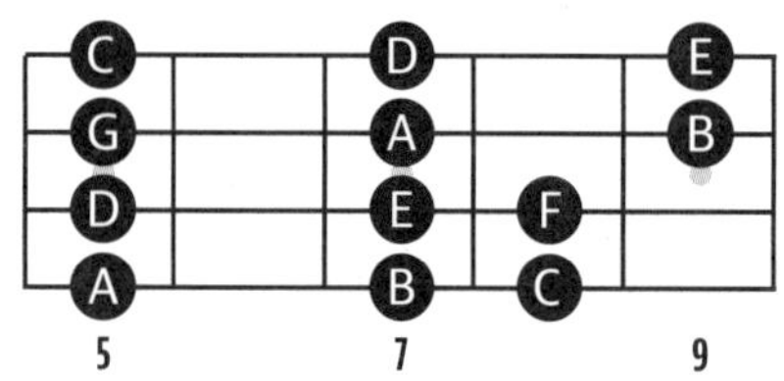

B♭ Aeolian

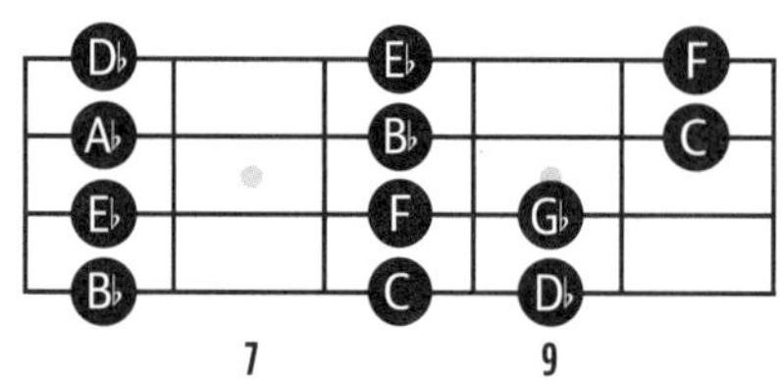

B Aeolian

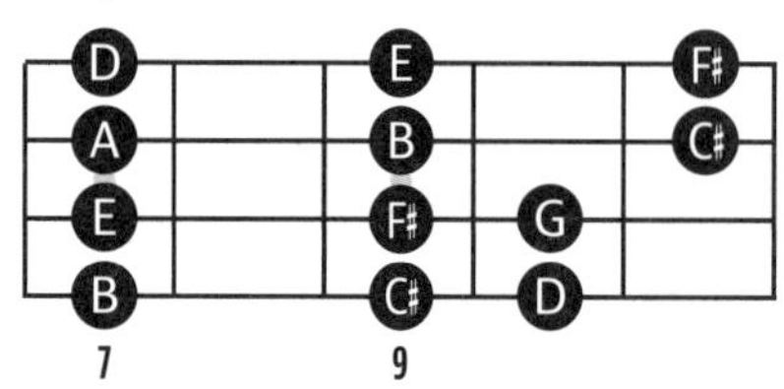

C Locrian

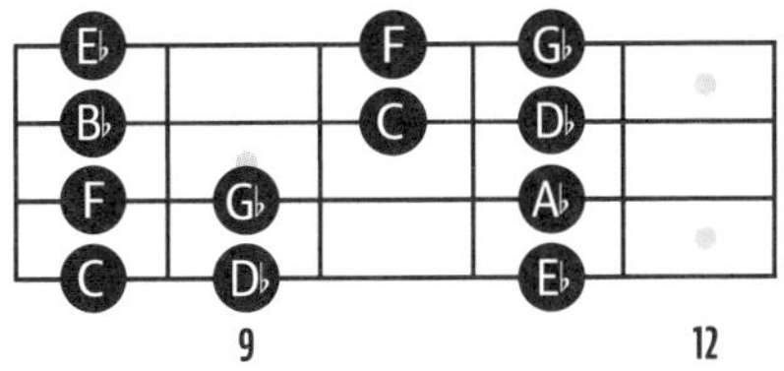

C♯ Locrian

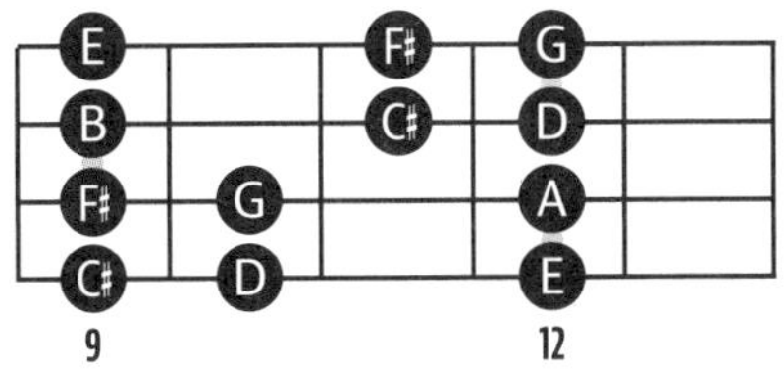

D Locrian

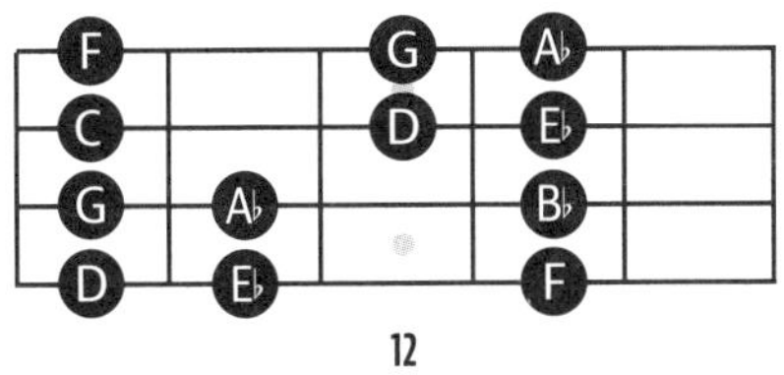

D♯ Locrian

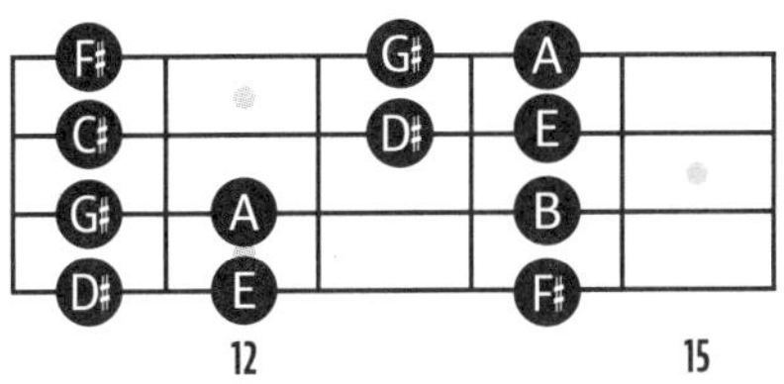

E Locrian

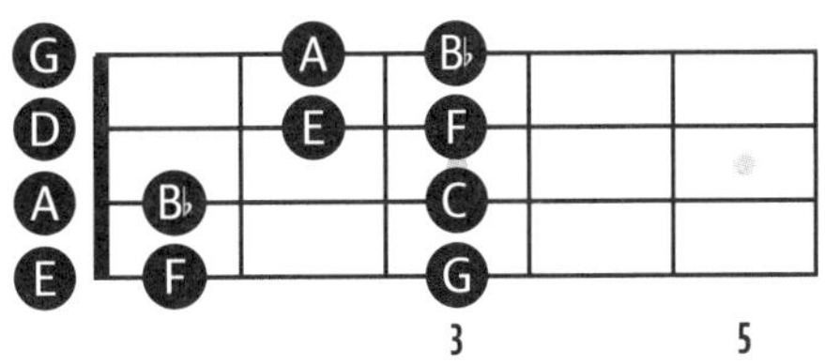

F Locrian

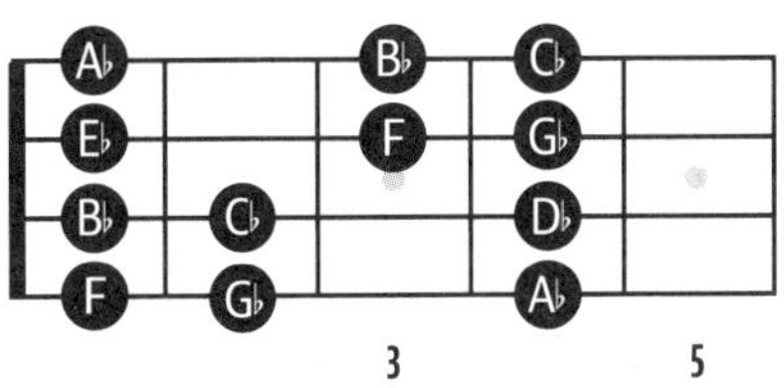

F♯ Locrian

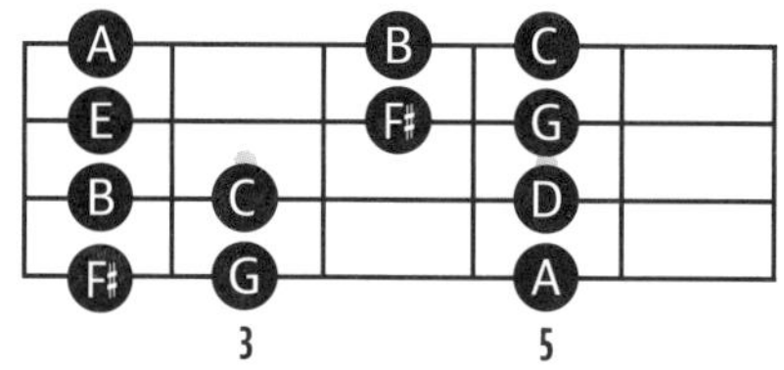

G Locrian

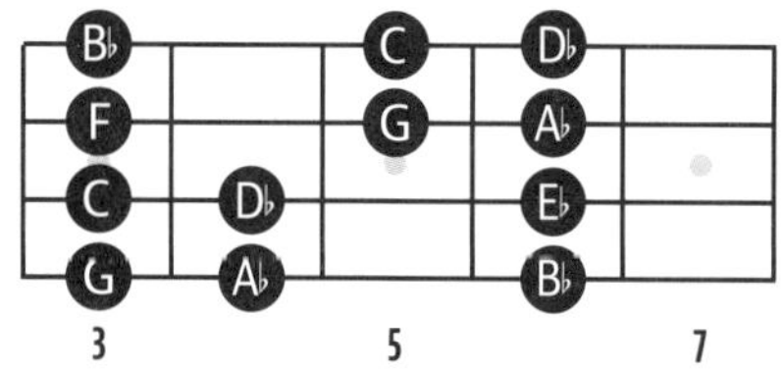

G♯ Locrian

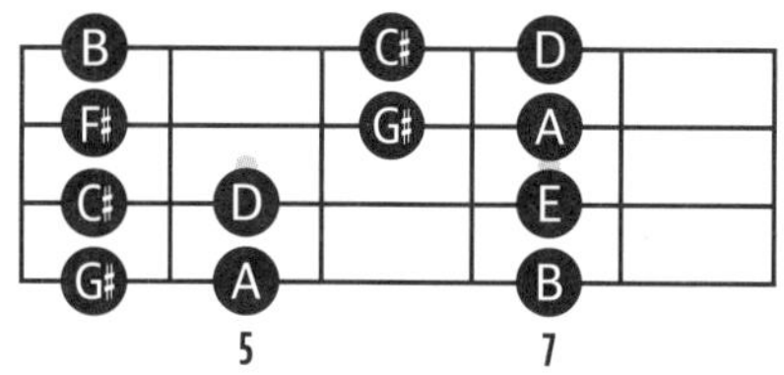

A Locrian

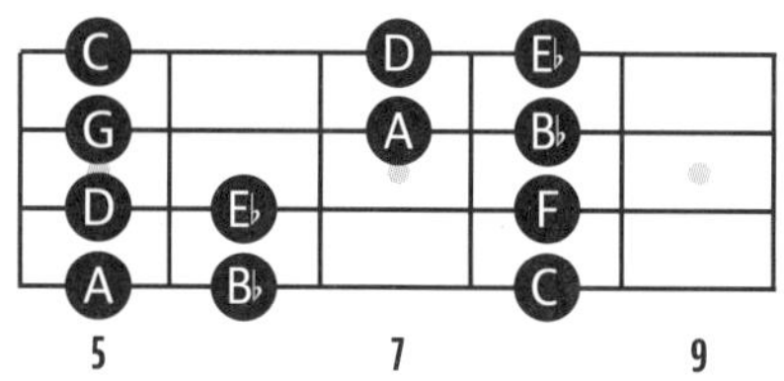

A♯ Locrian

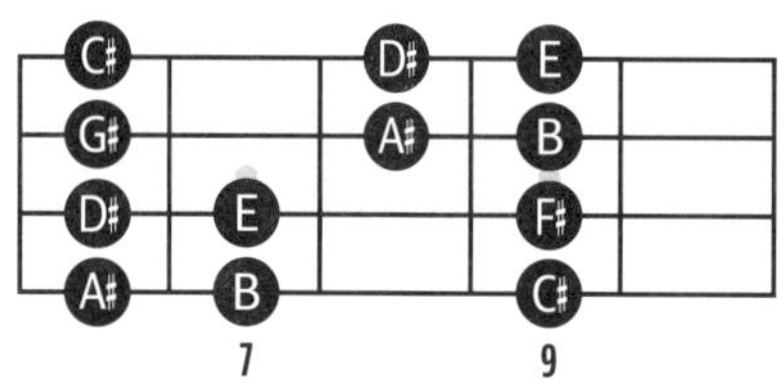

B Locrian

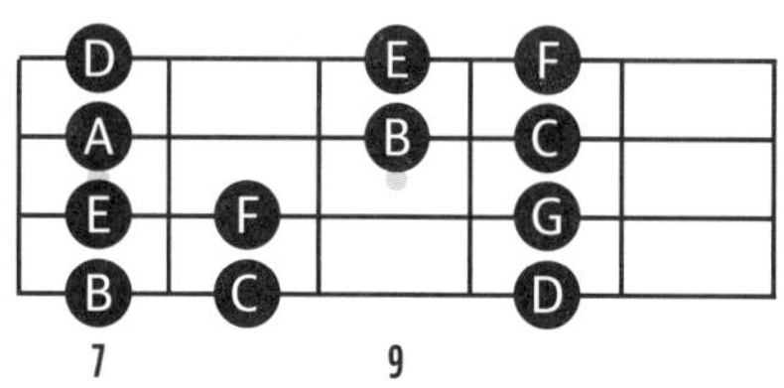

Pentatonic Scale Positions

C Major Pentatonic

Position 1

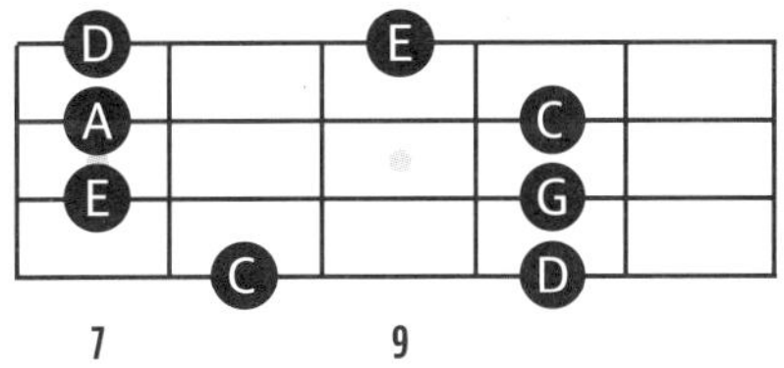

Position 2

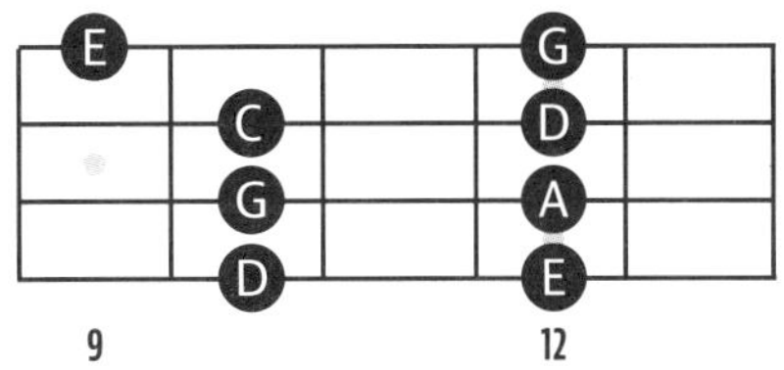

Position 3

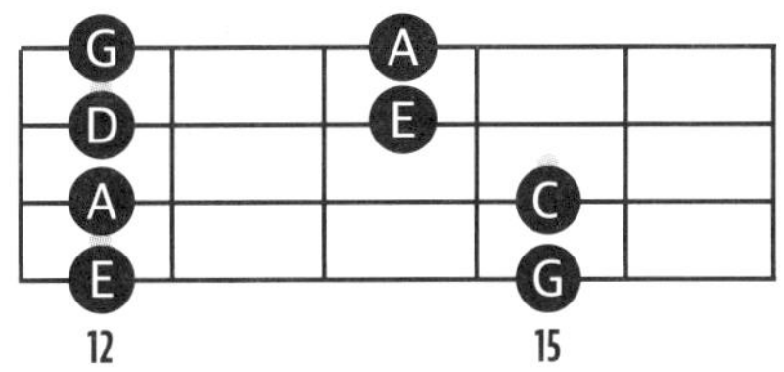

Position 4

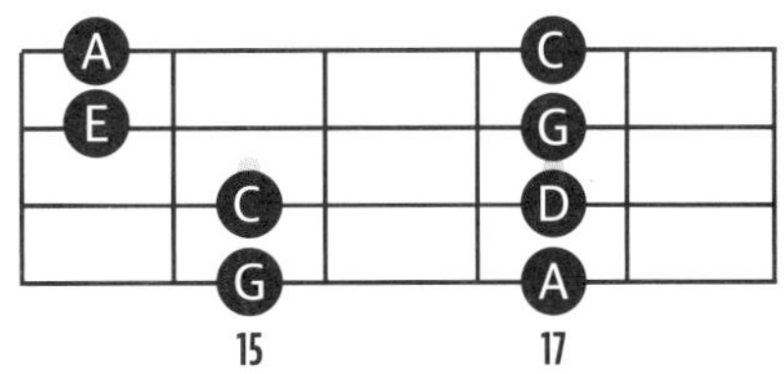

Position 5

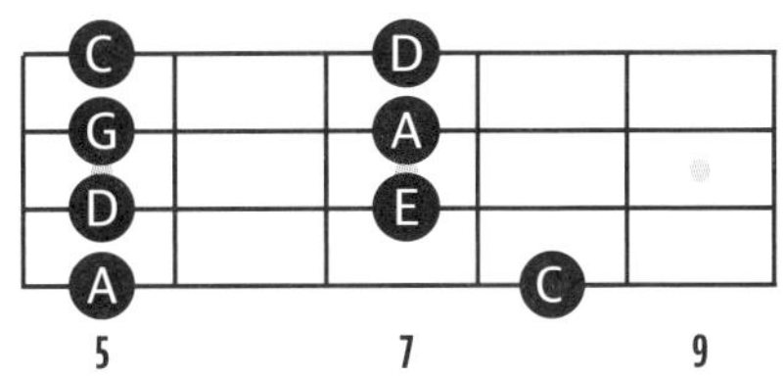

D♭ Major Pentatonic

Position 1

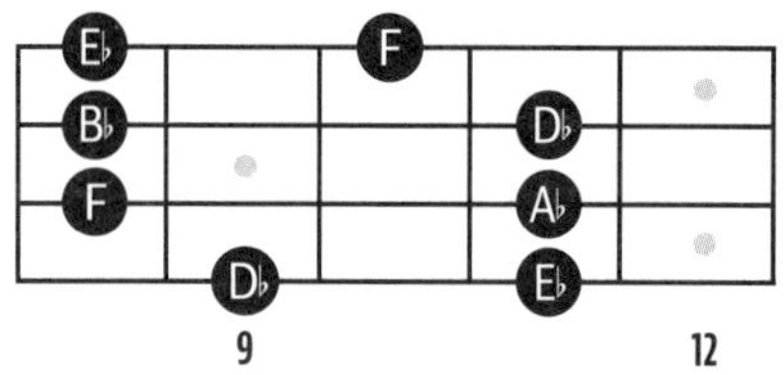

Position 2

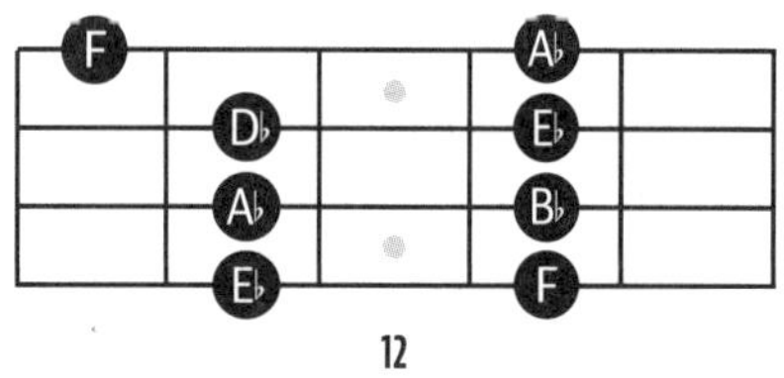

Position 3

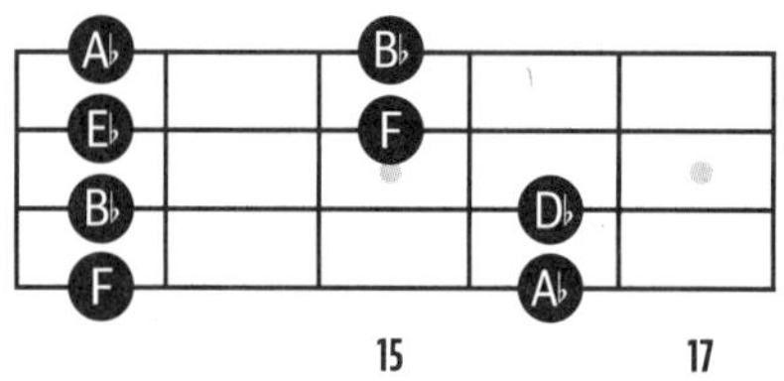

Position 4

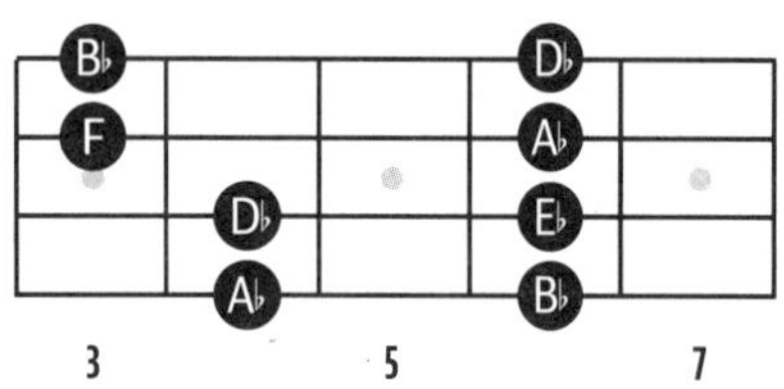

Position 5

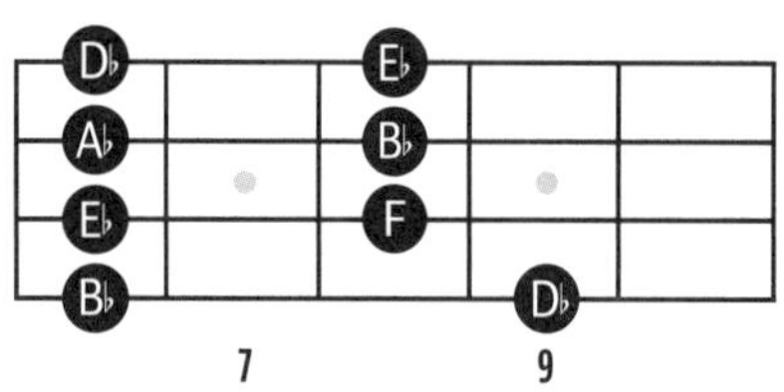

D Major Pentatonic

Position 1

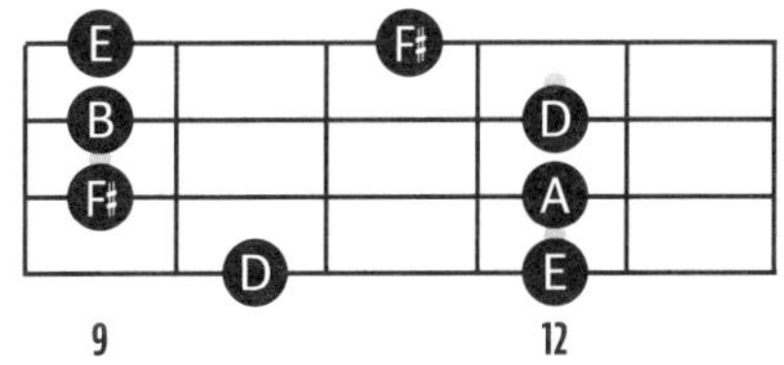

Position 2

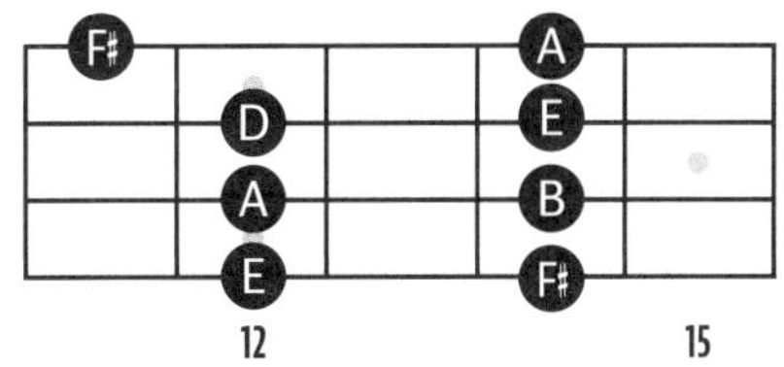

Position 3

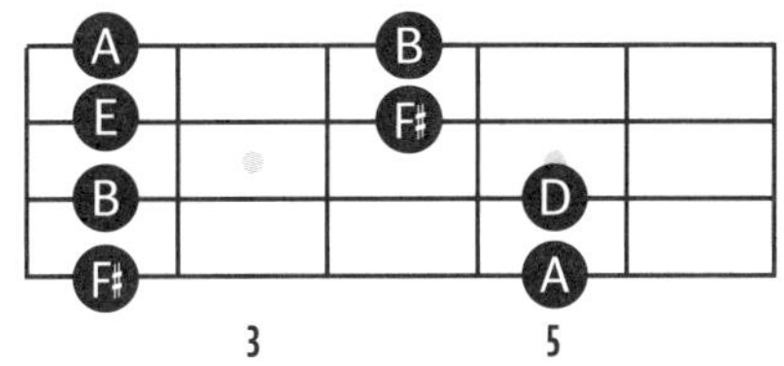

Position 4

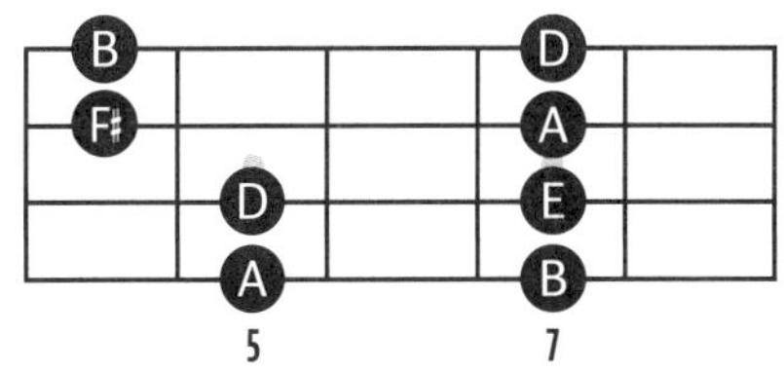

Position 5

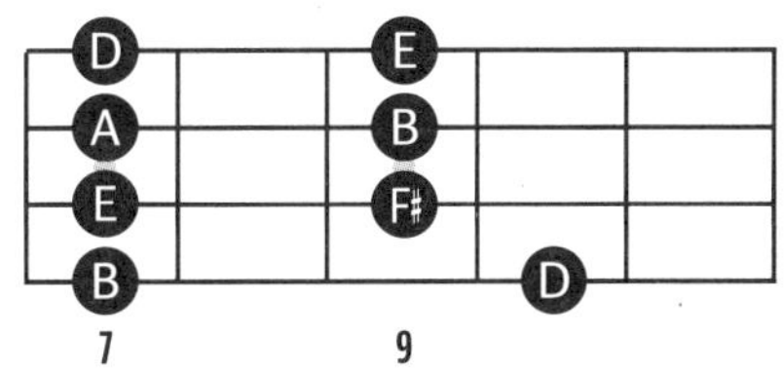

E♭ Major Pentatonic

Position 1

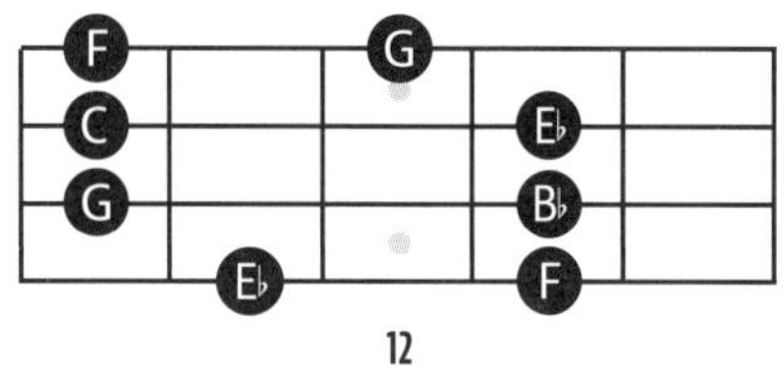

Position 2

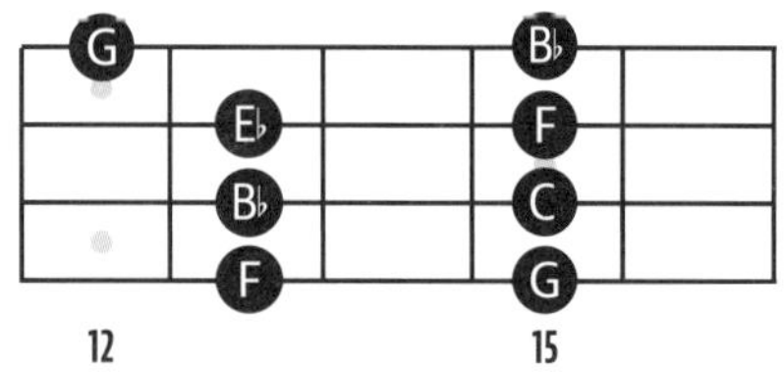

Position 3

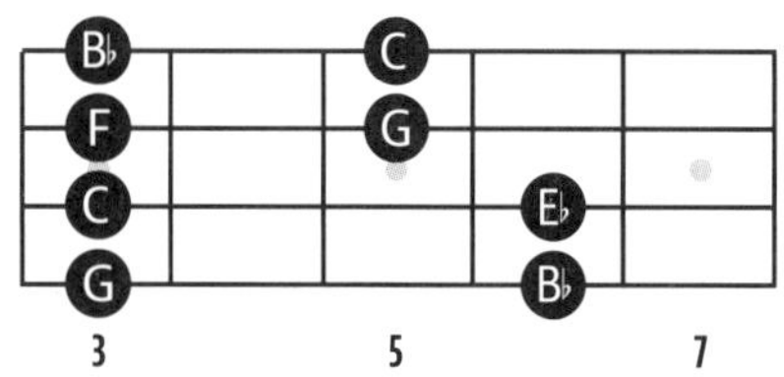

Position 4

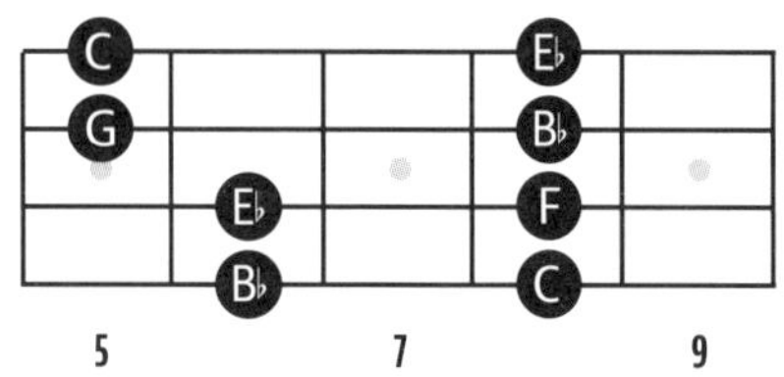

Position 5

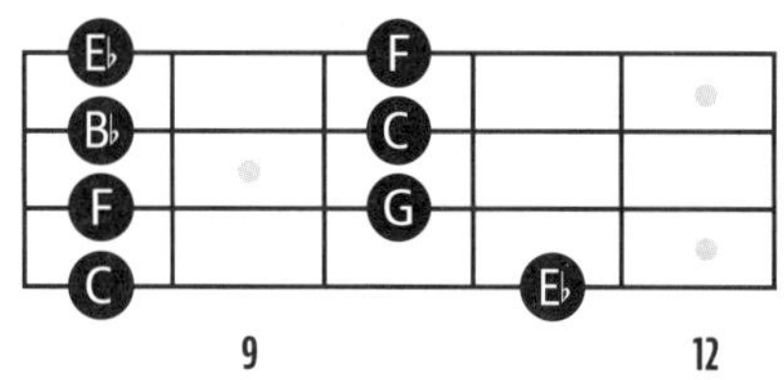

E Major Pentatonic

Position 1

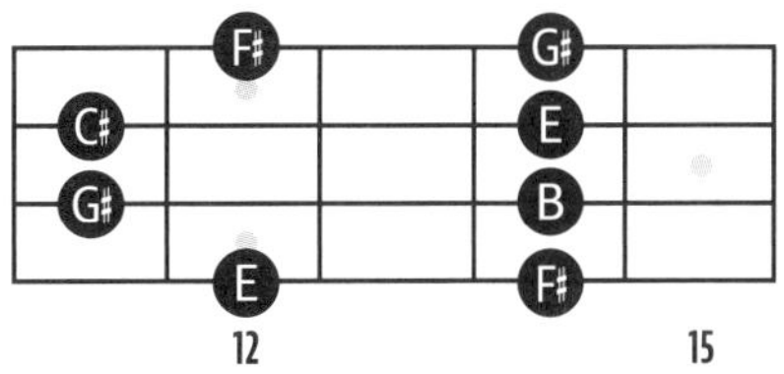

Position 2

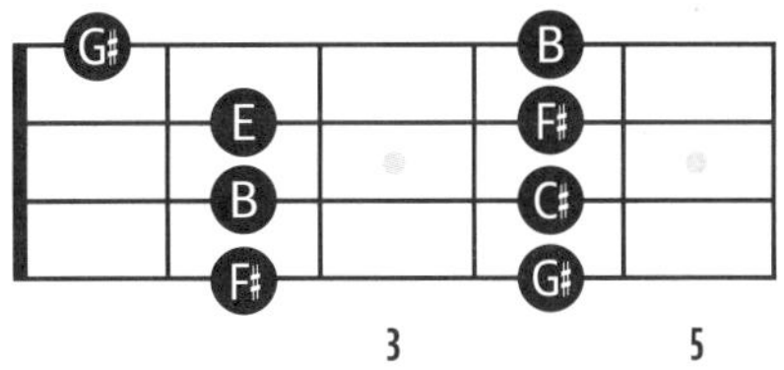

Position 3

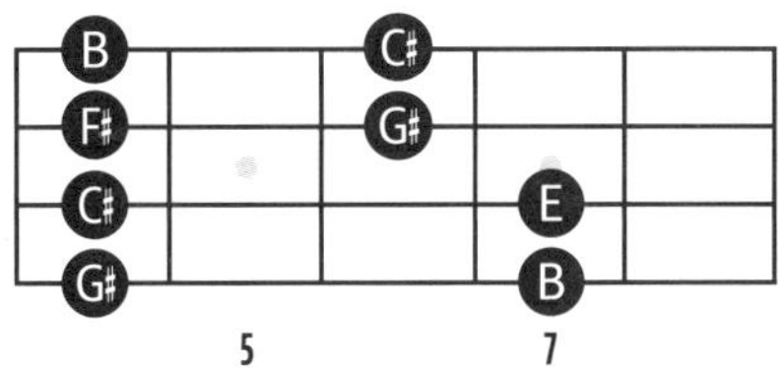

Position 4

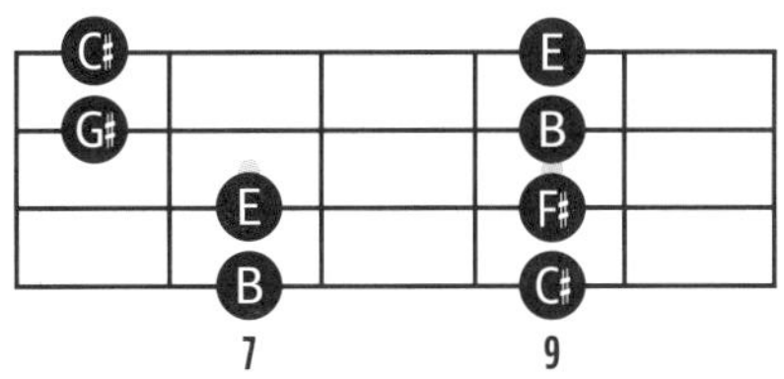

Position 5

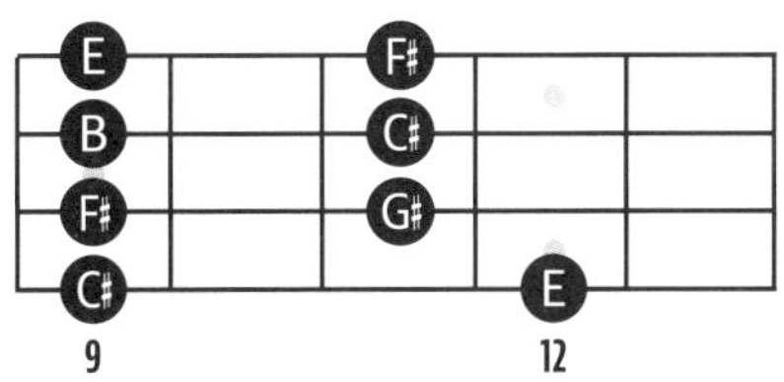

F Major Pentatonic

Position 1

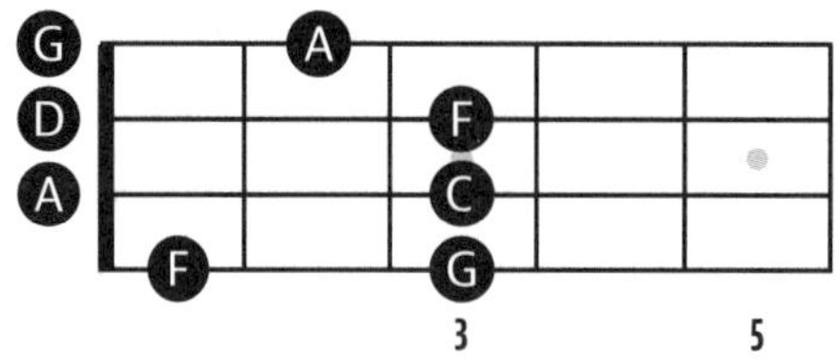

Position 2

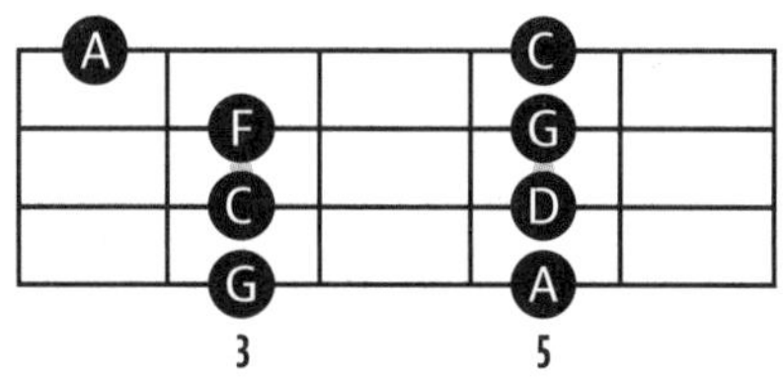

Position 3

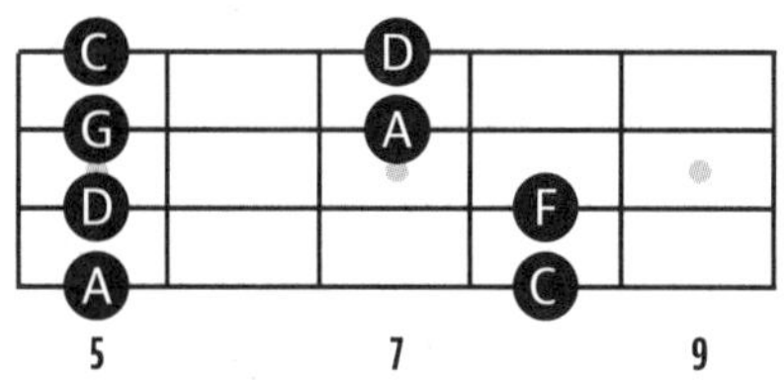

Position 4

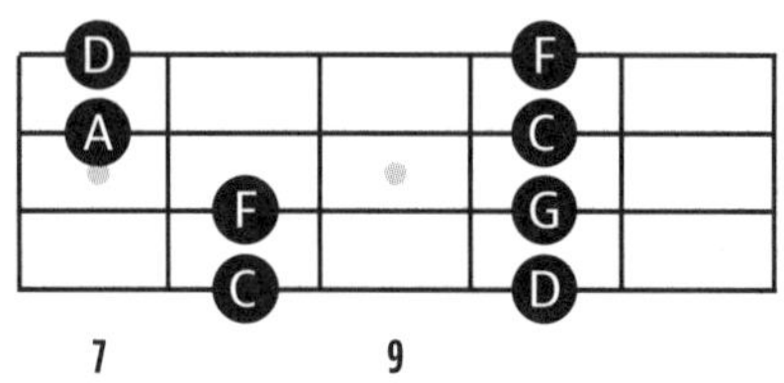

Position 5

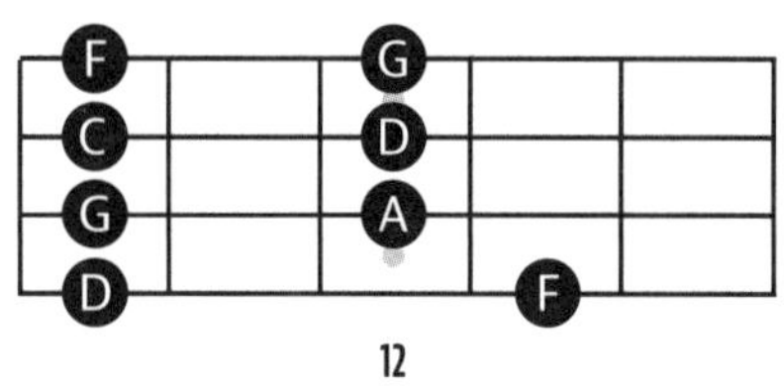

F♯/G♭ Major Pentatonic

Position 1

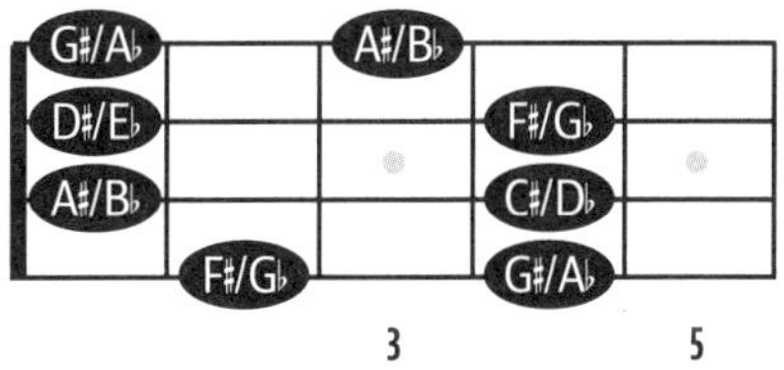

Position 2

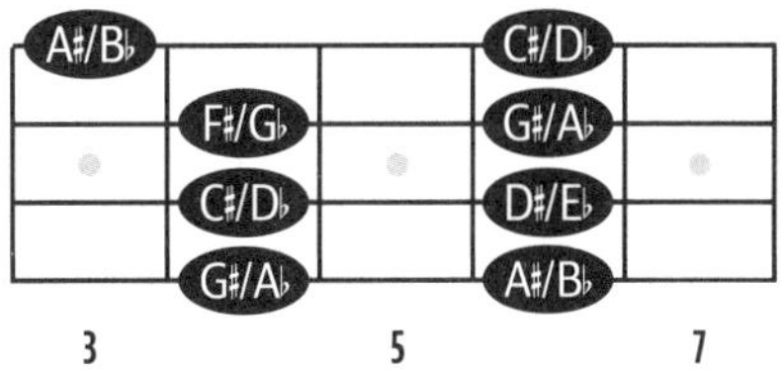

Position 3

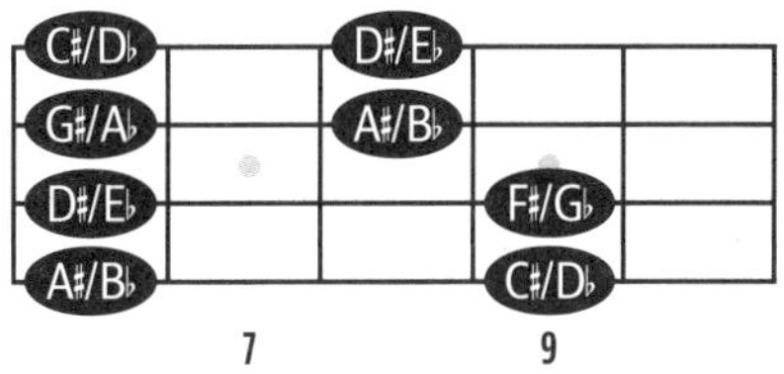

Position 4

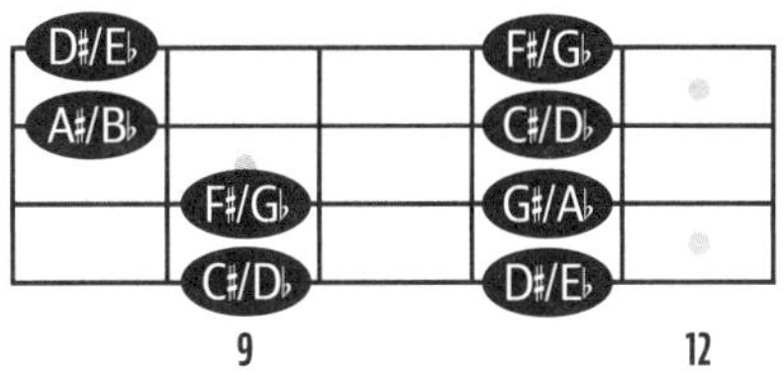

Position 5

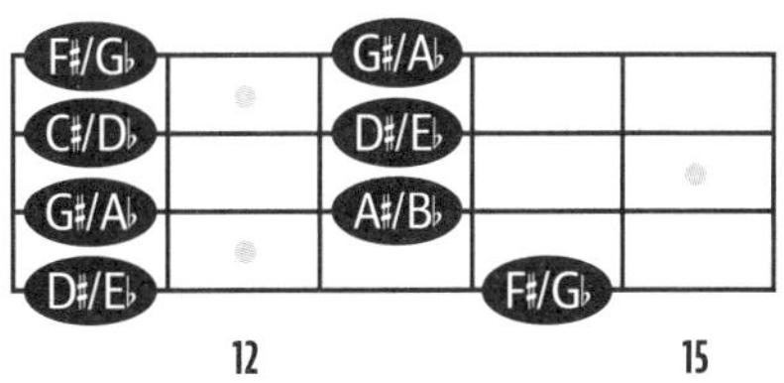

G Major Pentatonic

Position 1

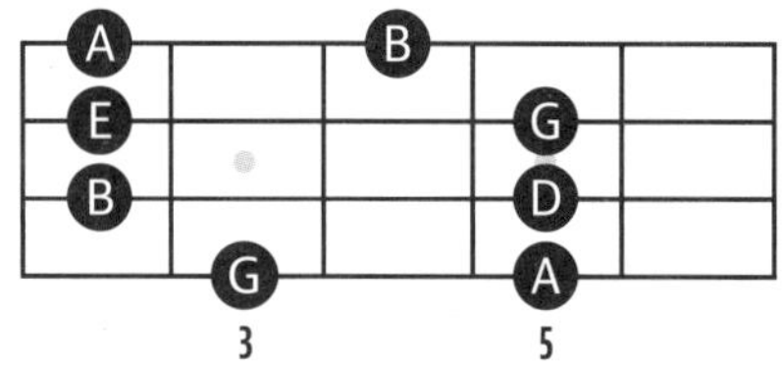

Position 2

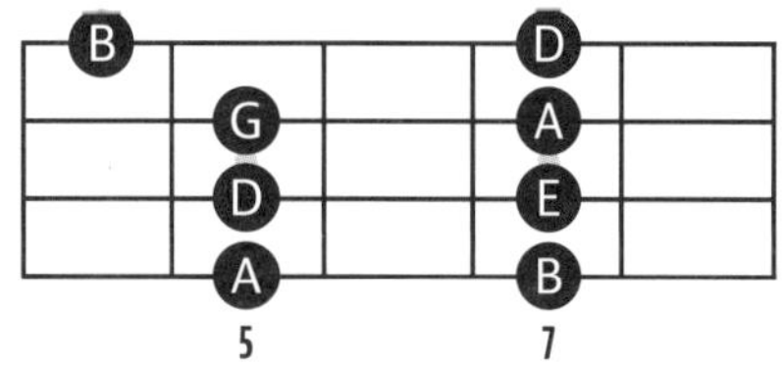

Position 3

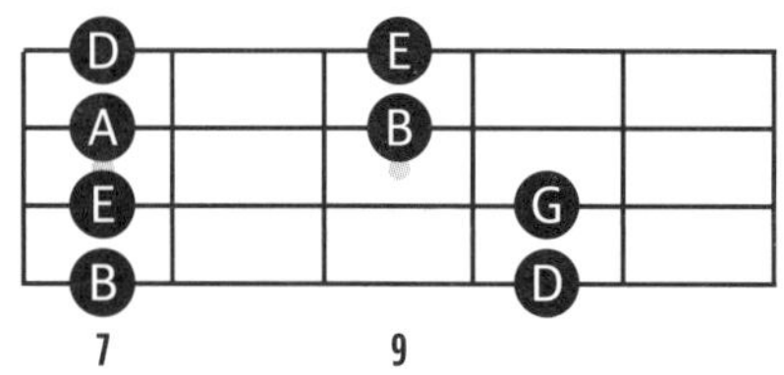

Position 4

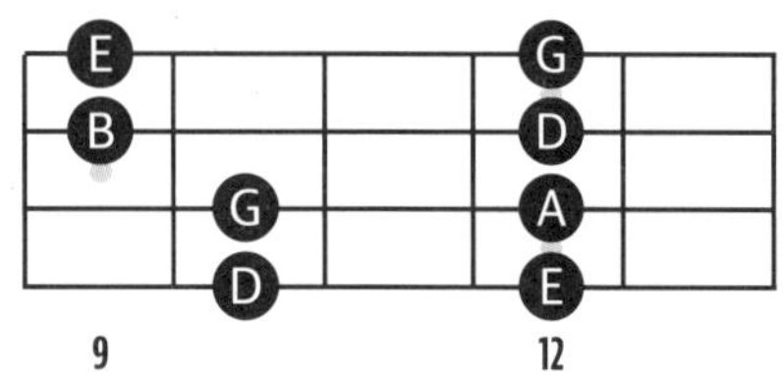

Position 5

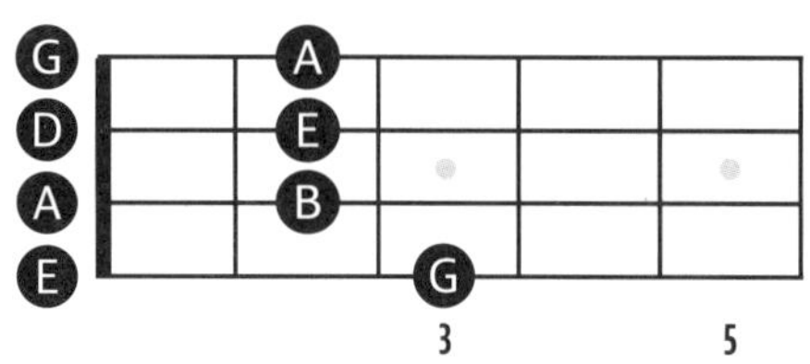

A♭ Major Pentatonic

Position 1

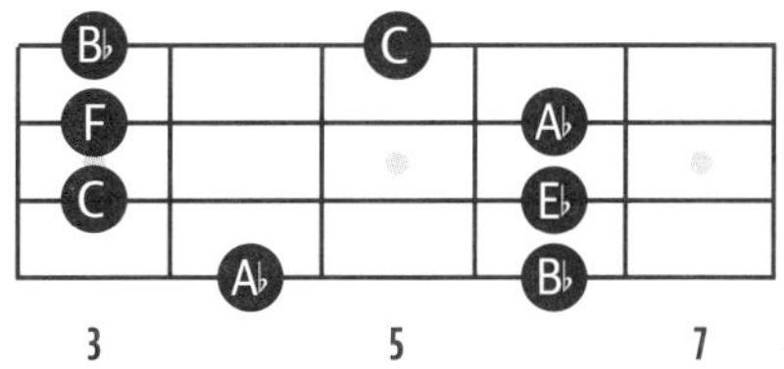

Position 2

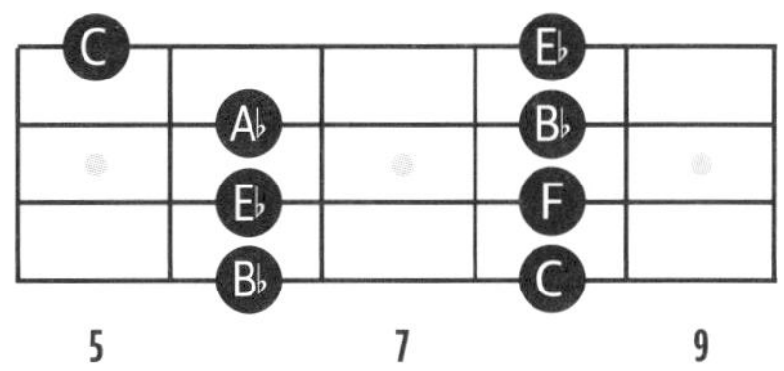

Position 3

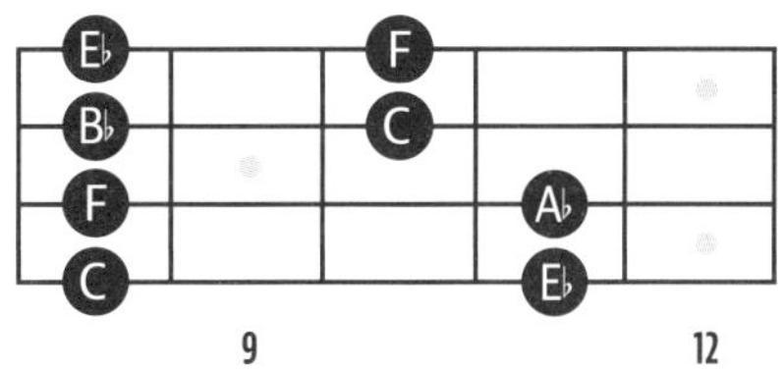

Position 4

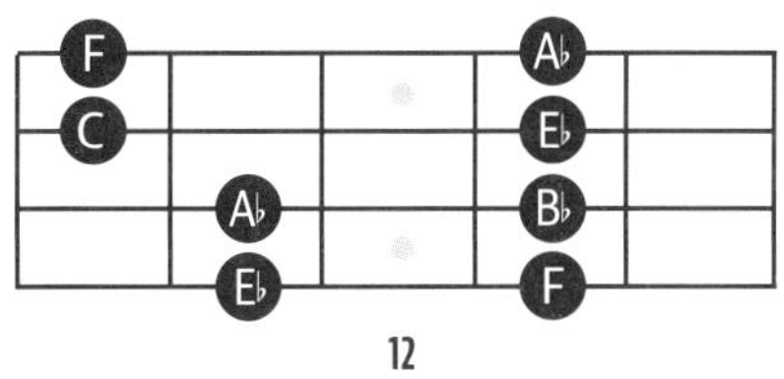

Position 5

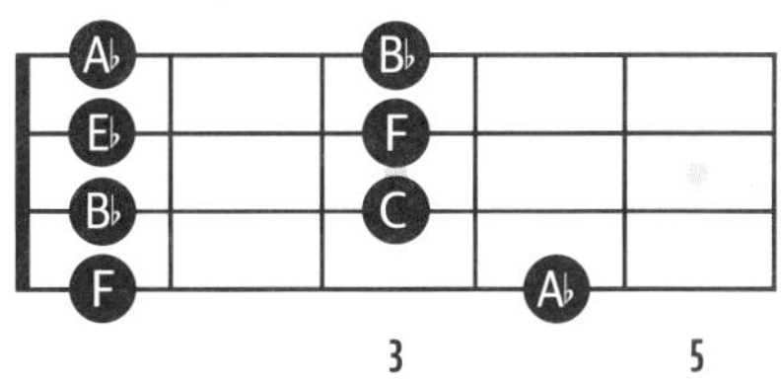

A Major Pentatonic

Position 1

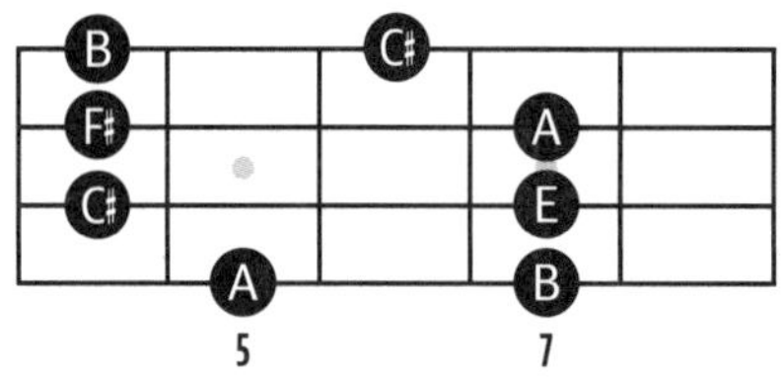

Position 2

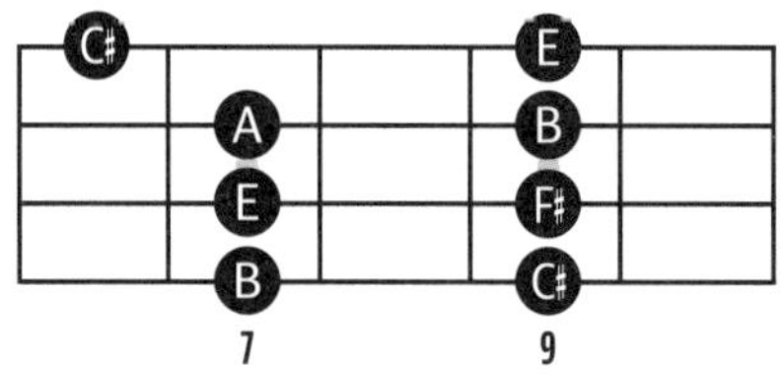

Position 3

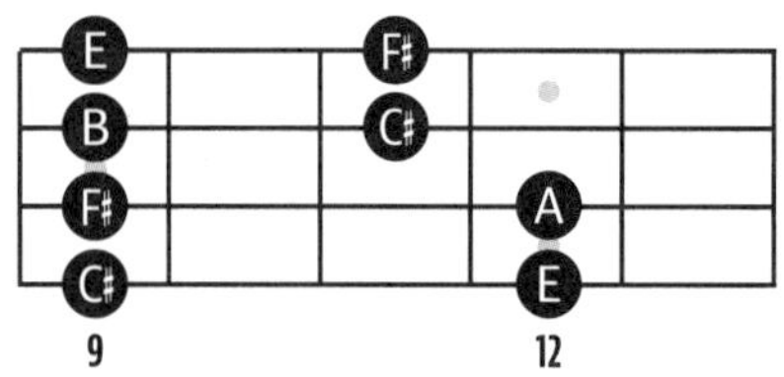

Position 4

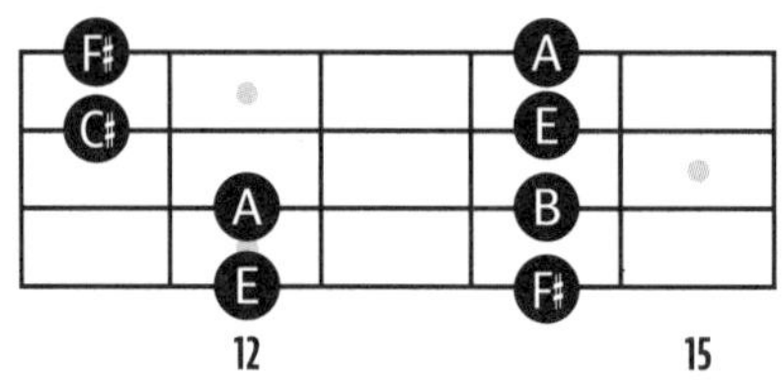

Position 5

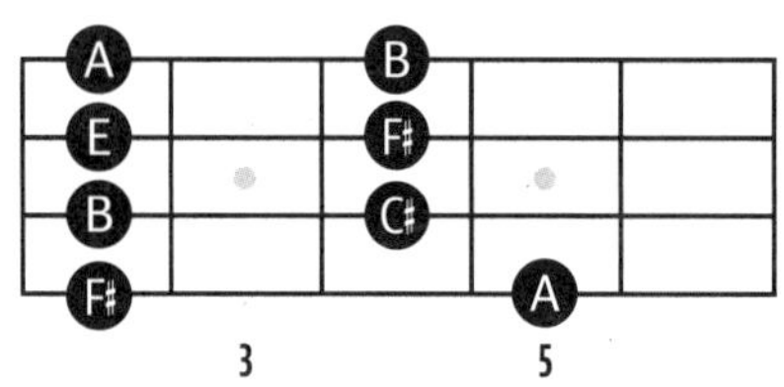

B♭ Major Pentatonic

Position 1

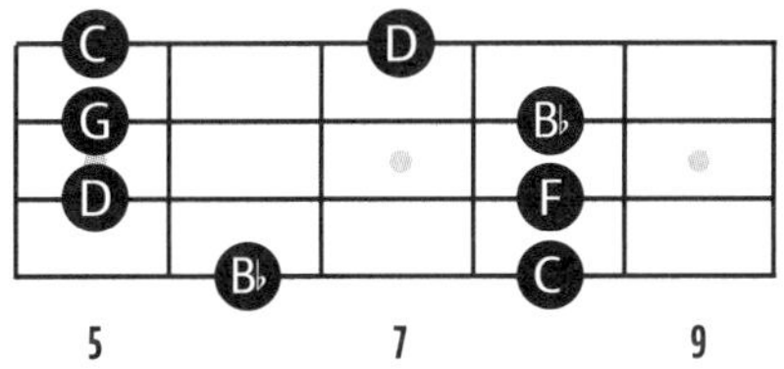

Position 2

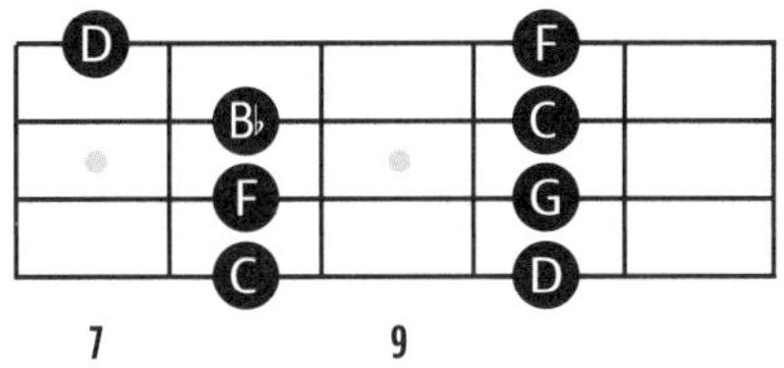

Position 3

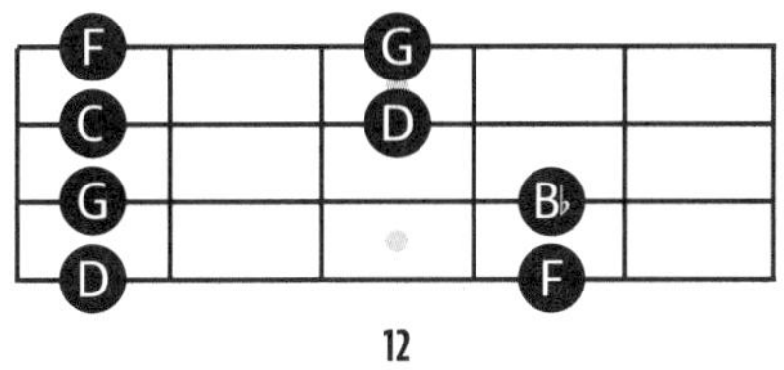

Position 4

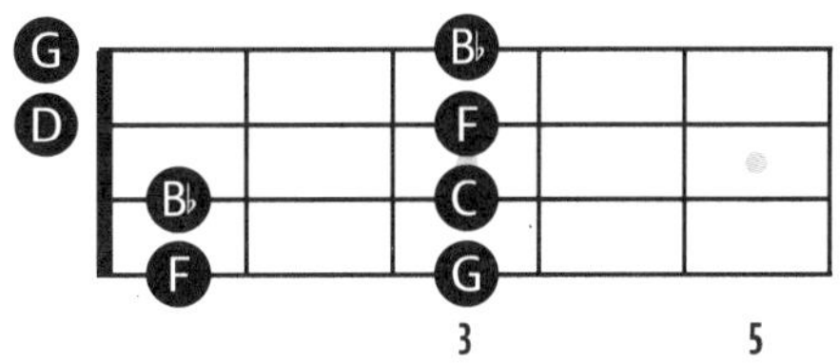

Position 5

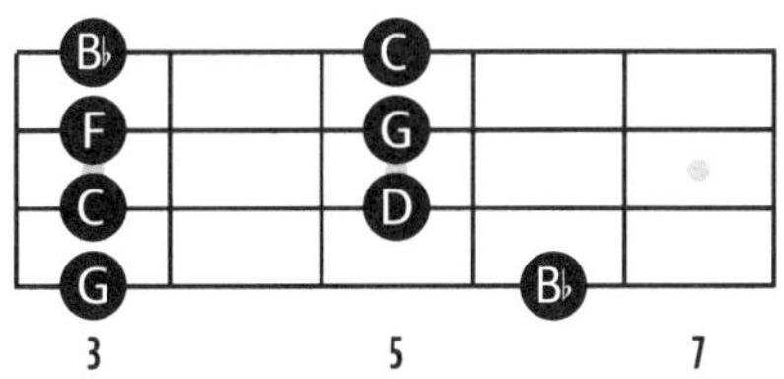

B Major Pentatonic

Position 1

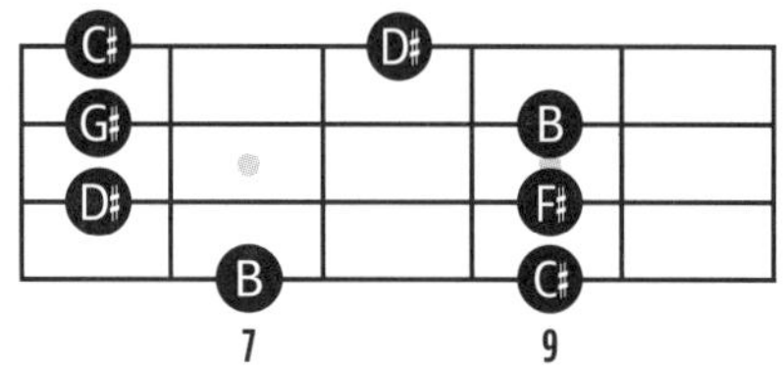

Position 2

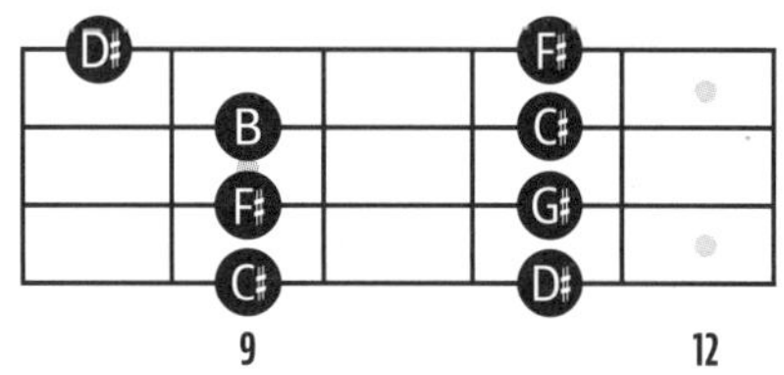

Position 3

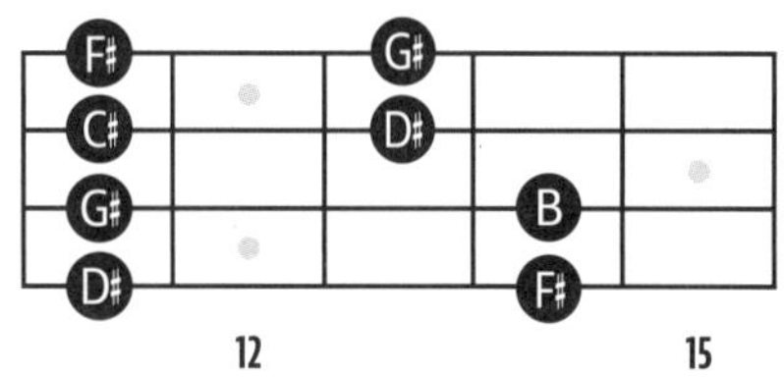

Position 4

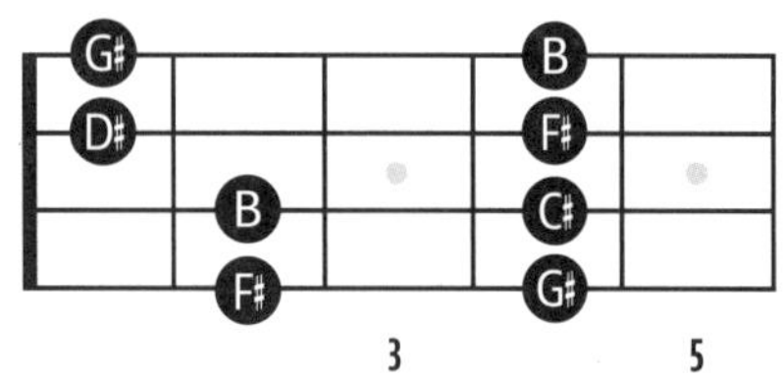

Position 5

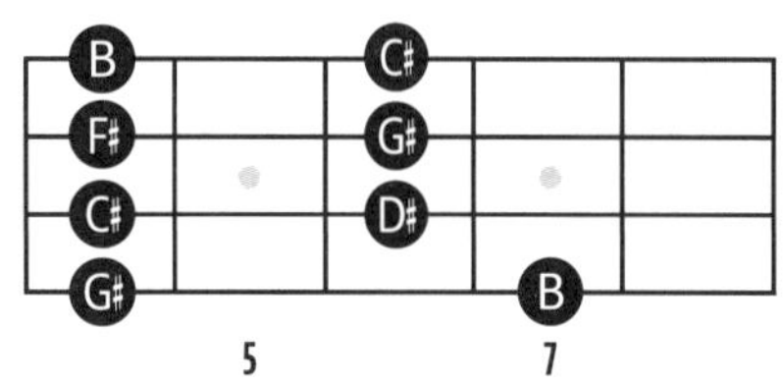

Appendix

Fretboard Quiz Answers

1. A
2. F♯ or G♭
3. A♯ or B♭
4. E
5. G
6. C♯ or D♭

Song Structure Quiz Answers

"Hollow" by Tori Kelly
Intro → Verse → Pre-Chorus → Chorus → Tag → Verse → Pre-Chorus → Chorus → Tag → Bridge → Chorus → Tag → End

"Blank Space" by Taylor Swift
Intro → Verse → Chorus → Verse → Chorus → Bridge → Chorus → End

"Let It Go" by James Bay
Intro → Verse → Pre-Chorus → Chorus → Intro → Verse → Pre-Chorus → Chorus → Intro → Bridge → Chorus → Outro → End

"Keep Your Head Up" by Andy Grammer
Intro → Verse → Pre-Chorus → Chorus → Verse → Pre-Chorus → Chorus → Bridge → Chorus → Outro → End

"Don't Start Now" by Dua Lipa
Intro → Verse → Pre-Chorus → Chorus → Verse → Pre-Chorus → Chorus → Instrumental → Pre-Chorus → Chorus → Instrumental → End

"Friends in Low Places" by Garth Brooks
Intro → Verse → Chorus → Instrumental → Verse → Chorus → Chorus → Chorus → End

"Love Me Now" by John Legend
Intro → Verse → Pre-Chorus → Chorus → Tag → Verse → Pre-Chorus → Chorus → Bridge → Chorus → Tag → End

"Sucker" by the Jonas Brothers
Verse → Pre-Chorus → Chorus → Verse → Pre Chorus → Chorus → Instrumental → Pre Chorus → Chorus → Outro → End

"Waiting on the World to Change" by John Mayer
Intro → Verse → Chorus → Verse → Chorus → Instrumental → Solo → Chorus → Tag → End

Nashville Number Quiz Answers

"DEAR MARIE" (Number Chart)

Words and Music by John Mayer

Tempo: 95bpm   Time Sig: 4/4   Key: A

Intro	1 1 1 1
V1	1 4 1 1 BASS IN
	4 4 1 1
	5 4 1 1
V2	1 4 1 1
	4 4 1 1
	5 4 1 1
V3	1 4 1 1
	4 4 1 1
	5 4 1 1
Gtr Solo	1 4 1 1
	4 4 1 1
	5 4 1 1
V1	1 4 1 1
	4 4 1 1
	5 4 1 1
	END

"AMAZING GRACE" (Number Chart)

Traditional American Melody

Words by John Newton

Tempo: 80bpm   Time Sig: 3/4   Key: C

V1	1 1 4 1 1 1 5 5 1 1 4 1 6⁻ 5 4 1
V2	1 1 4 1 1 1 5 5 1 1 4 1 6⁻ 5 4 1
V3	1 1 4 1 1 1 5 5 1 1 4 1 6⁻ 5 4 1
	END

"THINKING OUT LOUD" (Number Chart)

Words and Music by Ed Sheeran and Amy Wadge

Tempo: 79bpm   Time Sig: 4/4   Key: C

V1	1 <3 4 <5 1 <3 4 <5 :‖
Pre	1 <3 4 <5 1 <3 4 <5 :‖ BASS IN
	2- 5 <1 2- 5
	2- 5 <6- 2- 5
CH	1 <3 4 <5 1 <3 4 <5 :‖
	6- 5 4 3 4 5 <1
V2	1 <3 4 <5 1 <3 4 <5 :‖
Pre	1 <3 4 <5 1 <3 4 <5 :‖
	2- 5 <1 2- 5
	2- 5 <6- 2- 5
CH	1 <3 4 <5 1 <3 4 <5 :‖
	6- 5 4 3 4 5 <1
Outro	6- 5 4 3 4 5 <1 :‖ (repeat 3x)

"ALL OF ME" (Number Chart)

Words and Music by John Stephens and Toby Gad

Tempo: 120bpm Time Sig: 4/4 Key: G

Intro	6^- 4 1 5 :‖	PIANO INTRO
V1	6^- 4 1 5 6^- 4 1 5 :‖	
Pre	2^- 2^- 1 5 :‖	BASS IN
CH	1 1 6^- 6^- 4 4 5 5 :‖	
V2	6^- 4 1 5 6^- 4 1 5 :‖	
Pre	2^- 2^- 1 5 :‖	
CH	1 1 6^- 6^- 4 4 5 5 :‖	
Pre	2^- 2^- 1 5 :‖	
CH	1 1 6^- 6^- 4 4 5 5 :‖	
Outro	6^- 4 1 5 :‖	

Frequently Asked Bass Questions

How often should I change my bass strings?

How much you play the bass will determine how often you should change your strings. But if you are a beginner, I would say once or twice a year is sufficient because most beginners don't play outside of home.

If you are an intermediate to advanced player and play live with other people, I would say three to five months is fine, depending on the genre of music you're playing.

What kind of bass strings do I need to buy?
There are many bass string brands and types that you can purchase. Most brands are pretty good, but the type of string is what will determine the actual sound. Here is a short overview of the most common types you'll see when searching to buy strings.

- **Roundwound**: This is the most common type of string. They have a brighter tone and long decay when playing the notes. These strings have small ridges that you can feel under your fingers, and they are the type of string your first bass would most likely have come with.
- **Flatwound**: These strings have a smoother feel to the touch, which helps reduce finger noise while also having a warm and mellow tone. They are very different in sound and feel when compared to roundwounds.
- **Tapewound**: These are nylon-wrapped strings; they have a short decay and more of a "thud" sound when you play. These are not as common to see as a beginner.
- **Half-round**: If you want something between roundwound and flatwound in terms of tone and feel, then these are it. These are ground-down roundwound strings to give you smoother feel and warm tone, without being completely flatwound.

What is a good beginner bass guitar?
Similar to the many types of strings, there are a lot of great brands of basses out there to choose from. I would make sure to get either a new but affordable bass or a used, older bass that works well and has a discounted price. As a beginner, there are just a few questions you need to answer when searching for the right beginner bass: When you press down on the fretboard, can you hear each fret? When you plug it into an amp, does it make sound? When you cut the volume, is it "scratchy" sounding? Lastly, does it feel good in your hands when you play it?

If you are still unsure or have bought a bass that is used and don't know if it was a good purchase, I would consult with a guitar luthier or guitar repair shop in your area. Every time I have ever bought a bass, I would get what is called a *set-up* from a guitar repair shop. Basically, this means that they will go through your bass and make sure to answer those questions and fix what is potentially broken or problematic.

Should I get a four-string or five-string bass?
I have heard this question a lot over the years, but this is very subjective because it's really dependent on preference of style. In my opinion, when it comes to choosing one as a beginner, I would say a four-string bass would be the easiest to understand and learn on. I would suggest only getting a five-string after learning on a four-string because the learning curve between the two would be a lot smaller. The only difference between a four-string and five-string bass is that a five-string bass has an extra lower string, called the B string. The reason why people love five-string basses is to have access to lower notes that can't be reached on a four-string.

What are active basses versus passive basses? Which should I get?
Active basses are ones where the electronics or preamp are powered by a battery that gives basses more volume and control of tone. Passive basses are normal, run-of-the-mill instruments that don't need a battery to power the electronics. I would say that neither one is better than the other; it just depends on the musical style you play and the amount of control you would want to have on your bass.

Why is my bass making a buzzy sound when I play it?

This happens with most beginner basses, which is called *fret buzz*. This usually happens if you are not pressing down hard enough on the frets of the bass or if your bass's *action* (how high the strings are above the fretboard) is too low. If you are a beginner, then it's most likely because you aren't pressing down hard enough. If you are pressing down as hard as you can and it's still buzzing, you can take your bass to a guitar luthier or repair shop and get it checked.

How often should I practice?

Short answer: Every day. If you are an adult or have a very busy schedule, all I would stress to you is staying consistent with your practice schedule. The main issue I've had with students over the years is that they would practice for several hours one day, but then they don't practice the rest of the week. This caused them not to progress in their learning as well as they could have done. Remember this rule when practicing: "Practicing is about the quality, not the quantity." If you spend 30 minutes practicing every other day, set a timer and put your phone away and work on techniques that are hard for you to play. In the end, you will improve faster compared to spending hours practicing on just one day.

What kind of bass amp should I buy?

There are many brands that have great-quality bass amps, but I would suggest buying a combo bass amp—it's the simplest to set up and carry around with you.

Are effects pedals essential for playing bass?

Short answer: Kind of. In my opinion, bass pedals are very subjective, depending on the sound and genre of music you play. However, there are three types of pedals I think that every bass player should have: a direct box/preamp, a tuner, and a distortion pedal.

Over my years of playing in the professional music industry, these three types of pedals are what have been essential for most genres of music. My general rule, when it comes to bass pedals, is to save up and spend the money on one or two good pedals rather than four or five cheap pedals.

As a bass player, you don't need many pedals to achieve a good tone; sometimes, just one is good enough. Although this isn't always the case, how much you spend on bass pedals can determine the quality of sound from it. This is usually because the more expensive units have higher quality components and are given greater attention to detail when being made. However, if your pedal is affordable and sounds great, then go for it!

How much should I spend on a bass pedal?

Well, it really depends on what you have to spend. Nowadays, a good, mid-range direct box/preamp pedal would be anywhere from $300 to $600. When choosing how to manage your budget, I would advise you to spend the bulk of your money on a direct box/preamp pedal and chain your other less expensive pedals to it. The direct box/preamp can improve your overall tone, even with less expensive pedals in the signal chain.